Advance pr

GREEN, GREENER,

"Lori Bongiorno shows how we can reconnect ourselves with the ecologic cycle with *Green, Greener, Greenest* by highlighting how what we eat, buy, wear, build, and clean has a direct link to the health of the environment and the health of ourselves and our families. For anyone who has struggled to figure what to do to make a difference, this book offers a clear and concise map to a more connected future."

—Walker Wells, AICP LEED AP,
Sustainable Cities Program Director, Global Green USA

"Lori Bongiorno's book synthesizes helpful information about how consumers can green their lifestyles through a range of simple choices, from energy and water conservation to grocery shopping, and breaks it down in an easy-to-understand way. Gone are the days when people can claim they just don't know what they can do to help protect our planet. As this book explains, making a difference is much easier than consumers might think."

—Tensie Whelan, Executive Director, Rainforest Alliance

"In one portable volume, *Green, Greener, Greenest* covers all the bases for those seeking a greener lifestyle. From food to clothing to energy use and transportation, Lori Bongiorno's book is an invaluable reference for living in today's world."

—Ronnie Cummins, National Director,
Organic Consumers Association

continued…

"Lori Bongiorno's handbook to what's good, better, and best for the environment provides consumers welcome, clear, and highly readable advice on how to be as eco-smart as you want to be."

—Dan Becker, Former Director,
Sierra Club Global Warming Program

"'Going green' has never been easier now that Lori Bongiorno has helped us sort out the real information from the hype. There is something here for everyone, from those with a casual interest to those who would like to green every aspect of their life."

—Patti Wood, Executive Director,
Grassroots Environmental Education

"This is a useful and up-to-date compendium of the best resources for the eco-conscious. It will save you time in your quest for personal responsibility—time that can be spent in the greenest of all ways, by joining the political battle for sweeping, society-wide change."

—Bill McKibben, author of *Fight Global Warming Now*

"*Green, Greener, Greenest* is an excellent compilation of good information, briefly and accessibly presented, and a very useful handbook for green-minded people who mean business."

—Peter Matthiessen, author of *Shadow Country*

"From diamonds to diapers and cars to gardens, Lori Bongiorno provides an easy-to-read primer for making small changes that can make big differences in the health and lives of millions. A book like this could initiate a shift toward improved product safety long before governments step in and do their job."

—Theo Colborn, PhD, President, The Endocrine Disruption Exchange (TEDX); Professor, University of Florida

"Becoming green or sustainable takes time and some effort, but *Green, Greener, Greenest* makes the process much easier. From food and beverages to personal care products and pest control, Lori Bongiorno gives us practical suggestions to minimize our exposure to potentially harmful substances and to lessen our impact on the environment."

—Diane Hatz, Founder/Director, Sustainable Table

"Hopeful, helpful, and packed with well-researched tips, *Green, Greener, Greenest* is a great family guide to living the genuinely good life. Whether you are feeding your kids; gardening; or choosing cars, clothing, or cleaning products, you'll find the information you need to make wise and livable choices."

—Ann Lovejoy, author and sustainability educator

A PRACTICAL GUIDE TO MAKING ECO-SMART CHOICES A PART OF YOUR LIFE

Lori Bongiorno

A PERIGEE BOOK

A PERIGEE BOOK
Published by the Penguin Group
Penguin Group (USA) Inc.
375 Hudson Street, New York, New York 10014, USA
Penguin Group (Canada), 90 Eglinton Avenue East, Suite 700, Toronto, Ontario M4P 2Y3, Canada (a division of Pearson Penguin Canada Inc.) • Penguin Books Ltd., 80 Strand, London WC2R 0RL, England • Penguin Group Ireland, 25 St. Stephen's Green, Dublin 2, Ireland (a division of Penguin Books Ltd.) • Penguin Group (Australia), 250 Camberwell Road, Camberwell, Victoria 3124, Australia (a division of Pearson Australia Group Pty. Ltd.) • Penguin Books India Pvt. Ltd., 11 Community Centre, Panchsheel Park, New Delhi—110 017, India • Penguin Group (NZ), 67 Apollo Drive, Rosedale, North Shore 0632, New Zealand (a division of Pearson New Zealand Ltd.) • Penguin Books (South Africa) (Pty.) Ltd., 24 Sturdee Avenue, Rosebank, Johannesburg 2196, South Africa

Penguin Books Ltd., Registered Offices: 80 Strand, London WC2R 0RL, England

"How to Talk to Your Local Farmer" on page 5 was adapted from an article by Lori Bongiorno that was originally published in *The Green Guide*, www.thegreenguide.com, on June 30, 2004.
"Electronic Waste" on page 279 was adapted from an article by Lori Bongiorno that was originally published in *Verdant* in April 2007.
Cover art and design by Pat Gibson
Text design by Tiffany Estreicher

First edition: April 2008

Library of Congress Cataloging-in-Publication Data

Bongiorno, Lori.
Green, greener, greenest : a practical guide to making eco-smart choices a part of your life / Lori Bongiorno.
p. cm
Includes bibliographical references and index.
ISBN 978-0-399-53403-4
1. Environmental responsibility. 2. Sustainable living. 3. Alternative lifestyles. I. Title.
GE195.7.B66 2008
333.72—dc22 2007048031

PRINTED IN THE UNITED STATES OF AMERICA

10 9 8 7 6 5 4 3 2

Green, Greener, Greenest is printed on 100 percent post-consumer recycled paper certified by the Forest Stewardship Council (FSC), processed chlorine-free, and manufactured using Biogas Energy.

For Brent, Eliza, and Andy

ACKNOWLEDGMENTS

Maria Gagliano; Andy Barzvi; Sarah Weir; Frances Beinecke; Michelle Brady; Jessica Smith; Jessica Osserman; Kim Bonnell; Ellyn Spragins; Elise Pettus; Elizabeth Cahill; Abigail Bedrick; Roland Lange; Eric Simonoff; Catherine Milne; John Adams; Jenny Powers; Patti Wood; Sarah Janssen; Philip Dickey; Kay Rumsey; Monica Gilchrist; Dan Becker; Roland Hwang; David Wallinga; Kathleen Schuler; Gina Solomon; Jonathan Kaplan; Rich Kassel; Nancy Evans; Elise Miller; Ted Schettler; Jennifer Sass; Darby Hoover; Ronnie Cummins; Craig Minowa; Alex Wilson; Jerelyn Wilson; Leslie Hoffman; Patricia Monahan; Audrey Chang; Joe Mendelson; Jane Rissler; Bill Prindle; Stacy Malkan; Patrick Kinney; David McBride; Maria Vargas; Evelyne Michaut; Allen Hershkowitz; Michael Replogle; John DeCicco; Vickie Patton; Charlie Miller; Jane Houlihan; Hema Subramanian; Jovana Ruzicic; Stephen Ashkin; Herbert Buxton; Patricia Whisnant; Susan Inglis; Barbara Haumann; Emily Mitchell; Taryn Holowka; Scott Pactor; Laurie Howell; Joanna Jordan; India Baird; The Chajet family; Liza Gilbert; Andi Phillips; Sid Ray; Allison and Connor Coffey; Margaret Page; Amir Sadovnik; Deborah Cheadle; Andy and Marianna Price; RoseMarie Landolphi; Lisa Bongiorno; Danielle Bongiorno; MaryAnn Bongiorno; and Frank and Corinne Bongiorno.

CONTENTS

FOREWORD

Frances Beinecke, President, Natural Resources Defense Council

There are many reasons why people choose a greener path in life. For me, the inclination began when I was a child. I was first introduced to the American West though family trips and got taken in by that grand landscape. I also love the Adirondacks and was later inspired by the foresight of citizens who acted affirmatively by protecting those wild places 100 years ago in the New York State constitution. I became involved through a very personal connection to the natural world, and that connection grew to encompass many of the everyday decisions in a life that is also very urban. For others, it might start on the dinner plate or in the backyard garden, or because of concerns about personal health. Of course, that translates to the health of the planet, too. Your personal actions ensure that you and your family will stay healthy, which ultimately impacts the world around you in positive ways.

Regardless of the reason, it's clear that we all can, and indeed must, make changes to avoid the repercussions of global warming and other environmental challenges. The first step is to make more sustainable choices in our personal consumption and lifestyle patterns. Until very recently it was hard to find alternatives, and it's still difficult to know where to start. *Green, Greener, Greenest* provides all the information you need in one place so you don't have to hunt for it. Like everyone else, I'm doing my part bit by bit. As more green choices become available, I am making them, but I wouldn't say I am as squeaky clean green as I'd like to be. When hybrid cars became an option, I got one. I've also been able to switch to bio-fuels to warm my home. Being able to buy compact fluorescent bulbs at Target and finding organic foods at the local grocery store makes these changes easier. I am very grateful for the fact that I live in the city and can take public transportation. That's a huge plus when I look at my carbon footprint.

Consumers have enormous clout. The organic food market, for example, is the fastest growing sector of the grocery market because of increasing concerns about individual health. But we need more green under the sink and in the gas tank as well as in the refrigerator. Use this book as a tool to help you to make positive choices, and, if your local shop is lacking, be a messenger by asking them to supply sustainable items. And if you want to send a message to the boardroom, the cash register is an important place to begin.

Start small and try out some of the simplest "green" suggestions in *Green, Greener, Greenest,* and before you know it, you'll be inspired to take on the "greenest" challenges and get active. It is collective action that moves markets and moves leaders. Every community has engaged citizens whom you can seek out. If you live in the city, you might join with others to save a local park. In the suburbs, maybe it's promoting a "no idling" policy in the carpool line in front of your kids' school. In the country, it might be about ridding farmland of pesticides. *Green, Greener, Greenest* lists plenty of nonprofits you could volunteer for and puts you in touch with organizations that lobby the government for change. In order to make the changes we need at a corporate and political level, demand has to come from the grassroots.

But let's back up. Next time you need to replace a lightbulb use a CFL. Share a ride to work a couple of times a week. Take a walk to the local farmers' market instead of the supermarket to buy your fruits and vegetables. Or try another of the hundreds of suggestions offered in this book. Remember that every small step you take down that greener path moves you toward helping to create a more sustainable world for us all to live in.

INTRODUCTION

It's easy being greener, although it can be difficult to know where to start. I certainly didn't when I first became concerned about the links between the health of my family and that of the environment nearly a decade ago. I was confused by the media's conflicting messages of what constitutes an eco-friendly lifestyle. Instead of being motivated into action, I found the sometimes hysterical, oftentimes conflicting reports about mercury, pesticides, and climate change paralyzing. I believed that if I wasn't willing or able to make radical, self-sacrificing changes, then I may as well not even try. Besides, let's say I wanted to consider some of those changes. Where would I even start? It took time and a lot of digging for answers to figure out what worked for me.

I approach the topic of healthy and environment-friendly living both as a journalist and as a mother. I didn't even consider myself particularly "green" when I started writing about these topics—I had spent most of my career reporting about business. I was motivated to switch to health journalism after my husband's death in 2000 following a two-year battle with melanoma. During his illness, I pored through medical studies and tracked down doctors from all over the country to help determine the best treatments for him. It became bracingly clear to me how much better it is to prevent disease than to have to deal with it. At the same time,

I was caring for two very small children, so I had begun to consider issues like what kind of milk my children should drink and whether or not I should freely slather them with sunscreen.

It was when I was assigned a story on chemicals in breast milk that I became convinced that personal health and the health of the planet are inextricably linked. Although I was initially motivated by health issues, as I have learned more, I've begun to worry about the world we are leaving behind to our children if we don't start taking steps now to protect the environment. Policy changes and corporate initiatives are the real key to reversing big issues like global warming, which is why I am donating a portion of my proceeds to some of the charitable environmental organizations that are fighting for legislative and corporate solutions to our most pressing problems. We can't, after all, buy the much more fuel-efficient cars that we need to combat climate change unless they are available at the car dealer. Still, there are many things each of us can do depending upon what our interests and concerns are. I find that health (both that of my family now and in the future) is still the primary motivator when it comes to making lifestyle changes—although my growing concern about climate change is a close second. For you, it may be different. It may be the safety of our food system or an interest in sustainable building that sparks your interest.

But, it's hard to know where to start, even for the experts. At one point, when my kids were still toddlers, I stopped cooking fish for several months because I was overwhelmed by the incessant news reports warning of the dangers of eating PCB- or mercury-laden fish. I literally couldn't keep track of all the different things I was supposed to worry about. The reporter in me knew there must be plenty of safe options out there and that it was foolish and extreme to eliminate fish from our diet entirely. On the other hand, as a mother, I had read enough about the harmful effects of mercury on developing nervous systems to know that I didn't want to make any mistakes with my young children.

I promised myself I would sit down at my computer and sort through all the reports and studies to find the safest fish options for my family. After all, during my six years on staff at *Business Week* magazine, I had had to track down much more obscure information. How difficult could it be to figure out healthy fish to eat? Not very hard—if only I could find the time to actually do it. Researching safe fish remained on my lengthy "To Do" list as I dealt with the more pressing issues of my daily life earning a living and being a mom.

Luckily for my family, I soon started freelance writing for *The Green Guide*, an environmental health newsletter that strives to be the *Consumer Reports* for people who are concerned about personal health and the environment. I discovered the resources to help get to the bottom of the healthy fish question and my many other concerns, such as pesticides in produce and the health risks of using Teflon cookware. I also realized that I didn't have to dramatically overhaul my lifestyle to make a difference. I learned that small changes made at your own pace do help, especially when lots of others join in. Just changing one standard lightbulb to a CFL, for example, is hardly going to save the planet, but if every U.S. household did so, it would be the equivalent of taking 1 million cars off the road for one year.

Things have changed since I first became interested in living a greener life. As Diana Vreeland might have said, "Green is the new black." Celebrities have traded Hummers for hybrids. Hip organic clothing is making its way onto fashion must-have lists. There are excruciatingly long lines at Whole Foods Market. We've embraced an organic and all-natural lifestyle, and there are more products than ever available for conscious consumers to choose from (including a growing array of green books). However, all the product claims and the choices make it even more important for us to get reliable information and know where our time and money are best spent. Thanks to the Internet and to the media spotlight on environmental issues, we have an endless stream of data, but it is becoming increasingly hard to sort through it all and figure out what is legitimate and what's not.

That is why I decided to write *Green, Greener, Greenest*. It is the book I would have liked to have had on my bookshelf when I first started searching for answers. My aim is to provide time-pressed consumers with one thorough, streamlined guide that shows the full spectrum of possibilities. It will help you make practical, reasonable choices at your own pace and according to your own budget because there isn't one "right" way to make a difference. Anything you can do is worthwhile.

I've structured *Green, Greener, Greenest* to make it ultra user friendly. The book's graduated "green-greener-greenest" approach allows you to find the exact information you are seeking at the level of commitment that works for you. Each chapter opens with an overview that briefly explains a particular topic and its impact on personal health and the environment and then breaks down the topic according to specific products or issues. For example, Chapter 1 has subsections on produce, meat, poultry and eggs, and fish, among others. In each case, there is a concise description of the issues surrounding each product along with practical, realistic, bite-size suggestions of what you can do to purchase and eat the best possible food listed under "Green," "Greener," and "Greenest." "Green" tips lay out the easiest products to buy and behaviors to change and typically don't require any additional time or money. The "Greener" suggestions are for those who are willing to spend a little extra money or time on the issues they really care about. Readers who have the time, budget, and inspiration to fully take on an issue can turn to the "Greenest" suggestions for guidance. It's all about picking and choosing what makes sense for you.

Throughout the book you'll find many "Decoding the Labels" boxes aimed at helping you determine which labels are meaningful for a particular product and which are not. For example, "organic" means different things for different products. Don't bother spending extra money on organic seafood because there aren't U.S. standards to back up the claim. In *Green, Greener, Greenest,* you'll learn the definitions of a growing array of terms such as "grass-fed," "sustainable," "biodegradable," and many others so you know exactly what the labels guarantee and what they don't.

In putting together this book, I conducted interviews with doctors, public health officials, environmental advocates, and various other experts and read the latest studies to get the most up-to-date information available. In order to offer you manageable suggestions that can be implemented at your own pace, I've tried to keep things relatively brief and focus on the basics. A friend was recently going camping and was concerned about the safety of bug spray so I emailed her a multiple-page report on the subject. She sent it back and asked me for the "one-pager." This book is a series of one-pagers. There are additional resources listed throughout each chapter for those who want to learn more.

Today, scientists are beginning to discover connections between environmental degradation and a long list of medical problems such as allergies, asthma, learning difficulties, development delays, birth defects, many cancers, declining sperm counts, and others—some studies show blatant links, others are more theoretical. Toxic chemicals are showing up in mothers' breast milk, and now we know that we all have cocktails of multiple man-made chemicals in our blood, some of which have been linked to human health risks. Children are more sensitive to these chemicals because their organs and immune systems are still developing, and pound for pound, they are ingesting more chemicals than adults. There is also increasing evidence that fetuses are exposed to pollutants while still in the womb, a time of rapid development.

Just because a product is on a store shelf does not mean it has been tested properly or is completely safe for use. Many of the synthetic chemicals in existence have not been vigorously assessed for their effect on human health, especially their effects when people are exposed to them in combination with one another on a daily basis over a long period of time. That's good enough reason for me to make changes in some of the products I use when I can find safer replacements that work. When I learned that the major chemical in my favorite cleaning product was a liver and kidney toxicant that gets absorbed into the body through the skin, it was easy for me to switch to a brand without the chemical—so I did it. For me, it makes sense to switch to less potentially toxic products while the scientists are still doing the research rather than waiting it out. You may feel differently. Ultimately, I know that I can't realistically avoid everything that might be bad for my family's health, but I attempt to minimize the things that I can control.

The good news is that, armed with the right information, we can all take steps that will positively impact our own health and that of the planet. It makes sense to pick and choose your battles.

In many states you can call your local utility and switch to green power, if you are interested in supporting renewable energy. If you are concerned about using Teflon cookware, you could invest in new pans or take precautions like keeping the heat low and disposing of old pans with peeling coatings. If reports on toxic chemicals leaching out of plastic baby bottles are keeping you up at night, then you can use glass bottles or buy plastics without the questionable chemical.

Making informed choices is empowering. A few years ago, I needed to buy strawberries for my daughter's kindergarten class. I was on my way to the health food store to buy organic strawberries because I knew the conventional types are riddled with pesticides. On my walk, I passed a farmers' market and saw the most beautiful strawberries, but I didn't know if I should buy them because they weren't labeled organic. What's better: the organic berries at the store or the ones grown at the local farm? I wished then that I had a book like *Green, Greener, Greenest* to turn to for advice. The answer happens to be local if they are grown without pesticides. Now you'll have one comprehensive, easy-to-use resource to answer such questions and help you move toward a healthier and more environment-friendly life. You won't have to spend your time searching for answers; instead you will be putting it toward making a difference.

1 FOOD

Deciding what to eat for dinner is harder today than ever before. The average supermarket sells around 40,000 different products featuring a wide array of labels such as "organic," "free-range," and "all-natural," some meaningful, others bogus. You can shop in a variety of stores ranging from Wal-Mart, the largest and cheapest purveyor of food, to upscale natural food chains like Whole Foods. What's more, if you don't want to you don't even have to visit an actual store. Farmers' markets are proliferating as are opportunities to buy food online.

If you thought fat, calories, and cholesterol were more than enough to keep track of when choosing wholesome food, how about the worries over unhealthy additives and other chemicals we keep hearing about? The list of dangers to consider is seemingly endless—mercury and polychlorinated biphenyls (PCBs) in fish, arsenic and antibiotics in chicken, hormones in meat, genetically modified ingredients, mad cow disease, trans fats, and so on.

Concern about health is one of the driving forces behind the rapid expansion of organics, the fastest growing segment of an otherwise sluggish food industry. In some ways organic has become a victim of its own success. Agribusiness is gobbling up the very farms that started as a reaction to the industrialization of America's food supply. Small organic farms rebelled against conventional farming methods that relied on synthetic pesticides and other toxic chemicals that deplete the soil and pollute water, but there were other aspects to the organic movement that got lost when the U.S. Department of Agriculture (USDA) implemented organic standards in 2002. Organic farmers wanted to veer away from the large corporate farms that grew only one crop, say corn or wheat, and move back to the old way of farming with diverse crops and livestock all coexisting. They envisioned small regional farms supplying Americans with local, seasonal, whole foods. However, as organic farms grew they started to look a whole lot like their conventional counterparts, minus the harsh chemicals.

Even as critics claim that organic has been "industrialized" and co-opted by big business, there is no question that a lot of good has come out of the organic movement. The conversion of land into organic has been great for the environment. It has enabled consumers to have more access to fruits and vegetables grown without pesticides and to meat from animals raised on healthier feed. However, food still often has to travel thousands of miles from farm to table, the average distance for produce being about 1,500 "food" miles. One researcher, Louise Pape, director of Climate Today, found that wheat traveled 5,110 miles from a farm in Nebraska to a Wal-Mart in New Mexico, stopping in four other locales on its journey from field to a box of cake mix.

Organic foods are expensive, usually commanding a 20 to 50 percent price premium, depending on the product and whether it's in season, and they aren't always available. It can be especially difficult to find certified organic meat. This is all likely to change as Wal-Mart adds a substantial amount of well-priced organic foods to its shelves, much of it packaged organic versions of conventional foods like boxed macaroni and cheese and breakfast cereals. Wal-Mart's appetite for organic will surely result in the conversion of hundreds of thousands more acres of farmland to organic. The land won't necessarily be in the United States, but it's good news that consumers will have more access to organic.

There are also worries that the constant pressure to weaken the organic standards will only increase as big business gets more involved. That said, for now, when you buy organic you are voting for a more environmentally friendly kind of agriculture, one that supports a planet with richer soil and a cleaner water supply. You are also eating food that is increasingly thought to be better for your health.

As the meaning of "organic" is diluted, some farmers go "beyond organic" by using words like "local" and "sustainable" in reaction to the industrialization of organic. There's no official definition for "sustainable," but it's essentially a way of raising food that's healthy for those who eat it as well as the farms that produce it—the animals, the farmers, and the land itself. Chemical pesticides are minimally used, animals have access to pasture, and the farm itself is viewed as an extension of the local community. What's taken out of the environment is put back in so that it can be maintained indefinitely and available to future generations. Local food is fresher, doesn't have to travel thousands of miles to reach you, and is less expensive when you buy it directly from the farmer. It's also better for your local economy. (Critics of Wal-Mart's entry into the organic market are concerned that food dollars will be denied to local economies and redirected to the company's headquarters in Arkansas.) When you choose local you are supporting conservation of fuel resources, economic viability of local communities, freshness, and better taste. Eating locally and in-season foods is also a more traditional way of eating. The downside to local is that unless it's certified organic you have to do all the work yourself to figure out what went into its production.

The connection between what we eat and our health is well established. Americans eat too much in general and as a result are getting fatter as a nation. However, while we can directly connect the obesity epidemic to growing health problems such as diabetes, it's harder to measure the more subtle relationship between environmental toxins and health. Toxic pollutants can contribute to the development of many health-related problems, including learning and behavioral disabilities, declining sperm counts, and diseases such as cancer, Parkinson's, and others. Some of our exposure to industrial chemicals, pesticides, and heavy metals comes from the foods we eat. Many of these chemicals haven't been fully tested for their effects on human health. Bear in mind that the level and timing of exposure to chemicals, the mixture of chemicals to which one is exposed, and one's own genetic predisposition are all contributing factors to health problems, so it is difficult to tie specific chemicals to certain illnesses.

Health advocates argue that the United States should err on the side of caution and minimize exposures to pesticides and other industrial chemicals until they are proven safe. Pregnant women and young children have to be especially careful. Fetuses and children are more vulnerable because their systems are still developing. Children's bodies are smaller, so pound for pound they ingest more chemicals than adults, and their organs are still developing.

Arming yourself with enough information to make healthy

choices is crucial, especially when local, organic, well-priced food is not available.

How to Talk to Your Local Farmer

Knowing what to buy at farmers' markets can be tricky because it's not always easy to find certified organic products; a certified organic label is the only guarantee that produce wasn't doused in pesticides or chickens weren't fed antibiotics or animal by-products. Chances are good that the farmers you encounter at markets are from small local farms that practice sustainable farming. The best way to find out what they are up to is to ask them directly, so here are some questions (and ideal answers) to get the dialogue started. Keep in mind that it's hard to come up with blanket questions because different crops require different questions. Ultimately, developing a relationship of trust is your best guarantee.

WHAT TO ASK ABOUT FRUITS AND VEGETABLES

Have you grown this produce yourself? Farmers don't have control over vegetables and fruits from neighboring farms.

Is your farm open to the general public to visit? Farmers who have nothing to hide will often be happy to have people visit.

Are you trying to grow organically? If you get a flat-out no, there is probably no need to continue questioning. If you hear that they are trying, you should ask more detailed questions. Many farmers will say that getting certified costs too much money. You might want to point out that they can get more money for organic crops because it protects the health of consumers and farmers, and the environment.

What practices do you use to control pests, disease, and weeds on your farm? What do you use to rejuvenate soil to keep it healthy and fertile? Farmers who are paying attention to these issues and trying to make positive changes will be using some of the following techniques:

- Encouraging wildlife population by using bat and owl houses, bees in the area, and beneficial insects to control bugs
- Diversifying the crops that they grow
- Planting flowers and complimentary crops. For example, growing certain crops next to each other can help control bugs.
- Rotating crops, not planting the same crop in the same place each year
- Hand-hoeing weeds
- Growing cover crops, such as buckwheat or alfalfa, in the off-season to put minerals back into the soil
- Applying only botanical substances made from other plants or minerals to control pests, weeds, and diseases
- Applying only over-the-counter chemicals when they have a real problem, and not harvesting for three or four days after.

WHAT TO ASK ABOUT MEAT, CHICKEN, AND EGGS

Does your feed have antibiotics in it? The answer should be *no.*

What kind of feed do you give your animals? Best answers: cracked corn for chickens, and pasture and hay for beef and dairy, perhaps supplemented in winter with organic whole grain or whole corn (although that's controversial). You don't want to hear that they just get feed from the grain mill. You also want to know if the feed has animal by-products in it.

Are hens caged? Do they go outside, and do they have enough room to take dirt baths and get grass outside? Eggs will lack beneficial omega-3 fats unless chickens get to peck the dirt.

PRODUCE

Fresh fruits and vegetables are the epitome of healthy food—low in calories and loaded with vitamins, minerals, disease-fighting phytochemicals, and fiber. But before you reach for that box of beautiful conventionally grown strawberries on the supermarket shelf, you should know that the berries may also contain up to eight different pesticides and other synthetic chemicals used to kill unwanted bugs, weeds, fungi, and other "pests." Studies have linked pesticide residues, found in a wide range of conventional produce, to health hazards such as cognitive impairment, nervous system damage, reproductive effects, and some cancers in animals. There isn't much data on the impact of pesticide residues on humans, although the adverse affects of pesticides on farmers are well documented. Any impacts, of course, depend on a number of factors, including level and timing of exposure, and an individual's vulnerability.

It makes sense to avoid pesticides when possible while we wait for more human data, especially for babies and young children, who are particularly vulnerable. Buying organic fruits and vegetables is a good way to minimize exposure; studies show that organic produce has fewer pesticides than conventional and that people who eat organic have fewer residues in their bodies than those who don't. A 2005 study funded by the Environmental Protection Agency (EPA) showed that feeding children organic food can significantly lower their exposure to certain pesticides. On a similar note, a University of Washington report found that children who were fed organic fruits and vegetables had lower levels of pesticides in their urine than their counterparts who ate purely conventional diets. What's more, organic produce may be more nutritious because it absorbs more minerals and vitamins from soil that hasn't been depleted by harsh chemicals.

The best bet for your health, the environment, and the local economy is to buy fruits and vegetables that are organic, locally produced, and therefore, in season. Local produce doesn't have to be shipped long distances, so it's usually fresher, tastes better, and is more nutritious (produce starts losing nutrient quality after it's picked, so the closer you eat to harvest time the better). Local food is often cheaper when you are buying directly from the farmer, and if it isn't labeled organic you can ask the farmer whether he or she uses synthetic chemicals. It gets a little murkier when you have to choose between conventional local produce and shipped organic. If your primary concern is health, then go for the organic. If you are worried about health as well as sustainability, the local economy, and climate change, and you think your local farmer is responsible, then local is probably best.

All conventional produce is not created equal. Pesticide levels vary depending on the fruit or vegetable, so it makes sense to choose conventionally grown varieties with the least amount of residues and save your organic dollars for the most contaminated varieties when possible. According to the Environmental Working Group (EWG), an environmental research and advocacy group, the following fruits and vegetables have the most pesticide contamination: peaches, apples, sweet bell peppers, celery, nectarines, strawberries, cherries, lettuce, imported grapes, pears, spinach, potatoes, carrots, green beans, hot peppers, and cucumbers.

Those with the least residues include onions, avocado, frozen sweet corn, pineapples, mango, frozen sweet peas, asparagus, kiwi, bananas, cabbage, broccoli, and eggplant.

DECODING THE LABELS

USDA Certified Organic. Fruits and vegetables labeled organic are grown without synthetic chemicals, sewer sludge, genetically modified organisms (GMOs), or irradiation. There are also strict regulations regarding the composting of manure and when it can be applied. Organic produce is certified by the USDA's accredited independent certifying agencies.

Demeter Certified Biodynamic. This label guarantees that no synthetic pesticides and fertilizers were used. Farmers are committed to the principles governing biodynamic agriculture, such as viewing the farm as a self-sufficient entity. See www.demeter-usa.org to learn more about biodynamic farming and what the label means.

Fair Trade Certified. This label aims to protect farmers in developing nations and is a guarantee that strict economic, social, and environmental criteria have been met. Farmers and farmworkers get a fair price for their products and receive other economic support. Products with this label are grown by small-scale producers who follow sustainable farming methods, such as limited pesticide use. This label can appear on bananas, mangoes, pineapples, and grapes. For more information visit TransFair USA's website, www.transfairusa.org.

Food Alliance Certified. Farmers who get this third-party certification must subscribe to pesticide-reducing strategies, soil and water conservation, and safe and fair working conditions. For more information see www.foodalliance.org.

Rainforest Alliance Certified: The Rainforest Alliance aims to promote tropical conservation; the label certifies that certain fruits such as bananas, guava, pineapple, passion fruit, and plantains meet strict standards for worker welfare, farm management, and environmental protection such as reducing pesticide use. Visit www.rainforest-alliance.org for more info and for a list of certified providers.

For more information on labeling go to www.greenerchoices.org/eco-home.cfm.

GREEN

- Wash and peel produce.
- Eat a wide variety of produce to get all the nutrients you need and to protect yourself from exposure to the same pesticides.
- Feed babies and small children organic whenever possible.

GREENER

• Buy organic versions of the most contaminated produce (see page 9). For the Environmental Working Group's full results go to www.foodnews.org. An EWG simulation of thousands of consumers shows that people can lower their pesticide exposure by almost 90 percent by avoiding the top twelve most contaminated fruits and vegetables and eating the least contaminated instead.

• Buy organic versions of whatever foods you eat most often.

• Buy local whenever possible. To find a farmers' market nearby, visit www.ams.usda.gov/farmersmarkets or www.localharvest.org.

GREENEST

• Buy as much local and organic as you can afford or have access to regardless of pesticide-residue levels.

• Join a Community Supported Agriculture program. At the beginning of the growing season you buy a "share" in a local farmer's harvest. Each week you receive a share of the crops. To find one near you visit the Robyn Van En Center at Wilson College's website, www.wilson.edu/csasearch/search.asp.

• Food co-ops are another place to find well-priced local and organic foods. Most of them require members to work a monthly shift. Visit www.localharvest.org to find one near you.

• Grow your own produce. Don't use pesticides and check lead levels in your soil. See page 226 for information on how to get your soil tested.

- Get active. See "Food Activism" on page 38 for ideas.

Bionic Foods: What Are GMOs, Anyway?

The term "genetically engineered food" may conjure images of giant strawberries from Woody Allen's film *Sleeper*—but the results and issues are far more subtle than that. Also known as genetically modified organisms (GMOs), these foods are created when scientists take a gene from one plant or animal and insert it into the DNA of an unrelated organism. The genes are manipulated to give the plants and animals desirable traits such as the ability to repel insects or weeds. Some environmental and health advocates question whether there is enough information available to know if genetically engineered foods are safe for humans to eat and for the environment.

While there are no reports that people are getting sick from eating genetically engineered foods, that can be somewhat misleading because such foods aren't labeled, says Jane Rissler, senior scientist at the Union of Concerned Scientists. This is of particular concern to those with food allergies because in creating GMOs, scientists could take an allergenic protein from one food and introduce it into another. Without proper labeling, food-allergic individuals would not know to avoid that food (which is the only way to prevent allergic reactions). There's also concern that traditional crops can be contaminated by genetically engineered seeds or pollen. A 2004 Union of Concerned Scientists study found that large percentages of conventional seeds were already contaminated with genetically engineered seed.

For now, the vast majority of genetically engineered foods that you're likely to encounter are corn (including products such as corn syrup and corn oil), soy (and products such as soy lecithin and soy sauce), and canola and cottonseed oils. According to the Center for Food Safety, it's been estimated that 70 to 75 percent of processed foods on supermarket shelves contain genetically engineered ingredients, but because they aren't labeled as such it's difficult to know what's been genetically altered. However, if you see corn or soy products or canola and cottonseed oils listed among a food's ingredients, chances are the food contains GMOs.

WHAT YOU CAN DO

- Certified organic foods are not allowed to contain genetically engineered ingredients, so buying organic is your best bet if you decide you want to avoid them. You also may see GMO-free labels on products. There aren't any government regulations for use of the label, so it's up to you to decide if you trust it or not, says Rissler.

- The True Food Shopping List, www.truefoodnow.org, lists foods that contain GMOs as well as those that do not.

- Get active. Check out the Campaign to Label Genetically Modified Foods, www.thecampaign.org. The Center for Food Safety, www.centerforfoodsafety.org; Greenpeace, www.greenpeace.org/usa; and the Union of Concerned Scientists, www.ucsusa.org, also have fairly strong anti-GMO programs in which you can become active.

CHOCOLATE

Studies showing that a little good-quality dark chocolate may be good for your health are welcome news for chocolate lovers. Unfortunately, conventional cocoa plant–growing methods aren't so great for the planet or the farmworkers who grow it. Traditionally, cocoa was grown in the shade, but to get higher yields farmers have switched to new varieties that require sun, which is bad news for the animals that relied on cocoa farms for habitat. What's more, some pretty toxic pesticides are used to grow cocoa, and their residues can show up in chocolate. Most of the small farmers who grow cocoa aren't paid fairly, and in some cases, farms use forced child labor (this happens mostly in Western Africa). But all the bad news is no reason to banish chocolate from your diet. Just try being more selective about the chocolate you buy. In fact, by buying chocolate with the labels in the following list, you'll be supporting small farms and sustainable agriculture—some more good reasons for the occasional indulgence.

DECODING THE LABELS

USDA Certified Organic. This label is a guarantee that cocoa was grown without using synthetic fertilizers and pesticides.

Fair Trade Certified. Products with this label are grown by small-scale producers who follow sustainable farming methods, including limited pesticide use. For more information on the Fair Trade Certified label, see pages 9–10. Visit www.transfairusa.org to find Fair Trade Certified brands and stores that sell them. Dagoba Organic Chocolate and Green & Black's are some widely available options.

Rainforest Alliance Certified. Chocolate with this label meets strict standards for worker welfare, farm management, and environmental protection such as reducing pesticide use. Visit www.rainforest-alliance.org to find retailers that sell Rainforest Alliance Certified chocolate or buy online at eChocolates, www.echocolates.com; K Chocolat, www.kchocolat.com; or Birds and Beans, www.birdsandbeans.ca.

POULTRY AND EGGS

The old saying "You are what you eat" also applies to the animals we consume. That's not great news for conventional chickens or the people who eat them. Your average chicken feed contains some not-so-appetizing ingredients such as arsenic and rendered animal by-products. One thing you don't have to worry about is added hormones since it's against USDA regulations to feed them to any bird.

Many of the packaged birds we see in grocery stores were raised indoors on factory farms where thousands of chickens are crowded into small cages filled with the horrible stench of piled-up feces, rarely cleaned from the floors. Disease can spread easily under such confined conditions, so to prevent illness conventional chickens are routinely fed low dosages of antibiotics and arsenic, which also helps to fatten them up as quickly and cheaply as possible.

All the low-dose antibiotics administered aren't changing the fact that many chickens and eggs have salmonella and other bacteria that can make you sick if the food isn't cooked properly. Preemptive antibiotics found in poultry are also causing a rise in drug-resistant bacteria in the humans who eat them, so when people get sick with certain types of illnesses, common antibiotics may not work. Arsenic, a poisonous metal, causes cancer and may contribute to heart disease, diabetes, a decline in mental functioning, and hormone disruption, says the Institute for Agriculture and Trade Policy's David Wallinga, who also points out that these health effects are dose dependent—the higher the exposure level, the higher the risk. Feed containing animal by-products can also be contaminated with dioxins and PCBs, probable carcinogens that accumulate in the fat of animals and get passed up the food chain.

Raising poultry and eggs can be tough on the environment, the animals, and the people who work on factory farms. Chicken waste becomes pollution; manure contaminates rivers and groundwater, and ammonia emissions from it can pollute the air. A lot of grain, water, and fossil fuels are used when raising chicken and eggs, although if they are raised locally at least they don't have to be shipped across the country. Animals are typically raised inhumanely, and workers aren't always treated well.

DECODING THE LABELS

USDA Certified Organic. Chickens are fed 100 percent organic vegetarian feed, and eggs come from hens that eat organic. There are no animal by-products, antibiotics, or arsenic in feed, and irradiation and genetic modification of animals is against regulations. Farms must maintain safe composting standards for animal waste. Chickens need to have access to the outdoors, and farms are inspected to make sure these rules are followed.

Certified Humane Raised and Handled. Animals were raised humanely and not routinely fed antibiotics, although antibiotics can be used to treat sick animals. Humane Farm Animal Care's standards must be met. Visit www.certifiedhumane.org for more information.

Raised Without Antibiotics or No Antibiotics Administered. This label does not apply to eggs. There is no third-party verification to assure that poultry hasn't received any antibiotics.

Free Range or Free Roaming. These claims on eggs are not regulated. For poultry, the government requires daily access to the outdoors for an "undetermined period of each day," which can be as little as five minutes a day—hardly the open air existence the name conjures.

Natural. Minimally processed, no artificial flavoring, coloring, chemical preservatives, or artificial or synthetic ingredients. This label is misleading: these are the minimum standards for *all* industrially produced chickens, and there is no third-party verification controlling this label.

For more information on labeling go to www.greenerchoices.org/eco-labels/eco-home.cfm.

GREEN

- Remove skin from poultry to avoid any fat-soluble toxins such as dioxins or PCBs.

- Buy poultry from companies that say they have stopped using arsenic or that had low levels in the Institute for Agriculture and Trade Policy's report, www.iatp.org/food and health.

- Wash hands, countertops, and cutting boards in hot, soapy water after handling raw poultry. Thoroughly cook eggs and poultry and throw out cracked or dirty eggs. See the USDA's Safe Food Handling Fact Sheet for more suggestions, www.fsis.usda.gov/Fact_Sheets/Basics_for_Handling_Food_Safely/index.asp.

GREENER

- Buy organic whenever possible. Look for poultry with the Certified Humane Raised and Handled label or birds raised without antibiotics when organic is not an option. You can also look for local sources of chicken and eggs, which will likely taste better if they've been raised well, but there are no guarantees without the USDA Certified Organic seal of approval. See "How to Talk to Your Local Farmer" on pages 6–7 for questions to ask when buying locally.

- Ask your local supermarket and butcher to carry more organic poultry and eggs if they don't already have a selection.

GREENEST

- Cut down on or eliminate poultry and egg consumption. According to the USDA guidelines, most of us eat too much meat. If we ate less meat, says Wallinga, we'd have less exposure to persistent pollutants.

- Take action. Go to www.keepantibioticsworking.com to find out what you can do to preserve the effectiveness of antibiotics. See "Food Activism" on page 38 to find other organizations involved in assuring a safe and healthy food supply.

FISH AND SEAFOOD

It's daunting for even the most sophisticated seafood consumers to figure out what healthy and sustainable fish to eat. On the one hand, fish is filled with many beneficial nutrients, especially the omega-3 fatty acids that can reduce the risk of cardiovascular disease. On the other hand, there are countless reports and advisories on the contaminants found in fish—most notably mercury, PCBs, and dioxins. It's not always easy to balance the health benefits of fish against the potential harm caused by toxins. Then there are the sustainability issues, such as the deleterious impact of overfishing as well as fishing methods that sometimes catch and destroy unintended marine life.

Mercury, one of the most common fish pollutants, is released into the air from coal-fired plants and ends up in rivers, lakes, and oceans. It's then transformed by bacteria into methylmercury, a highly toxic compound that can harm the developing nervous systems of fetuses, infants, and young children. There is mounting evidence that it may also contribute to cardiovascular disease. It's still unclear how much mercury causes serious health problems in adults, but it's not a bad idea to limit consumption while this issue is being sorted out. In general, bigger predatory fish have higher mercury levels and other toxins because they are high up on the food chain and have eaten more contaminated fish than their smaller counterparts. Mercury accumulates in the muscle tissue of fish, so there is no way of escaping it in contaminated fish. The FDA and EPA recommend that women who are pregnant, likely to become pregnant, or nursing, and young children should not eat shark, swordfish, tilefish, and king mackerel. Albacore tuna (white flesh) should be limited to no more than 6 ounces per week and less for smaller children. (Some environmental groups think even that limit is too high). Up to 12 ounces of fish with lower mercury levels such as shrimp, salmon, pollock, and catfish can be eaten each week for these "higher risk" groups, according to the agencies.

The image of farm-raised salmon has taken a huge hit thanks to the discovery that fatty tissue and skin can contain PCBs and dioxins, which aside from being probable carcinogens, have been proven to damage developing nervous systems and impair learning. Farm-raised salmon has more fat than wild salmon, and their feed has high levels of PCBs and dioxins. It's important to note that PCBs, dioxins, and some pesticides are also present in wild fish, especially bottom-dwellers like striped bass, blue fish, American eel, and others, but levels tend to be lower than those of farmed salmon.

Fish farms can take the pressure off of dwindling fish supplies, but they are not without their costs to public health and the environment. Farmed fish can escape pens and wreak havoc on wild fish by passing on disease and competing with them for food. Fish feed can contain ground-up wild fish, polluted fish oils, and other chemicals that can cause toxic chemicals to accumulate in fish, as is the case with salmon. It's unclear whether colorants used to make farm-raised fish look like their wild counterparts are harmful to health. That said, there are plenty of farm-fish choices that have a low impact on the environment, such as catfish, U.S. tilapia, U.S. shrimp, mussels, and bay scallops.

How exactly do you pick out healthy and sustainable fish to eat? The best way to navigate the fish market is to use one of the several fish lists designed by environmental organizations published with the express purpose of helping consumers make wise decisions. A number of organizations compile these lists, and each one is a little different depending upon whether the primary concern of the organization is health or sustainability. The Fish List is a joint effort by three of these groups—Environmental Defense,

Blue Ocean Institute, and Monterey Bay Aquarium Seafood Watch (each of which has its own fish list)—to consolidate their recommendations. You can find it at www.thefishlist.org along with some helpful health information. You might also try Environmental Defense's Pocket Seafood Selector, which states very clearly both health and sustainability issues. The organization's website, www.oceansalive.org, also offers a separate list of how many servings per month women, men, and children can eat of certain fish along with fish buying tips.

DECODING THE LABELS

Organic. There is not an official USDA standard for organic seafood certification so this is not a meaningful label. The USDA has discussed possible standards for fish and seafood but as of press time there were no proposals. Some fish and seafood do come with an organic certification from overseas organizations, but they typically rely on livestock guidelines, which aren't necessarily the safest rules for fish.

Marine Stewardship Council. This organization certifies fisheries that are well managed and promote sustainable fishing practices. The guidelines are vague, and it's also important to remember that the label doesn't take into account toxic chemicals in fish.

For more information on labeling go to www.greenerchoices.org/eco-labels/eco-home.cfm.

GREEN

• When eating canned tuna, buy chunk light—not albacore tuna, which has about three times the mercury as light tuna. This is because albacore are larger and live longer than the skipjack species that often make up canned chunk light tuna, says David McBride, a toxicologist at the Washington State Department of Health. However, Environmental Defense says its best to limit tuna because some light tuna may have yellowfin tuna, which is also high in mercury. Use the Environmental Working Group's Tuna Calculator, www.ewg.org/tunacalculator, to see how much canned tuna you can safely eat each week based on the FDA's guidelines. All you have to do is enter your gender and your weight.

• The way you cook fish can reduce the levels of PCBs, dioxins, and pesticides that accumulate in fatty tissue. Follow these recommendations from Environmental Defense: remove skin before cooking, let the fat drain away when cooking, and avoid fish drippings. Grilling, broiling, or poaching allows the fat to drain away. Limit frying, which seals in chemical pollutants that might be in a fish's fat. Remove the skin and fillet fish before you smoke it. This doesn't work for methylmercury, which is found in the muscle tissue, not the fat of fish steaks and fillets. The only way to reduce mercury exposure is to eat less contaminated fish.

GREENER

• Find a reliable fish source that you can trust. Bring a fish advisory card with you when you shop and ask lots of questions. See pages 20–21 for different types of fish lists. You should be able to find out whether a fish is farmed or wild caught, where it comes from, and whether it is definitely the kind of fish advertised. A knowledgeable fishmonger should be able to help you figure out how to make fish substitutions.

• Choose wild and canned Alaskan salmon over farm-raised salmon.

• Check the EPA's local fish advisories when eating sport fish. Go to "Where You Live," www.epa.gov/waterscience/fish/states.htm, and click on the map or type in your ZIP code.

GREENEST

• Get active. Seafood Choices Alliances, www.seafoodchoices.com, and Monterey Bay Aquarium, www.seafoodwatch.com, offer ideas on how to get involved in promoting a healthier and more sustainable fish supply.

• Urge your elected officials to support legislation aimed at reducing mercury in the environment. If we get rid of the fish toxicants, then we don't have to worry about eating less fish.

• If you are worried about mercury exposure (especially if you are considering getting pregnant) you can measure how much mercury you've been exposed to with a hair-sampling kit from www.sierraclub.org or www.greenpeaceusa.org. These kits are not as reliable at measuring current exposure as are blood tests administered by a physician. The good news is that avoiding fish with high mercury levels can make a difference in a relatively short period of time because the half life of methylmercury is only about 60 to 90 days. If you are planning a pregnancy, David McBride from the Washington State Department of Health recommends reducing consumption of fish with higher levels of mercury for six to twelve months beforehand.

MEAT AND DAIRY

Like poultry, most cows, sheep, and pigs are raised in dirty, crowded conditions on factory farms also known as "concentrated animal feeding operations" (CAFOs). Their feed usually contains antibiotics and other unappetizing additives, which can show up in the meat we eat. As with chickens, the USDA prohibits the use of hormones when raising hogs, so at least your pork won't have added hormones. Not so for cattle and sheep. According to the Center for Food Safety, the beef industry pumps growth hormones into more than 80 percent of beef cattle raised in the United States each year to boost growth rates and increase body mass. Six hormones are approved for use, and two in particular, estradiol and zeranol, are likely to have negative human health effects, including cancer and impacts on child development, according to the Center for Food Safety.

When it comes to hormones in dairy products, recombinant growth hormone (rBGH), also known as recombinant bovine somatotropin (rBST), used to increase production in dairy cows, is a concern for both the health of the cows and the humans who consume dairy products. The hormone is banned for use in Canada and Europe. Cows on rBGH are more susceptible to mastitis. As a result, more antibiotics are needed to fight the infection. According to the Center for Food Safety, cows given rBGH produce milk containing insulin growth factor-1 (IGF-1). What's concerning is that numerous studies show that IGF-1 is linked to breast, prostate, and colon cancers. Despite claims that a product is antibiotic or hormone free, the organic label is the only real guarantee that rBGH wasn't administered. Joseph Mendelson, legal director of the Center for Food Safety, however, thinks that as the issue heats up, dairy farmers will continue to voluntarily abandon their use of rBGH.

Bovine spongiform encephalopathy (BSE), also known as mad cow disease, has become a concern ever since it was discovered in a cow in the United States. Humans who eat contaminated meat are at risk of contracting the brain-degenerative and fatal variant Creutzfeld-Jacob disease (vCJD). Mad cow is primarily spread by feeding infected nervous system tissue to other animals. The Center for Food Safety says that the tissue from infected cows' central nervous system is the most infectious part of the cow and may be found in hot dogs, taco fillings, bologna, and other products containing gelatin and ground or chopped meat. Organic is safer, says Mendelson, because there are barriers in the feeding practices that lessen the risk.

If you eat beef, it's a good idea to look for meat from grass-fed cattle. Most cows are fed grain (primarily corn) rather than the grass their bodies were designed to eat. This fattens them up more quickly, but it also makes them sick and more in need of antibiotics—the overuse of which can contribute to antibiotic resistance in humans. There are other benefits as well. "Greener

Pastures: How Grass-fed Beef and Milk Contribute to Healthy Eating," a 2006 report from the Union of Concerned Scientists, analyzed many studies and determined that beef and milk from animals raised entirely on pasture have higher levels of beneficial fats. Milk from grass-fed animals contains more of the omega-3 fatty acid alpha-linolenic acid (ALA), which scientists have demonstrated reduces the risk of heart disease, according to the report. It also found that beef and milk from grass-fed cattle are higher in conjugated linoleic acid (CLA), a fatty acid shown in animal studies to protect against cancer. The report stated that raising cattle on grass can reduce water pollution, one of the industry's several major environmental impacts.

According to a 2006 United Nations Food and Agriculture Organization report titled "Livestock's Long Shadow—Environmental Issues and Options," livestock are one of the most significant contributors to today's most serious environmental problems, such as climate change and land and water degradation. Cattle rearing, for example, produces large amounts of carbon dioxide, nitrous oxide, and methane, all greenhouse gases that contribute to climate change; and ammonia emissions are significant contributors to acid rain. Animal wastes, antibiotics, hormones, and the pesticides and fertilizers used on feed crops contribute to water pollution. Deforestation is another big problem, especially in Latin America where some 70 percent of former forests in the Amazon have been turned over to grazing. The authors of the report conclude that measures need to be taken to lessen the effect of livestock on the environment, especially because people are eating more meat and dairy products than ever and consumption is expected to double by 2050.

At press time, there were a couple of crucial issues concerning meat that remained undecided. The FDA is considering allowing food from cloned livestock into the food supply. The jury is still out on whether this will happen and if cloned milk and meat will be labeled so consumers can choose for themselves whether they feel safe eating it. Cloning will not be allowed for organic milk or meat, says Mendelson. You can also ask your butcher and supermarket if the meat and dairy they are selling comes from cloned animals and express your opinion about whether or not you want to buy products from cloned animals.

Another concern is food irradiation (exposing foods to high doses of radiation to kill bacteria), which currently isn't used very much, and when it is, the food label must say so. The FDA is now considering a change that would loosen the labeling standards and allow packaging to state that meat is "pasteurized" rather than "irradiated," which could be confusing to consumers. The Center for Food Safety is opposed to irradiation for many reasons, saying it creates fundamental changes to the food, affects its nutritional properties, and creates a false sense of freshness. Organic is your best bet to ensure that meat is not irradiated. If labeling changes do occur, be wary of labels that state the meat is pasteurized if you are trying to avoid irradiated food.

DECODING THE LABELS

USDA Certified Organic. Synthetic pesticides, fertilizers, antibiotics, hormones, genetic engineering, irradiation, and sewer sludge are prohibited. Animals must eat 100 percent organic feed, which isn't allowed to contain animal by-products, and they must have access to the outdoors. Third-party certifiers verify that farms are following the USDA's guidelines.

No Antibiotics Administered. Animals were raised without antibiotics, but there isn't an independent organization certifying this claim.

Certified Humane Raised and Handled. Animals raised for dairy and beef are treated in a humane manner without the use of growth hormones or antibiotics in feed. The farms are inspected. For more information visit the Humane Farm Animal Care's website at www.certifiedhumane.org.

Demeter Certified Biodynamic. This certification prohibits synthetic pesticides and fertilizers, animal by-products, and genetic engineering. Farms must adhere to biodynamic principles such as applying a holistic approach to farm management. For more information visit www.demeter-usa.org.

Free Roaming or Free Range. There is no standard definition of this term for beef, so it doesn't mean anything on its own.

Grass-fed. If you see the label along with the USDA Process Verified Program seal, then it's a guarantee that ruminant animals were fed 100 percent grass (forage) for their entire lives, with the exception of milk consumed before weaning. Animals aren't fed grain or grain by-products and have continuous access to pasture during the growing season. Farms are audited to make sure the guidelines are met. The label isn't a guarantee that antibiotics and synthetic growth hormones weren't used.

If you see the label along with the American Grassfed Association's seal, then it means that animals were fed a 100 percent grass (forage) diet and had access to pasture all year round. Antibiotics and synthetic growth hormones are prohibited. Farms are inspected to verify that standards are being met.

If you see the grass-fed label without the USDA seal or American Grassfed Association's logo, then claims weren't verified by a third party.

Hormone Free. All pork is free of added hormones regardless of whether it is labeled as such. It does imply that there aren't any added hormones in beef, but there isn't an independent organization verifying this. There is no government definition for dairy products.

Natural. Meat was minimally processed and doesn't contain artificial flavoring and other additives. There isn't a verification system in place to back up this claim. There is no government definition of this for dairy.

GREEN

- Minimize exposure to fat, which contains toxic chemicals such as dioxins. Dioxins are unintentional by-products of industrial activities that are released into the air and considered a human carcinogen by the World Health Organization. They settle on grasslands where grazing cows ingest them, according to the Institute for Agriculture and Trade Policy, which also warns that fetuses are at greatest risk from exposure to dioxins, which cross the placenta during pregnancy and can be toxic to growing, developing brains. Choose meats that are lean and cut off any additional fat, suggests the Institute for Agriculture and

Trade Policy, and use lower-fat cooking methods including broiling, grilling, roasting, or pressure cooking because cooking and preparation methods can reduce dioxin levels by up to half. Your cooking method can also impact climate change. According to the Sierra Club, barbequing on a gas grill emits half as much carbon dioxide as using charcoal briquettes.

• Buy low-fat milk and dairy products to avoid possible toxins that accumulate in fat (however, children under two need full-fat dairy for brain development).

• Wash hands, countertops, and cutting boards in hot soapy water after handling raw meat.

• Thoroughly cook meat. See the USDA's Safe Food Handling Fact Sheet for more suggestions, www.fsis.usda.gov/Fact_Sheets/Basics_for_Handling_Food_Safely/index.asp.

GREENER

• Buy organic when possible—it's your best bet that animals were raised without antibiotics, hormones, genetic engineering, irradiation, and other harmful practices, although it's no guarantee that animals were fed grass. Organic meat is more expensive than conventional meat and can be hard to find. Right now demand outstrips supply, but hopefully prices will decline as supply catches up. One way to handle the price differential is to buy better quality meat, but less of it. Organic dairy is easier to find, but the Cornucopia Institute says all organic dairy is not created equally and some of it is produced on factory farms that skirt organic regulations. See the institute's Dairy Report, which explains the issues and rates dairy producers around the country, at www.cornucopia.org.

• Choose grass-fed when possible. Grass-fed beef is leaner, so you may need to cook it differently. It also tastes different from corn-fed meat so it might take a few tries before you get used to it. The American Grassfed Association has a list of producers on its website, www.americangrassfed.org.

• Buy local meat and dairy. If you can't find local meat, then try to purchase domestic meat to avoid supporting the deforestation of South American rain forests.

• Eat less meat and dairy. There are many painless ways to achieve this: make one day a week completely meatless; only eat meat for one meal per day; limit the amount of meat on your plate and fill up on more vegetables and grains. Be creative!

• Ask your supermarket to carry more organic and grass-fed meat and dairy products.

● GREENEST

• Eliminate meat entirely from your diet. If you'd like to take it a step further, try going vegan and avoid animal products altogether. Make sure you learn about how to replace essential vitamins and minerals in your diet.

• Get active. See page 38.

FOOD SOURCING ON THE NET

The Internet is a great tool for finding local and sustainable foods. Check out the following websites:

- **Eat Well Guide,** www.eatwellguide.org: This is a free online directory of sustainably raised meat, poultry, dairy, and eggs from farms, stores, restaurants, hotels, and online. Just enter your ZIP code to find local products.
- **Local Harvest,** www.localharvest.org: Use the website to help you find farmers' markets, family farms, and other sources of sustainably grown food in your area.
- **GreenPeople,** www.greenpeople.org: This directory of eco-friendly products includes several food sources.

FOOD PREPARATION AND STORAGE

While it's pretty obvious that what you eat and drink can impact your health and that of the planet, the way you prepare, serve, store, and transport your food are also worth considering. Sustainable options such as bamboo cutting boards and bowls are widely available as a renewable alternative to wood. Recycled glass is another eco-friendly option you're likely to encounter. A customer favorite on green-living retailer Gaiam, www.gaiam.com, is a countertop bag dryer that makes it easy to reuse plastic bags—a great way to cut down on Ziploc use and a definite plus for the planet!

There is a lot of confusion about the safety of Teflon. The

bottom line is that cooking with nonstick-coated pans may release toxic gases if the pans reach too high a temperature. DuPont, Teflon's manufacturer, says the pans are safe with normal use. An Environmental Working Group study found that preheating cookware coated with Teflon and other nonstick surfaces can exceed safe temperatures, which causes the coating to break apart and emit toxic particles and gases that have been linked with bird deaths and human illnesses. In lab tests *Consumer Reports* found very little perflourooctanoic acid (PFOA) in the air when nonstick pans were heated below the manufacturer's recommendation of 500 degrees. That's reassuring; however, most of us don't know how hot our pans are getting. In 2005, an EPA advisory panel recommended that PFOA, also known as C8, a chemical used to make Teflon, be named a likely human carcinogen. The following year the EPA signed a voluntary agreement with DuPont and other companies to reduce the chemical's use by 95 percent by 2010 and to aim for total elimination by 2015.

Plastic containers are a popular way to store food. It is well known that they are an eco-nightmare because most of them are made from petroleum, a nonrenewable resource. Hazardous gases are emitted in their production. Many containers ultimately end up clogging landfills. What isn't usually publicized is that storing food and beverages in some plastic containers can potentially harm human health. You can differentiate plastic by looking at the recycling code number that appears inside a triangle at the bottom of many containers. Polycarbonate, code 7; polyvinyl chloride (PVC), code 3; and styrene, code 6, have all been shown to leach toxic chemicals that can contaminate food. This doesn't mean

PLASTICS TO AVOID

Polycarbonate is most commonly used for five-gallon water bottles, "sport" water bottles, and in white linings of canned foods. It can leach bisphenol-A (BPA), a known endocrine disruptor (see page 86).

PVC has added "plasticizers" to make it soft and flexible. PVC cling wrap, for example, contains diethychydroxylanine (DEHA), which can leach into oily foods when heated. According to Schuler, this substance can cause liver, kidney, and spleen problems, as well as negatively affect bone formation and body weight. It's also a possible human carcinogen.

Polystyrene, used in Styrofoam, can leach styrene, especially when in contact with acidic and hot foods. Animal and worker studies have shown styrene is toxic to the brain and nervous system.

that other plastics are entirely safe; they just haven't been studied as much, says Kathleen Schuler at the Institute for Agriculture and Trade Policy. For now, stick with those that are considered safest for food storage: polyethylene terephthalate (PETE), code 1; high-density polyethylene (HDPE), code 2; low-density polyethylene (LDPE), code 4; and polypropylene (PP), code 5. For those not labeled, call the manufacturer or avoid them altogether.

● GREEN

- Don't microwave food in plastic because chemicals are more likely to leach out when they are heated. Use glass or lead-free ceramic containers instead. "Microwaveable plastic" doesn't guarantee that chemicals won't leach, says Schuler. Use wax paper or a plate to cover foods in the microwave instead of plastic, and if you must use plastic wrap, make sure it doesn't touch the food. Let foods cool before storing them in plastic containers.

• Choose plastic wrap made from polyethylene rather than PVC. If the box is not labeled, call the manufacturer.

• Take good care of plastic items by not washing them with harsh chemicals, and dispose of scratched and worn containers. Research has shown that older, scratched polycarbonate bottles will leach more, says Schuler.

• Dispose of any Teflon-coated pans that are peeling, cracked, or otherwise showing signs of age. Don't preheat empty Teflon pans. The Environmental Working Group recommends that bird owners stop using them since the gases can poison birds. It's also a good idea to use ventilation when cooking with Teflon pans.

● GREENER

• Try not to buy brands of canned food lined with white plastic coatings. At the moment, the best way to figure this out is by trial and error.

• Avoid plastic when possible. Use lead-free glass or ceramics to store leftovers and wax paper to wrap sandwiches. Recycled aluminum foil is becoming available, but it's more expensive than conventional.

• Ask your local store to start using bio-based plastic containers made from starches such as corn for prepared foods and to sell bio-based disposable utensils and cups.

• Use alternatives to Teflon, whenever possible. Cast iron and enameled cast iron are two great nonstick alternatives. Stainless steel is another healthy alternative, but some foods such as eggs may stick. *Cook's Illustrated,* www.cooksillustrated.com, and *Consumer Reports,* www.consumerreports.org, both have ratings on cookware.

• Chemicals in the Teflon family can be present in food packaging such as microwaveable popcorn bags, according to Jane Houlihan at the Environmental Working Group. She suggests using plain brown bags instead for cooking popcorn.

• Use stainless steel or aluminum bottles to transport beverages instead of reusable or disposable plastic bottles. Klean Kanteen, www.kleankanteen.com, offers reusable stainless steel bottles, and you can buy lined aluminum from SIGG, www.mysigg.com.

● GREENEST

• For plastic-wrapped deli foods, slice off a thin layer where the food came into contact with the plastic, suggests Schuler. For more information on using plastics safely see the Smart Plastics Guide at www.healthobservatory.org.

• Bring your own refillable containers when you purchase

take-out food or if you are a member of a food co-op with the option to buy products like dish soap in bulk.

• If cost is not an issue, then banish Teflon-coated pans from your kitchen just to be on the safe side.

THE ETERNAL DILEMMA: PAPER OR PLASTIC?

In a perfect world, the answer is neither, but for those times when bringing your own canvas bag is just not an option, the not-so-short answer is that it all depends on the circumstances. If the bag is made from post-consumer recycled fiber, then you can't go wrong using paper, says Allen Hershkowitz, director of the Natural Resources Defense Council's National Solid Waste Project. (See if the bag is labeled as such or ask at the store.) You should also choose paper if you are in a location where there is a risk that the plastic might end up in a large water body like an ocean, river, or lake. Plastic waste is a huge threat to aquatic species, which can ingest it or get entangled in bags. Paper is biodegradable and doesn't pose the same risk.

If the paper is not made from post-consumer recycled fiber, but instead is made from timber and you aren't in a location that risks entanglement or digestion by a water animal or bird, then you are better off using plastic, according to Hershkowitz. Plastic is also a good choice if you can reuse it and your paper option isn't recycled. What should you do with them when you're done? Recycle paper. If you don't reuse plastic bags, then find out if they can be recycled in your area, or better yet, see if you can get a recycling program started if there isn't already one established nearby. See Chapter 12 for more ideas on recycling.

Food Activism

If you want to take an active role in shaping food supply issues, then visit the websites of these organizations regularly to stay up-to-date, connect with like-minded people, and find out how you can help influence policy decisions:

Center for Food Safety, www.centerforfoodsafety.org, aims to protect human health and the environment by promoting organic and other forms of sustainable agriculture. You can sign up for "Action Alerts" or regularly check the website.

Organic Consumers Association, www.organicconsumers.org, has a comprehensive website that provides background information on many issues; offers links to sources of organic, local, and sustainable products; and is a great source of current news and campaigns to promote change. Sign up for the biweekly *Organic Bytes* newsletter, which is filled with ideas for activism.

Slow Food Movement USA, www.slowfoodusa.org, supports and celebrates the food traditions of North America. It considers heirloom varieties of fruits and vegetables, Cajun spices, handcrafted wine and beer, farmhouse cheese, and other artisanal foods part of our cultural identity. The movement was born in Italy as a reaction to the opening of McDonald's in Piazza di Spagna in Rome in 1986 and aims to counteract the global industrialization of food.

Sustainable Table, www.sustainabletable.org, is a website created by the nonprofit organization GRACE to help consumers understand the problems with our food supply and offer viable solutions and alternatives. It's a great place to go to find more information and for ways to get active.

Union of Concerned Scientists, http://ucsaction.org, offers a free email newsletter called FEED that will keep you informed about food production and safety issues and tell you how you can help enact change. Go to the website to subscribe.

2 BEVERAGES

These days, you can find countless options for local, organic, and sustainable food sources. In fact, organic food has been the fastest growing segment of the food industry for at least a decade because of consumer concerns about personal health and the environment. But let's not forget that what we drink can also have an enormous impact on our health and that of the planet. It's important to be aware that many of our beverages originate on farms—beer is made mostly from barley and wine is composed of grapes, for example.

Organic and sustainable drinks are coming into their own thanks to heightening awareness and an expanding array of products. Take coffee: there's already considerable choice for those looking for alternatives to conventionally grown coffee. Organic coffee is one of the fastest growing segments of the organic beverage market, according to the Organic Trade Association. This is a boon for coffee farmers as well as the other species of plants and animals that coexist on plantations where coffee is sustainably grown.

You'll also find a wide selection of organic juices, made from organic fruits and vegetables, at health food stores, Whole Foods, and some grocery stores. There is some confusion about whether organic juices are unpasteurized, but about 98 percent of the juice (organic or otherwise) sold in the United States is pasteurized, according to the Centers for Disease Control and Prevention (CDC), which means it's heated to high temperatures for a short time to kill pathogens (germs) such as E. coli 0157:H7, salmonella, and cryptosporidium. Prepackaged, untreated juice has a warning label, and the CDC recommends that young children, the elderly, or people with weakened immune systems avoid it. Keep in mind that while juice contains beneficial nutrients, it's not a replacement for eating fruit, which has fiber. Experts point out that drinking an excessive amount of any kind of juice or soda adds empty calories to our diets.

Of course, the beverage most essential to good health is safe, clean drinking water. In Americans' quest for well-being and convenience, sales of bottled water have skyrocketed. However, be warned that bottled water is not necessarily any better in terms of flavor or safety than what comes out of your tap, especially if you live in a place with good-quality municipal water. We reach for bottled water in part because we associate it with images of unspoiled nature—cool springs and refreshing waterfalls—but in fact, the production and disposal of millions and millions of plastic bottles each year, not to mention transporting that water, takes a tremendous toll on the environment.

WATER

The quality of your tap water depends on where you live. The list of potential water contaminants is long. Some are naturally occurring, such as arsenic. Others are man-made: agricultural pollutants, such as pesticides and factory-farm waste; sprawl and urban pollutants that run off roads or pesticide-laden lawns; industrial pollutants; and even by-products of the chemicals used to treat drinking water to make it safe. The Environmental Protection Agency (EPA) regulates several contaminants and limits how much of certain compounds can be in drinking water. However, the Environmental Working Group points out that a considerable number of chemicals are still unregulated and no safety standards have been established for their presence in drinking water.

Here's a small sampling of common tap-water contaminants as well as information on which kinds of filters will remove them. For more information on filters see page 47.

Arsenic is naturally occurring or enters the water supply through runoff from orchards or industrial waste and may result in skin damage, problems with circulatory systems, and increased risk of getting cancer, according to the EPA. Charcoal filters, reverse osmosis filtration systems, and distillers can all remove arsenic.

Atrazine enters the water supply through runoff from herbicide used on row crops. It may affect the cardiovascular system or cause reproductive problems, according to the EPA. Atrazine can be removed with charcoal filters.

By-products of the water disinfection process, such as **haloacetic acids** and total **trihalomethanes**, can cause increased risk of cancer, according to the EPA. Charcoal filters can remove these types of contaminants.

Lead can enter water from corrosion of pipes. Lead exposure can result in delays in physical or mental development in children. Lead can be removed with a simple carbon filter as well as reverse osmosis and distillation.

Pathogens, such as **cryptosporidium**, which comes from human and animal fecal waste, can cause gastrointestinal illness. People with compromised immune systems need to be particularly careful. Carbon filters and reverse osmosis can remove pathogens.

Perchlorate is the primary ingredient of rocket fuel. The Environmental Working Group reports that it's in the water of 26 million Americans, primarily in Texas, California, Minnesota, and Pennsylvania. At press time, its presence in water is not regulated by the EPA, but this is under consideration so it may change. Reverse osmosis filters out perchlorate.

For more information on water contaminants

- Visit the EPA's Safewater website, www.epa.gov/safewater, and click on "List of Contaminants."
- Access the Environmental Working Group's National Tap Water Quality Database at www.ewg.org/tapwater. It gives extensive information on contaminants that are regulated by the EPA as well as on those that are not. It also gives good regional information.
- Read the "What's on Tap" report by the Natural Resources Defense Council (NRDC). Available on the NRDC website, www.nrdc.org, the report has lots of useful information including data and grades for specific cities.

Although it is important to the health of you and your family to be aware of possible water contaminants, it shouldn't scare you away from drinking tap water. The important thing is to know your water source. Many experts concur that most tap water is safe and that it's preferable to bottled water. Environmental Defense's president Fred Krupp says tap water is best as long as it is clean because it saves money and isn't transported long distances. He also points out that municipal water supplies are oftentimes cleaner than bottled water.

Researchers at the NRDC agree. After a four-year intensive study of the bottled-water industry they concluded that there is no assurance that bottled water is any cleaner or safer than tap water. In fact, approximately 25 percent or more of bottled water simply comes from the tap; sometimes it's further treated, sometimes it's not. Buyers should beware when it comes to bottled water, says the Environmental Working Group's vice president for research Jane Houlihan, who points out that the safety standards for bottled water aren't any more stringent than those for tap water. She adds that some bottles can leach chemicals into the water. Polycarbonate plastics, for example, can leach bisphenol-A (BPA), a potent hormone-disrupting chemical, into bottled water. Indeed, eight of the ten 5-gallon polycarbonate jugs that *Consumer Reports* tested in 2000 left residues of BPA in the water.

Bottled water also negatively impacts the environment. Bottles are made from fossil fuels. According to Earth Policy Institute, making bottles to meet Americans' demand for bottled water requires more than 1.5 million barrels of oil annually—that's enough to fuel about 100,000 cars for one year! In addition, transporting the water requires a tremendous amount of energy and many bottles end up in landfills. Being aware of the realities of bottled water can make that prettily packaged and expensive product shipped from halfway around the world seem a lot less refreshing and glamorous.

GREEN

- Minimize your consumption of bottled water. It's a good way to save money since bottled water can cost up to 10,000 times more than tap water—selling for as much as $2.50 per liter ($10 per gallon), it costs more than gasoline, according to the Earth Policy Institute. If you do buy bottled water, Houlihan suggests looking for information about how that water was treated and where it came from. If you frequently buy the same kind of water call the company and ask for results from their water-quality report.

GREENER

- Always drink tap water at home if you have access to clean municipal sources. Get your water tested and install an appropriate filter if necessary (see pages 47–49). See the next page for tips on making sure your well water is safe to drink.

GREENEST

- Eliminate all bottled water if you have access to a healthy supply from your tap. Purchase and carry a reusable bottle filled with tap water.

- Lobby to have a filtration system installed in your office.

- Get active. Sign up for Clean Water Action's email activist list at www.cleanwateraction.org. Visit the websites of the NRDC, www.nrdc.org; the Environmental Working Group, www.ewg.org; the Sierra Club, www.sierraclub.org; and the Clean Water Network, www.cleanwaternetwork.org for updates and opportunities for taking action to help your water supply.

Drink Clean: Finding the Best Filter

There are different types of water filters, and they don't all reduce the same contaminants. The first step in determining the best filter for your home is figuring out what's in your tap water. Here's how:

SAFE WELL WATER

About 15 percent of Americans rely on their own private drinking water, according to the EPA. While the EPA regulates public water, private well water is not subject to its standards, although some state and local government laws may apply. Ultimately, it's up to you to make sure your well is providing safe drinking water. The EPA's Safewater website has an extensive section on well water that provides a wealth of information on different types of drinking-water wells, guidelines for proper installation, potential health risks, and many other topics. Visit www.epa.gov/safewater and click on "Private Wells." The site also provides information about how often you should have your well water tested (which is annually if not more often depending upon your circumstances), suggestions for which labs to use, and other useful testing information. Water contamination can vary depending upon where you live, so discovering your local issues can help you figure out what to look out for in your own supply.

• Each year by July 1 you should receive a Drinking Water Quality Report or Consumer Confidence Report (CCR) in the mail from your water supplier that will tell you where your water comes from and what's in it. You can also find it online by visiting the EPA's website, www.epa.gov/safewater, and clicking on "Local Drinking Water Quality." Read this report carefully and read it all the way to the end, suggests Houlihan of the Environmental Working Group, who notes that the report leads with the good news so you need to dig a little further to really find out what's going on. The NRDC wrote a guide to reading this report called "Making Sense of Your Right to Know Reports," which is available at www.safe-drinking-water.org.

• You can also get your water tested. Lead, for example, can leach from your pipes into your water. You can buy a simple, reliable test online or at your local hardware store. Some cities and towns provide free lead-testing kits. Go to your state or municipal government website to find out if this is available in your area.

Once you know what's polluting your water it's a matter of choosing a filter that will get rid of those particular contaminants. There's a whole range of styles available, from the commonplace carafe, which is good for small amounts of drinking water but can be slow and prone to clogging, to filters you can mount on your faucet, countertop, or under your sink. There are even whole-house models. Buy water filters that are certified by NSF International, an independent nonprofit that certifies food- and water-related products; you can look for the NSF mark on a product, or you can visit www.nsf.org/consumer (click on "Search for NSF-Certified Products" and then on "Drinking Water Treatment Units") and search by manufacturer or by the type of contaminant you are trying to reduce.

Determining which filter to buy can certainly be confusing if you are trying to get rid of more than one contaminant, and the NSF can be a valuable resource for helping you sort out which product will work best for you. Make sure you change your filter as recommended by its manufacturer. Good maintenance is crucial to the performance of your filtration system no matter how simple or complicated it is.

Here's the lowdown on water filters:

Carbon filters are an inexpensive and common solution for many water contaminants. They are usually found in pitchers and some faucet-mounted models. Carbon attracts and absorbs many impurities such as lead, disinfection by-products, parasites, some pesticides, radon, and volatile organic chemicals, according to the NRDC. These models don't work for everything, so check the label before buying to make sure it removes what you need it to.

Distillers boil water and recondense the purified steam. According to the NRDC, they get rid of heavy metals, arsenic, barium, fluoride, selenium, and sodium.

Reverse osmosis systems get rid of most contaminants, but they can be expensive and they waste a substantial amount of water. They're sometimes used with a carbon-based filter.

For more information on specific filters see *Consumer Reports'* Greener Choices website, www.greenerchoices.org, for ratings.

Healthwatch: Fluoridated Water

The Centers for Disease Control and Prevention (CDC) calls the fluoridation of drinking water to prevent dental decay one of the great public health achievements of the twentieth century. Not everyone agrees with that statement. The subject of adding fluoride to the public water supply is controversial, especially because we are also exposed to it elsewhere, including in food, beverages, and toothpaste, so some people may be ingesting too much of it. Recent studies suggest that exposure to fluoride may cause various health problems, but so far it's not enough to convince the government to change direction. In 2006, the National Research Council recommended that the EPA reduce the amount of fluoride added to municipal supplies because excessive fluoride exposure can damage teeth in children, weaken bones, and may increase the risk of fractures. Fluoride may also negatively affect the endocrine system and the brain. A controversial 2006 Harvard University study reported that boys exposed to fluoridated water had a higher rate of a type of bone cancer called osteosarcoma, although more studies are needed to support this. The jury is still out on whether the addition of fluoride to public water is a good or bad thing, but it's definitely an issue to watch.

There isn't a lot you can do if fluoride is added to your municipal water supply. It's a good idea to get your family dentist's take on the issue, but here are a few suggestions to minimize your and your family's exposure:

- The American Dental Association has issued an interim warning for infants' drinking formula. It suggests that parents feed infants ready-to-feed formula or use water that has no or low levels of fluoride, such as water that is labeled purified, demineralized, deionized, distilled, or reverse osmosis–filtered water.

- Avoid bottled water with added fluoride in it if you are concerned about fluoride.

- If you're worried about fluoride, consider filtering with a reverse osmosis system or distillation to reduce exposure.

- Get active. Visit the Fluoride Action Network, www.fluoride alert.org.

COFFEE AND TEA

A morning cup of coffee or tea is an important daily ritual for many Americans. But what we really need to wake up to is the fact that much of the coffee and tea we drink comes from developing countries where struggling farmers don't get paid fair prices for their labor and product. These farmers are also exposed to poor working conditions including high levels of synthetic pesticides and fertilizers. The good news is it is increasingly possible to purchase great-tasting fair trade and organic coffee and tea.

Traditionally, coffee was grown under the shade of tree canopies, which provided habitat for migratory birds, insects, and other natural inhabitants. These coffee plantation methods were safer for farmers and the environment because they required fewer synthetic pesticides and fertilizers. In an effort to get higher coffee yields, however, traditional coffee-growing methods have been abandoned in many cases and trees are being cut down so coffee can be grown in the sun. As a result, more synthetic chemicals are needed to control pests and promote growth, and the habitat for a number of plant and animal species is disappearing.

Growing tea also has numerous environmental impacts such as soil erosion and degradation, the conversion of forest habitat into tea farms, and the use of harsh pesticides and other synthetic chemicals.

DECODING THE LABELS

USDA Certified Organic. Coffee and tea labeled organic is grown without synthetic pesticides and other prohibited substances. Decaffeinated organic coffee must go through a certified organic decaffeination process that maintains the organic integrity of the beans, according to the Organic Trade Association, which says the Swiss Water process, which uses only water to remove caffeine, is most commonly used. The USDA Certified Organic label means that at least 95 percent of the ingredients are organic.

Bird Friendly. This label was created by the Smithsonian Migratory Bird Center to assure that coffee is grown using strict shade management practices and other sustainable practices. The label appears only on products that are certified organic. Looking for this label is one way for consumers to move beyond organic and support both synthetic chemical–free coffee production as well as shade-grown methods. Visit the Smithsonian National Zoological Park website, http://nationalzoo.si.edu, and do a keyword search for "bird friendly" for more information and for local sources of bird friendly coffee.

Fair Trade Certified. This label guarantees that strict economic, social, and environmental criteria have been met. Farmers and farmworkers get a fair price for their products and receive other economic support such as access to credit. Products with the label are grown by small-scale producers who follow sustainable farming methods such as limited pesticide use. Approximately 85 percent of all Fair Trade Certified coffee sold in the United States is also certified organic, according to the Organic Trade Association. For more information, visit TransFair USA at www.transfairusa.org.

Rainforest Alliance Certified. The label certifies that coffee and tea meets strict standards for worker welfare, farm management, and environmental protection such as reducing pesticide use. Visit www.rainforest-alliance.org for more information and for a list of certified providers. You'll also find a list of online coffee retailers that sell its certified products. Some examples: Boyd Coffee Company, www.boydscoffeestore.com; White Rock Coffee, www.wrcoffee.com; and straight from Northeastern Brazil, Café Sombra, www.cafesombra.com.

There are many sources of sustainably grown coffee and tea online and in local markets. It is available at many national retailers such as Whole Foods, Trader Joe's, Safeway, and Target as well as specialty coffee and tea shops including Starbucks, Peet's Coffee and Tea, and Caribou Coffee.

For more information about coffee and tea labels, visit www.greenerchoices.org/eco-labels/eco-home.cfm.

GREEN

- When brewing coffee, use reusable filters. If you have to use paper filters choose unbleached. For tea, try an infuser instead of bags. Cusp Natural Products, www.cuspnaturalproducts.com, makes reusable coffee filters and tea bags from hemp, a fiber that's stronger than cotton.

• If you can find affordable coffee or tea that's USDA Certified Organic, Fair Trade, Bird Friendly, or Rainforest Alliance Certified, buy it. If it's a little pricier than you prefer, make an effort to buy it just once a month.

GREENER

• Buy USDA Certified Organic, Fair Trade, Bird Friendly, or Rainforest Alliance Certified whenever possible. Look for the labels on pages 52–53 or go online to find more options.

• Ask your local grocery store and coffee bar to start stocking sustainable coffee and tea.

GREENEST

• Buy and drink only USDA Certified Organic, Bird Friendly, Fair Trade, or Rainforest Alliance Certified coffee and tea.

• Only patronize coffee shops that serve sustainably grown coffee and tea.

• Get active. The Organic Consumers Association, www.organicconsumers.org, is a good place to start.

WINE AND BEER

Conventional wine and beer production can be hard on the environment. The grapes used to make wine and the grains used to make beer are grown with a cocktail of synthetic chemicals that are highly polluting. Large amounts of fossil fuels are used to ship finished products around the world. Alternative options are becoming more widely available.

When it comes to wine, there are several sustainably grown options that aren't necessarily certified organic. That's because the USDA doesn't allow organic wine to have any added sulfites, which are used as preservatives. This is good news for those who are sensitive to them, but the exclusion of sulfites can make some wine less stable, a problem when it has to travel long distances.

Beer is made from barley and hops, a perennial plant that adds bitterness and aroma. Small local breweries have become much more common over the years, so you are likely to have some options nearby. Organic beer is harder to come by, but that's changing as demand grows. It's one of the fastest growing categories of organic beverages.

DECODING THE LABELS

USDA Certified Organic. Certified organic wine is produced from grapes that aren't grown with synthetic chemicals and don't have added sulfites. Wine that's labeled "Made with organic grapes" has small amounts of added sulfites (a reasonable option for those farmers who adhere to organic principles but feel their product needs the added stability of sulfites). Organic beer is made with at least 95 percent organic ingredients. If a label says that beer is "made with organic ingredients," then at least 70 percent of the ingredients are organically grown, that is, without the use of synthetic pesticides or fertilizers.

Demeter Certified Biodynamic. Like organic, this label (which applies only to wine) certifies that wine is free of synthetic pesticides and fertilizers. However, it goes further to assure that farms adhere to biodynamic principles such as applying a holistic approach to farm management. Unlike organic, it does allow for small amounts of sulfites to be added to wine. For more information visit www.demeter-usa.org.

● GREEN

- Support local breweries. Buying local reduces the amount of fossil fuels used to ship a product and supports local businesses. To find out what breweries are near you visit http://beeradvocate.com. Buy local wine when it's available. Look for it next time you visit your neighborhood farmers' market.

● GREENER

- Buy beer from a brewery that enforces sustainable practices. Brooklyn Brewery, www.brooklynbrewery.com, for example, is 100 percent powered by wind and gives its used grain to farmers for feed. New Belgium Brewery's facility is built sustainably and is also powered by wind; for more information visit www.newbelgium.com.

- Buy organic beer. Brands include Wolaver's Organic Ales, www.wolavers.com; Butte Creek Brewing Company, www.buttecreek.com; and Peak Organic Brewing, www.peakbrewing.com. Anheuser-Busch has jumped into the organic beer market with Wild Hop Lager, www.wildhoplager.com, and Stone Mill Pale Ale, www.stonemillpaleale.com. Visit the manufacturer websites to find out where you can find their products in your neighborhood.

- Buy organic and/or biodynamic wine. You can find it at most wine stores so just ask. Bonterra, www.bonterra.com, and Frog's Leap, www.frogsleap.com, are two widely available producers. (Frog's Leap uses certified organic grapes, but it doesn't say so on the label). Protect organic (and conventional) wine from heat and light. Appellation Wine & Spirits owner Scott Pactor suggests storing wine in the refrigerator during the peak summer months (if you don't own a wine refrigerator or have central air conditioning that keeps your house below 70 degrees). Make sure the wine won't freeze, and lay it on its side so that the cork stays moist. USDA Certified Organic wines do not have added sulfites so you have to take a little better care of them so that they don't turn, but Pactor says there are plenty of delicious stable options available. He also points out that most people have probably had organic wine and haven't even known it since producers don't always apply for certification. In fact, when shopping for wine you can ask your local store owner if he or she stocks wines that are made organically but that might not be certified. The Appellation website, www.appellationnyc.com, offers extensive information on storing and buying organic wines and also sells a wide selection. Union Square Wines & Spirits, www.unionsquarewines.com, and Astor Wines & Spirits, www.astorwines.com, also have organic and biodynamic wines that you can buy online.

For more information and wine reviews, check out the Organic Wine Journal, www.organicwinejournal.com.

GREENEST

- Brew your own organic beer. Seven Bridges Cooperative, www.breworganic.com, offers tips and supplies.
- Get active. Visit http://beeradvocate.com for beer ideas.

3 PERSONAL CARE PRODUCTS

Even the most low-maintenance person can easily use several personal care products every day—toothpaste, shampoo, moisturizer, and shaving cream for starters. When you factor in hair dye, anti-aging formulas, deodorant, makeup, blemish cream, and so on, the list can get pretty long. Even kids aren't exempt—we regularly slather them in diaper creams, powders, sunscreen, and various other lotions and potions. According to the Environmental Working Group, a watchdog organization that has done extensive research on personal care products, most people use about nine personal care products every day, encountering a combined average of 126 different ingredients. That's not a pretty picture when you consider the fact that we know very little about the chemicals we apply to our skin so freely. The Environmental Working Group reports that only 11 percent of 10,500 chemicals used in personal care products have been tested properly by Cosmetics Ingredient Review, an industry-funded panel. Some products, such as the active ingredients in sunscreen, are regulated by the Food and Drug Administration (FDA). But the vast majority of chemicals used in personal care products haven't been fully assessed because the

FDA doesn't require premarket testing or health studies before an item hits store shelves.

Not only is there limited information available on these products, but we also don't know much about the long-term health effects of being continually exposed to small amounts of chemicals, many of which accumulate in our bodies and can be passed on to the next generation. Personal care products can be absorbed through our skin, inhaled, and sometimes even ingested through lipsticks or when we put our hands in our mouths. Researchers working on the few chemicals that are tested are generally looking for acute effects—what happens immediately when you put something on your skin, such as a rash or burn. However, some of the most concerning health issues are those that may take a long time to show up. According to the Environmental Working Group, more than a third of all personal care products contain at least one ingredient linked to cancer. It's not just what happens to you today or tomorrow, but what happens down the line, says Hema Subramanian, an analyst at the Environmental Working Group.

The effects of our pursuit of beauty and wellness through personal care products are far reaching. What you lather up with can contaminate the planet as chemicals are washed down drains or disposed of improperly. A March 2002 U.S. Geological Study found that many household chemicals, including those found in personal care products, have made their way into the nation's streams. Excessive packaging clogs landfills. Animal rights groups such as People for the Ethical Treatment of Animals (PETA) have been trying to raise public awareness about the barbaric and often unnecessary tests performed on animals in creating these items.

This can all sound very depressing, but there are options. First, it's important to remember that you do ultimately have control over what you spread on your skin. To make real progress, we need better regulations so that new products are proven safe before they land on store shelves, rather than being investigated after problems arise. Public opinion can also encourage cosmetic companies to enact change from within. We have seen some positive steps taken by the industry in the past couple of years, but there is still a lot of work to be done, says Stacy Malkan, author of the book *Not Just a Pretty Face: The Ugly Side of the Beauty Industry* (New Society Publishers, 2007), which chronicles the history of the Campaign for Safe Cosmetics, the problem of toxic ingredients, and the availability of safer alternatives. She adds, "Companies are paying attention to consumer demand. Consumers have a lot of power to shift the market by choosing less toxic products and getting politically active." This chapter is filled with ways to help you navigate the personal care aisle. Here are some general suggestions for all product groups, including soap, shampoo, lotion, sunscreen, and cosmetics, with more specific product suggestions later on in the chapter.

GREEN

- Use fewer products. The best thing you can do is limit the number of products you use so you're exposed to fewer chemicals, suggests Nancy Evans, health science consultant at the Breast Cancer Fund.

- Avoid unnecessary products altogether, says Malkan. For example, synthetic bubble bath may feel pampering, but you don't need it.

- As with most consumer products, buy in bulk the ones you use most often—it saves money and packaging.

• Read the labels and don't be fooled by meaningless general claims (for tips see page 65). Try to avoid the most harmful chemicals. The following chemicals are all from Environmental Working Group's "What Not to Buy List." (For specific products that are made of these nasty chemicals and loads of other information see www.cosmeticsdatabase.com):

Placenta extracts from human and cow placenta used to condition skin and hair can give off hormones. (Also listed as "placental extract" or "placental protein").

Mercury is a known neurotoxin that's found in some mascaras and eye drops. (Also listed as "thimerosol").

Lead acetate is a known neurotoxin found in some hair dyes.

Animal parts such as mink and emu oil (fat scraped from the back hide of mink and emu) can be used as conditioning agents in sunscreen, shaving cream, hair spray, lip balm, and others.

Hydroquinone skin lightener can cause a skin-discoloring condition called ochronisis that in severe cases can be irreversible and disfiguring. There's also some evidence that it causes cancer in rats. The FDA issued a warning about skin lighteners containing hydroquinone.

Phthalates are male reproductive toxicants that can be present in some nail polishes and can hide in fragrances. See page 71 for more details.

GREENER

• The following ingredients are also listed on Environmental Working Group's "What Not to Buy List." They may be a little harder to avoid because they are in a variety of products or are difficult to identify, but it's worth the additional time and effort if you are able to avoid them:

Fragrances may contain harmful ingredients such as phthalates and neurotoxins, and they commonly trigger allergies.

Nanoparticles are super tiny particles that for the most part are untested, unregulated, and are not required to be labeled, but are present in several personal care products and are listed on some labels.

Petroleum by-products are listed as "petrolatum" and "petroleum distillates" on labels. Some can be contaminated with carcinogenic impurities such as 1,4-dioxane, a probable human carcinogen. The following ingredients may contain it: "sodium laureth sulfate" and ingredients with the terms "PEG," "xynol," "ceteareth," and "oleth." An easy solution is to use the Environmental Working Group's Skin Deep database, www.cosmeticsdatabase.com, and search for products free of cancer-causing impurities, because 1,4-dioxane can be in 56 different cosmetic ingredients. That's a lot for anyone to keep track of!

• Research the products you use most frequently. If they contain toxic ingredients, then find safer alternatives. The Environmental Working Group's Skin Deep database is the most exhaustive tool available to help you figure out what's in the products you're using and guide you to safer alternatives when necessary. The user-friendly database draws on the information in 50 toxicity and regulatory databases including those of Environmental Protection Agency (EPA), Centers for Disease Control and Prevention (CDC), and the European Union to provide safety ratings for all of the products it lists. You can search by product, ingredient, or category and compare brands when you visit the website at www.cosmeticsdatabase.com.

• Buy products from companies that have signed on to the "Compact for Safe Cosmetics," a pledge to formulate products that don't use ingredients that are known or suspected to cause certain health problems. To see the list visit Campaign for Safe Cosmetics at www.safecosmetics.org and click on "Safer Companies." Some examples of signees: Aubrey Organics, Avalon Natural Products, Burt's Bees, Jason Natural Products, and Weleda.

GREENEST

• Make your own products. Better yet, invite your friends over to make them with you. If you live in Massachusetts, you can contact the Alliance for a Healthy Tomorrow to help you host a Healthy and Beautiful Spa Party, where you and your pals can learn about some of the issues surrounding chemicals in personal care products while concocting your own treatments. If you live further afield or simply want tested recipes visit the Campaign for Safe Cosmetics website, www.safecosmetics.org, and download the Host a Healthy Cosmetics Spa Party kit created by the Alliance, which includes directions on all aspects of hosting a party as well as recipes. The website www.care2.com also provides recipes.

- Contact the manufacturers of your favorite products and ask them to sign the Compact for Safe Cosmetics if they haven't already done so. The more the companies hear from consumers, the more they are going to take these concerns seriously, says Malkan.

- Get active. See page 80.

DECODING THE LABELS

Reading cosmetic labels isn't exactly easy. Labels can be hard to find and often have print so small you need a magnifying glass. And not all of the ingredients are necessarily listed. Fragrance, for example, is often a mixture of many different chemicals, but because it's considered a trade secret you'll only see the word "fragrance" on the package. Ingredients are listed in order of volume, but amounts are not specified. The FDA does oversee ingredients that are considered drugs such as triclosan and the active ingredients in sunscreen and acne products. A drug label will list any ingredients vetted for safety by the FDA.

The following labels and marketing claims are often found on personal care products. Here's what they mean:

USDA Certified Organic. If the USDA Certified Organic label or the 100 percent Organic label is on the package, then it does mean that the agriculture-based ingredients are grown without synthetic pesticides and fertilizers and that there aren't any harmful or synthetic ingredients such as petroleum by-products added. However, if you just see the word "organic" either in the name of a product or without the USDA seal, then you need to read the ingredients list carefully to see how many of the ingredients are really organic and what else is in the product. The USDA label was developed specifically for food, and there are some things unique to personal care products, such as preservatives, that need to be addressed. The National Sanitation Foundation is working on standards developed specifically for personal care products. At press time, the standards were not published.

Natural. There is no standard definition of this term for personal care products, and there isn't an independent organization verifying that this claim is true.

Leaping Bunny. If you see the logo it means that the company has pledged to follow the standards outlined in the Corporate Standard of Compassion for Animals, which is an agreement not to conduct or commission any more animal testing of product ingredients. However, companies may continue to use ingredients that were tested on animals in the past. The standards were developed by the Coalition for Consumer Information on Cosmetics, an international group of animal protection organizations. Claims are independently verified. For more information on the label and on products not tested on animals, visit www.leapingbunny.org.

Fragrance Free. This doesn't necessarily mean that there isn't fragrance in a product. It means only that the product doesn't have a strong smell—fragrance can still be added to mask the smell of another ingredient. The only surefire way to avoid fragrance is to look at ingredients and confirm that the word "fragrance" is not listed.

Hypoallergenic. There is no official definition of this term or independent party to verify its use. The manufacturer decides when to use it, and there is no way of trusting its validity.

ECOCERT and **BDIH.** These are two reputable European certification programs with standards specifically designed for personal care products. If you see their labels stamped on a product, then strict standards have been met.

For more information on labels visit, www.greenerchoices.org/eco-labels/eco-home.cfm.

HAIR DYE

There is a lot of talk about the dangers of hair dye. Does it cause cancer? Unfortunately, there isn't a definitive answer. The good news is that according to the American Cancer Society, most of the available data doesn't show hair dyes to be a significant cancer risk. However, they do caution that the findings of published studies are inconsistent. Here are suggestions for those who want to take precautions until the science is more established:

GREEN

- Avoid dyes containing coal tar and ammonia.
- When you dye your hair, take these precautions recommended by the FDA: don't leave dye on your head any longer than necessary; rinse your scalp thoroughly after use; wear gloves; don't

mix different dye products because you may cause potentially harmful reactions; and don't dye your eyebrows or eyelashes.

- Avoid hair dye if you are pregnant, especially during the first trimester.

GREENER

- Stick to lower-impact hair dyes such as henna-based dyes and those that are semipermanent. There are plenty of lower- to moderate-impact product suggestions at www.cosmeticsdatabase.com.

GREENEST

- Avoid hair dye altogether.

ORAL CARE

One of the biggest factors affecting the type of toothpaste you decide to use is whether you want added fluoride. The American Dental Association recommends fluoride toothpaste, but since it's also found in many municipal water supplies, there is some concern that we are ingesting unsafe quantities of fluoride (see pages 50–51).

GREEN

- Don't swallow fluoride toothpaste. If your child is too young to spit properly, use a fluoride-free alternative.

• Check with your city to see if fluoride is present in your water supply so you can make informed decisions about whether to avoid fluoride in your toothpaste.

GREENER

• There are a wide range of chemicals that can be found in toothpastes, mouthwash, and other oral care products. Visit the Skin Deep database, www.cosmeticsdatabase.com, to find a product that meets your needs with the lowest toxicity ratings. There are plenty of natural products on the market, both with and without fluoride.

• Purchase a greener toothbrush. Preserve toothbrushes by Recycline, www.recycline.com, are made from 100 percent recycled plastics and can be sent back to the company in a prepaid mailer; they are available at www.drugstore.com.

• Use greener dental floss made with vegetable wax or essential oils. Brands include Nature's Gate and Tom's of Maine.

GREENEST

• Use a mixture of baking soda and water to brush your teeth.

• Avoid conventional mouthwash, which can have ingredients linked to cancer, development and reproductive toxicity, and allergies, according to the Environmental Working Group. The Skin Deep database, www.cosmeticsdatabase.com, has plenty of less toxic suggestions.

DEODORANT AND ANTIPERSPIRANTS

Several rumors have gone around in recent years discussing a link between deodorant and breast cancer. The American Cancer Society says that there isn't good scientific evidence to support this claim. More research needs to be done though, especially when it comes to parabens, a preservative used in many personal care products, including deodorants. A small study published in the *Journal of Applied Toxicology* in 2004 did find traces of parabens in breast tumors. This is potentially concerning because parabens contain estrogenlike properties, and estrogen is linked to an increased risk in some types of breast cancer. However, it's unclear whether the parabens in those tumors came from deodorants or from any of the many other products that contain them. Another issue with antiperspirants is the ingredient aluminum salts, which closes pores and reduces sweating. They can cause irritation, and aluminum is a heavy metal, which can accumulate in your body.

GREEN

- Avoid products containing parabens until more studies are done proving their safety. You'll see the word "paraben" listed on labels, but it often has a prefix such as "methyl," "propyl," "butyl," or "ethyl."
- Avoid antiperspirants, which contain aluminum salts.

GREENER

- Try a natural brand of deodorant, but be sure to check www.cosmeticsdatabase.com or read the label carefully to make sure a brand truly avoids toxic chemicals. There are mixed reviews on whether these products work as well as conventional deodorants and antiperspirants, and unfortunately trial and error may be the best way of figuring out what works for you.

GREENEST

- Instead of using conventional products, try one of the following alternatives: baking soda, rock salt, or crystal products (made from natural mineral salts).

Spotlight On: Phthalates

Phthalates are a group of chemicals that are commonly found in cosmetics and personal care products. They're also added to some plastics to make them more pliable and are found in lots of consumer products such as children's toys, air fresheners, some pharmaceuticals, building materials, and medical devices. The European Union banned their use in cosmetics in 2005 (and children's toys in 2003), but they are still used in the United States.

Phthalates are a known male reproductive toxicant. Animal studies have shown that exposure in the womb to low levels of phthalates causes a decrease in testosterone, which can lead to birth defects and compromised fertility later in life. Researchers are finding some of the same effects in humans. Some of the possible impacts of phthalates on boys and men include undescended testes, birth defects of the penis (hypospadias), lower sperm counts, and infertility. A 2003 Harvard University study showed an association between phthalates and poor semen quality among a group of men from couples seeking treatment at a fertility clinic in Boston. A study published in *Environmental Health Perspectives* in 2006 found that three-month-old baby boys whose mother's milk had high levels of phthalates had changes in testosterone levels. Women should be especially careful to avoid phthalates during pregnancy. When there is exposure in the womb it can set up a whole cascade of problems for developing boys since they need testosterone for the development of male sex characteristics and sex organs, says Sarah Janssen, MD, PhD, MPH, and a science fellow at the Natural Resources Defense Council (NRDC).

It's unlikely that you'll eliminate phthalates completely from your life because they can migrate into food through packaging that contains phthalates, and they can also contaminate water and air, but it makes sense to reduce your exposure when possible. Personal care products are one of the areas where you have the most control. You may want to eliminate products with added fragrance, especially if you are pregnant or nursing, as the chemical cocktail used to create many fragrances often contains phthalates. Children's toys are another area that you have some control over. Stick to wood and cloth when you can, and try to find plastic toys that are free of phthalates when possible. For more on this see page 100.

NAIL POLISH

Many companies have already removed some of the worst ingredients in nail polish, says Malkan, who refers to the ingredients dibutyl phthalate, formaldehyde, and toluene as the "toxic trio." Though finding safer nail polish is easier nowadays, nail polish is still not completely free of toxic chemicals, and since you can inhale the most harmful of these chemicals minimizing exposure can be difficult.

GREEN

- Avoid nail polish with any of the toxic trio ingredients. If a nail polish is unlabeled, do not use it.
- If you are pregnant, avoid polishing nails. If you must, then paint them outdoors or where there is good ventilation. Don't polish your kids' nails.

GREENER

- Try limiting nail polish use even if you aren't pregnant, and only frequent well-ventilated spas.

GREENEST

- Avoid nail polish entirely. Buff instead of polish.

SUN PROTECTION

Most of us are aware of the dangers of overexposure to the sun, and it's pretty common knowledge that we need to seek out "broad-spectrum" sunscreen—products that protect us from both the ultraviolet B (UVB) and ultraviolet A (UVA) radiation. However, a 2007 study by the Environmental Working Group says we may not be getting all the protection we need, even if we use sunscreens with high sun protection factor (SPF) ratings. That's not the only concerning news that came out of the EWG report. The bottom line: only 16 percent of the products on the market today are both safe and effective, meaning that they block both UVA and UVB radiation, remain stable in sunlight, and contain few if any ingredients with significant known or suspected health hazards. How is this possible? The FDA hasn't set guidelines for UVA protection, and the SPF factor is solely based on UVB protection. It's still important to consider SPF when buying sunscreen, but it's not a guarantee that you'll be protected from deeply penetrating UVA rays.

GREEN

- Use the best sunscreen to fit your needs. Because there are so many factors to consider when purchasing sunscreen and the stakes are high, the best thing you can do to find the safest and most effective products is to visit www.cosmeticsdatabase.com. The Environmental Working Group has done the hard work for you. Keep in mind that there isn't a perfect sunscreen available now. As the next generation of sunscreens hits the market, it's going to get increasingly difficult to sort through all the hype and figure out which are the best products. For now, your best bet is to stick with the tried and true and seek out those with the active ingredients zinc oxide and titanium dioxide, both of which provide broad-spectrum UVA and UVB protection. Many of these products contain nanoparticles, which haven't been tested properly and do raise some concerns. However, in the case of sunscreen, the Environmental Working Group says available studies show very little or zero penetration of these chemicals, a major concern with most nano materials; and the sun protection benefits are very high. If you have sensitive skin you might want to avoid para-aminobenzoic acid (PABA), although it's less likely to be in sunscreen these days.

• Use sunscreen correctly. The American Cancer Society suggests using a sunscreen with an SPF of 15 or higher, applying it about 20 to 30 minutes before going outside, and reapplying it every two hours. Once you reach SPF 30, there isn't a huge difference with higher SPF values. Don't skimp, either. An ounce of sunscreen should be used for an average adult. Don't use sunscreen on babies younger than six months—it's best to keep them out of direct sunlight.

• Avoid sunlamps and tanning booths.

● GREENER

Don't rely only on sunscreen. Follow this advice from the American Cancer Society:

• Limit exposure to direct sunlight from 10 a.m. to 4 p.m. when the sun's ultraviolet rays are most intense. The sun's rays are strongest if your shadow is shorter than you are. UV radiation can also pass through water and reflects off of sand and snow.

• Wear a hat with at least a two- to three-inch brim all around or shade caps, which look like baseball caps with a long piece of material draping down the sides and back.

• Wear protective clothing. Dark colors and tightly woven fabrics prevent more UV rays from reaching your skin than do lighter shades and loosely woven clothing. Some companies make sun-protective clothing. Check out Solumbra, www.solumbra.com, and Coolibar, www.coolibar.com, for extensive lines of clothes that block both UVA and UVB rays. There's also a growing array of protective swimwear available at mainstream retailers.

• Wear sunglasses that block 99 to 100 percent of UVA and UVB radiation. Glasses labeled "UV Absorption up to 400 nm," and "Meets American National Standards Institute (ANSI) UV Requirements" provide enough protection. Cosmetic glasses block only about 70 percent of the UV rays. Buy children smaller versions of protective adult sunglasses.

GREENEST

• Urge the FDA, www.fda.gov, to set mandatory sunscreen safety standards, develop UVA standards, and approve new effective and safe sunscreens in the United States.

FEMININE PRODUCTS

It's hard to imagine that women can do anything to green up in this area, but there are some options. Conventional tampons and sanitary pads are typically made out of cotton, which is sprayed with huge amounts of synthetic pesticides and fertilizers, and rayon, which is a synthetic fiber that possibly contains dioxin, a known human carcinogen. There's been debate over whether it is harmful to use tampons containing dioxin. So far the scientific evidence says no, although studies on the topic are minimal. A January 2002 *Environmental Health Perspectives* study by the EPA and University of Texas found trace amounts of dioxins in tampons but concluded that our primary exposure to dioxins is through food. Tampons and sanitary napkins are typically bleached with chlorine, a process which sends many harmful by-products, especially dioxin, into the air. When these chemicals settle on grasslands they are eaten and thereby introduced to the food supply.

The other issue to consider is that disposable products create a lot of waste and end up in landfills or flushed down toilets. Some of the reusable options on the market take care of that issue and also save you money.

● GREEN

- Buy chlorine-free 100 percent organic cotton tampons. You'll help keep some pesticides, fertilizers, and dioxins out of the environment, a good thing for your health and the planet. Products from Natracare, www.natracare.com, and Seventh Generation, www.seventhgeneration.com, are widely available at Whole Foods, natural food stores, select pharmacies, and online at www.drugstore.com and www.gaiam.com. They are more expensive than conventional products but are just as convenient and effective.

● GREENER

- Use washable menstrual pads. Lunapads, www.lunapads.com, makes 100 percent cotton menstrual pads and panties (with both organic and conventionally grown cotton) that you can throw in your washing machine.

GREENEST

- Try reusable menstrual cups. The Diva Cup is available at www.drugstore.com. Other choices include The Keeper, made of natural gum rubber, and The Moon Cup, made of medical-grade silicone, both available at www.keeper.com.

- Try natural sponges. They are available at some health food stores and online.

Healthwatch: Endocrine Disruptors

Throughout this book you'll see several chemicals referred to as endocrine disruptors. What exactly are they and what do they do? Endocrine disruptors are chemicals that can block, imitate, or alter levels of naturally occurring hormones in our bodies and may adversely affect our health. The endocrine system is responsible for orchestrating several important bodily functions, including regulating the nervous and reproductive systems.

The harmful effects of continuous low levels of endocrine-disrupting chemicals in lab animals and wildlife are scientifically well documented and raise concerns about human health. So far, it's been difficult to conclusively determine their impact on humans, but they are suspected of causing cancer, infertility, premature birth, and learning disorders, among others. Ted Schettler, science director of the Environmental Health Network, explains one reason it's so difficult to sort out: we study these chemicals one by one in a discrete lab setting when in the real world, people are exposed to multiple chemicals simultaneously. We test them separately and regulate them separately, but we aren't exposed to them separately.

While the jury is still out, the safest thing to do is avoid exposure when possible. Endocrine disruptors and other potentially hazardous chemicals are found in many consumer products that we encounter on a daily basis, such as personal care products, cleaning products, plastic bottles, toys, and pesticides. They also enter our food supply. Throughout the book you'll see suggestions for cutting down your exposure.

For more information about endocrine disruptors as well as many other topics having to do with environmental health see the following sources:

Environmental Health News, www.environmentalhealthnews.org, compiled by the nonprofit Environmental Health Sciences, is a comprehensive and user-friendly source of news. Updated daily, it's broken down into three columns: one with links to stories in the world press, another with links to the latest peer-reviewed studies being published, and the last with links to new reports from nonprofits and government agencies. You can also sign up for their daily newsletter *Above the Fold*.

Collaborative on Health and the Environment, www.healthandenvironment.org, is a coalition of individuals and organizations seeking to address the growing concerns about the links between human health and environmental factors. They provide readable, comprehensive reports on many different diseases such as asthma, Parkinson's, and some cancers, and on disorders such as autism and learning disabilities. There's also a database that you can search by disease or chemical.

Silent Spring Institute, www.silentspring.org, is a partnership of scientists, doctors, public health advocates, and others who aim to identify the links between women's health and the environment. In 2007, the nonprofit partnered with Harvard University, Roswell Park Cancer Institute, and the University of Southern California to assess the scientific evidence on environmental causes of breast cancer. The group identified 216 chemicals associated with mammary gland tumors in animals and also looked at hundreds of human epidemiological studies. The findings are summarized in two databases that you can access on the website.

The Breast Cancer Fund, www.breastcancerfund.org, is a San Francisco–based nonprofit that identifies the environmental causes of breast cancer and seeks elimination of preventable factors. On its website, you'll find numerous fact sheets and reports as well as ways for consumers to take action.

Get Active

The Campaign for Safe Cosmetics, www.safecosmetics.org, is a coalition of public health and environmental groups who want to protect the health of consumers and workers by requiring the health and beauty industry to replace toxic chemicals with safer alternatives. Visit the website for ideas and resources for getting politically active.

Environmental Working Group, www.ewg.org, follows the industry carefully. Visit its website periodically to see if there are any take-action alerts for personal care products. You can also sign up for biweekly email alerts with the latest policy news, shopping tips, and advice.

Register a complaint with the FDA. If you have a reaction to a product, you can report it to the FDA at www.cfsan.fda.gov. You can also file a complaint with the company that makes the product.

Get involved in state efforts. States can lead the way on change. California, for example, recently passed a law that requires any company selling a personal care product in California that contains a human carcinogen to disclose that information to the state. Here's a list of some of the most active organizations advocating for public policies and corporate practices that protect the public from unnecessary use of toxic chemicals in everyday products, not only in the cosmetics arena. If you don't live in one of these states, then contact one of them to ask if they know of any efforts in your home state:

- **California:** Californians for a Healthy and Green Economy (CHANGE), www.cehca.org/projects.htm
- **Connecticut:** Coalition for a Safe & Healthy Connecticut, www.safehealthyct.org
- **Maine:** Alliance for a Clean and Healthy Maine, www.cleanandhealthyme.org
- **Massachusetts:** Alliance for a Healthy Tomorrow, www.healthytomorrow.org
- **Michigan:** Michigan Network for Children's Environmental Health, www.mnceh.org
- **Minnesota:** Healthy Legacy, www.healthylegacy.org
- **New York:** Alliance for a Toxic-Free Future, www.toxicfreefuture.org
- **Washington:** Toxic-Free Legacy Coalition, www.toxicfreelegacy.org

4 BABIES AND CHILDREN

A parent's natural instinct is to protect her young. The truth is, you can drive yourself crazy worrying about all the potential harm lurking, and a lot of it is out of your control anyway. A less stressful approach is to take reasonable precautions to protect your child whenever you can. In the case of man-made toxic chemicals, there's plenty you can do and good reason to make changes when possible because babies and young children are more vulnerable than adults.

There are several reasons for this. They weigh less than adults, but they eat and drink more per pound of body weight and have a faster respiratory rate, so they breathe in more air than do grown-ups. Pound for pound, they receive proportionately larger doses of toxic chemicals than adults do. Gina Solomon, MD, MPH, and senior scientist at the Natural Resources Defense Council (NRDC) has an interesting way of illustrating it: you wouldn't give a child the same dose of Tylenol that you would take, but children are getting the same doses of pollutants as adults are.

Another factor is that children's bodies and brains are still growing. Their immune systems and other protective mechanisms may not be fully developed. What's more, if a child is exposed to a harmful chemical at a certain point in his or her development, it can have lasting impacts. According to Solomon, if you expose a child to a neurotoxin while the brain is still developing, it can irreversibly influence the way the structure of the brain grows. Children's behavior also works against them. Babies and toddlers crawl around and play on the floor and then put their hands in their mouths, exposing them to more toxins.

The science is becoming clearer every day, with new studies suggesting how various chemicals can influence children's health and development even in the womb, says Elise Miller, executive director of the Institute for Children's Environmental Health. Indeed, mounting evidence shows that babies are being exposed to toxic chemicals in utero, so pregnancy and even pre-pregnancy, when possible, is a great time to start taking these issues into consideration. A joint study of 10 babies born in 2004, carried out by the Environmental Working Group and Commonweal, found an average of 200 industrial chemicals and pollutants in their umbilical cord blood.

What might all this mean for kids' health? Research and statistics confirm that chronic childhood diseases and disorders such as autism, asthma, allergies, birth defects, obesity, learning and developmental disabilities, early puberty, and some childhood cancers are on the rise. There is also concern that prenatal and early life exposures to harmful substances may influence a child's susceptibility to disease later in life. In some cases the connections between toxic chemicals and illness are well established, while in others more research needs to be done. While we are waiting for scientists to give us definitive answers, proponents of the precautionary principle say it makes sense to take the "It's better to be safe than sorry" approach and avoid chemicals that are suspected of causing damage. That said, you're not going to be able to protect your baby from every threat, and most of the time it's going to be okay. It's crucial to remember that several factors come into play—timing, exposure levels and duration, and genetic predisposition.

We need to protect children from harmful substances in the environment, and at the same time, we need to protect the planet from all the stuff that babies and young children accumulate these days. Car seats, cribs, strollers, baby carriers, and toys are just a few of the items on any pregnant mother's lengthy shopping list. It's virtually impossible for all of it to be green. The sheer volume alone is anything but eco-friendly. In short, the best thing you can do for the planet is to use less stuff. Think about whether you can get by without some of the things you automatically assume you need. Our parents, for example, got along just fine without contraptions like the Diaper Genie. For items you really need, consider borrowing stuff from friends or buying used instead of new. (Be sure to check to see if a product has been recalled first.) It's great for the planet and your wallet, especially when you consider the fact that little ones outgrow things quickly, so most of your friends' castaways are in pretty good shape.

This chapter covers the basics specific to babies and children, but following the tips throughout this book will also help create a healthier environment for your child and protect the planet for future generations.

Spotlight On: Bisphenol-A

Bisphenol-A (BPA) is a controversial and widely used chemical that's used to make polycarbonate plastics and epoxy resins. It's primarily found in some of the popular clear hard-plastic drinking water bottles (labeled 7 on the bottom), baby bottles, the white linings found in many canned foods and beverages, bottle tops, and the lids of baby food jars. It's also used in some dental sealants that are applied to teeth to prevent cavities.

A 2007 consensus report published by thirty-eight scientists from around the world in the *Journal of Reproductive Toxicology* found that BPA is ubiquitous in our daily lives and that Americans are exposed at levels shown to cause harmful health effects in lab animals. The list of adverse health effects in animals is long: breast and prostate cancer, decreased sperm counts, reproductive abnormalities, neurobehavioral problems, early puberty in females, and others.

It makes sense to minimize exposure until we have more data on human exposure. Here are some ideas:

- Avoid polycarbonate drinking bottles. Try those labeled with code 5 or a stainless steel version.

- Buy baby bottles made from safer plastics or use glass bottles. See page 87.

- Avoid canned foods and beverages.

- Make your own baby food. The basic process is simple: steam or boil organic produce and then puree in a blender. Make large batches and freeze individual portions in ice cube trays.

- Call manufacturers of baby foods and canned foods that you use often and urge them to stop using BPA in the linings of cans.

- If your child's dentist wants to apply sealants to your child's teeth, ask him if the sealant has BPA in it. If the dentist doesn't know, get the brand name and call the manufacturer. Make sure your child spits well after sealant is applied.

BABY BOTTLES AND TRAINING CUPS

Sooner or later, most babies, even those who drink breast milk, come into contact with a plastic bottle. Inexpensive and convenient, plastic bottles are easy for busy parents to cart around without worrying about breakage. However, your average plastic baby bottles and training cups, made of polycarbonate (code 7) plastic, have a big downside. They can leach BPA (see page 86 for more information). BPA can seep into liquids when bottles are heated or scratched. Some baby bottle manufacturers have switched to safer plastics and more are likely to do the same as consumer awareness builds. Until they're off the market completely, here's what you can do:

GREEN

- Choose safer plastics. Buy bottles and training cups made from polypropylene (code 5) or polyethylene (codes 1, 2, or 4), which are safer than bottles made form polycarbonate plastic. See page 34 for more on plastics. Call the manufacturer if the packaging or bottle doesn't say which type of plastic a product is made from. Born Free sells BPA-free bottles and training cups. You can buy them online at www.newbornfree.com or at Whole Foods and Babies "R" Us. Don't forget about breast-milk storage bags and pump equipment. At press time, Medela, www.medela.com, sells polypropylene breast pump kits and milk storage bottles and polyethylene milk storage bags. For more information on safer plastic baby bottles see the Smart Plastics Guide at www.healthobservatory.org.

• If you have to use polycarbonate, discard old scratched bottles and "sippy" cups, suggests Kathleen Schuler, MPH, a senior associate at the Institute for Agriculture and Trade Policy. According to Schuler, plastic that shows signs of wear such as scratches or a cloudy, crackled appearance will more readily leach chemicals, and scratches can harbor bacteria.

• Do not warm plastic baby bottles in the microwave. You can heat liquids separately and pour them into the bottle when they are at a comfortable temperature, or place a bottle in a bowl of warm water to take the chill off.

• Choose clear nipples made from silicone rather than darker rubber, which may leach carcinogenic nitrosamines, according to Schuler. Always check for cracks where bacteria can accumulate.

GREENER

• Use tempered glass bottles when possible. They're healthier, better for the planet because they aren't made from petroleum (a nonrenewable resource), and they can be recycled. Of course, glass can break, so check regularly for cracks and chips and never let your baby walk around with a glass bottle. In fact, the American Academy of Pediatrics recommends parents not allow their babies to ever walk around with a bottle regardless of the material it is made of. If children fall while sucking a bottle they can get hurt, and sucking a bottle for long periods of time can cause baby bottle tooth decay.

● GREENEST

- Choose stainless steel sippy cups, available at www.kleankanteen .com. They're healthier for your child and the planet. They're also more expensive than conventional plastic training cups, but they're more durable, so you won't need to purchase as many.

Healthwatch: Chemicals in Breast Milk

The list of reasons why "breast is best" is long and continually growing. Nursing babies have fewer ear, respiratory, and gastrointestinal infections. Breast-feeding may also protect against sudden infant death syndrome (SIDS). What's more, the benefits appear to be long lasting. Many studies indicate that children who breast-feed are likely to have higher I.Q. scores and lower likelihood of developing allergies, asthma, diabetes, obesity, and even some cancers, says Solomon of the NRDC. It's great for moms, too. Those who nurse have lower rates of breast and ovarian cancers and fewer hip fractures after menopause.

While the American Academy of Pediatrics and other health groups tout the benefits of breast-feeding, it's hard for some mothers to ignore reports of unwanted substances in breast milk. It has been found to contain persistent organic pollutants such as pesticides, flame retardants, dioxins, polychlorinated biphenyl (PCBs), perchlorate, musk-xylenes (found in perfumes), and triclosan (an antibacterial agent found in a wide range of consumer products). Many of these chemicals make their way up the food chain and accumulate in human fat, a primary ingredient of breast milk. It's daunting to hear about the cocktail of chemicals present in some mothers' milk, but a wide range of experts concur that mothers should still breast-feed because the benefits outweigh the risks. The NRDC's Solomon sums it up: breast milk is advantageous in so many ways that it's the best thing parents can feed their babies. (That doesn't mean you should feel guilty if you can't breast-feed.) Solomon also reports that levels of certain chemicals in breast milk have dropped after countries such as Sweden have banned or regulated them. What can you do? Because many of these chemicals build up in our bodies over our lifetime, it's hard to make an impact over the short term. The best thing is to work toward ridding the marketplace and environment of harmful chemicals. Until then, it certainly wouldn't hurt for pregnant and nursing mothers to stay away from toxic chemicals such as pesticides and solvents, and eat a healthy diet, especially one with less animal fat. There are suggestions throughout this book on how to implement a healthier lifestyle, all of which are especially helpful for pregnant and nursing mothers trying to minimize their exposure to toxic chemicals.

To learn more or to get politically involved visit the following websites:

Making Our Milk Safe (MOMS), www.safemilk.org, was founded by nursing mothers after they discovered that perchlorate and other toxic chemicals were present in breast milk. Their goal is to protect babies' health by eliminating the growing threat of toxic chemicals in breast milk. They provide ideas for getting politically active and using your purchasing power to make a difference.

The Natural Resources Defense Council's "Healthy Milk, Healthy Baby" report explains the issues in detail and is available at www.nrdc.org/breastmilk.

DIAPERS

It is a common misconception that cloth is the holy grail of eco-friendly diaper options. That error is likely born out of the myth that "inconvenient" equals "green." The truth is, all diapers have an environmental impact, whether they are disposable or made from cloth. Disposable diapers, made from wood pulp (trees) and plastic (petroleum), end up clogging landfills. Disposable diapers are typically bleached with chlorine, a process that sends many harmful by-products, especially dioxin, into the air. When these chemicals settle on grasslands they may be eaten by livestock and thereby introduced into the food supply. A January 2002 *Environmental Health Perspectives* study by the Environmental Protection Agency (EPA) and University of Texas found dioxins in trace amounts in diapers but concluded that our primary exposure to dioxins is through food. The problems with cloth diapers include the enormous amounts of toxic pesticides and fertilizers that are used to make conventional cotton, and the energy, water, and chemicals that are required to wash them.

What to do? Many experts say that you should just pick

whatever is convenient for you and save your time and energy for greening up some of the other areas of your life where you can really make a difference. One thing you can take into account when making the diaper decision is where you live. If your local landfills are especially crowded, consider cloth diapers if they work with your lifestyle (some day care centers may not allow them, for example). If your water is in short supply, it may be better to go with disposables. You also don't have to pick one method. Some people use cloth during the day and disposable at night, or mix strategies in other ways.

GREEN

- If you use disposables, empty contents into the toilet before tossing soiled diapers. Untreated fecal matter can potentially contaminate ground water if it leaks from landfills.

GREENER

- If you go for disposables, consider a "natural" brand such as Seventh Generation, Tushies, Tendercare, or Nature Boy & Girl. Seventh Generation and Tendercare are made without chlorine bleach. Tushies doesn't have the superabsorbent padding common in most disposable diapers that can turn into gel and end up on your baby. Nature Boy & Girl is labeled biodegradable, but you'll need to have access to commercial composting facilities in order for the diapers to break down. Call your local waste management authority to find out if this is an option in your community. As of press time, a chlorine-free, gel-free, biodegradable diaper isn't available, so the best option is to pick the product that addresses the issue most important to you and that works best on your baby. Drugstore.com has a wide selection of alternative diapers, or look for them at Whole Foods or your local health food store.

• If you decide on cloth, then you have a few different options. You can wash them at home or send them out to a diaper service. Washing them at home with hot water without chlorine bleach is the most eco-friendly way to go. It's even better if you buy organic cotton and unbleached diapers and plastic-free diaper covers. You can find organic cloth diapers at Ecobaby Organics, www.ecobaby.com. The other option is to rent diapers from a service that washes them for you every week. You can find a local diaper service in the Yellow Pages or visit the National Association of Diaper Services website, www.diapernet.org.

GREENEST

• Try gDiapers, a unique product that is a hybrid of sorts. Just snap a flushable insert into cloth pants. You can compost wet inserts if you have home composting, or flush the insert down the toilet. Nothing goes to the landfill. You can wash and reuse the pants and waterproof snap-in liners, but this doesn't require as much water and energy as traditional cloth diapers. The product is Cradle to Cradle Certified by innovative product and design firm MBDC (see page 171). You can buy gDiapers at Whole Foods, Wild Oats, and some natural food stores, or online at www.gdiapers.com or www.drugstore.com.

• If you are up for an adventure and have a lot of time to spend with your baby, go diaper-free. The Elimination Communication

Method (also known as Natural Infant Hygiene or Infant Potty Training) is gaining some pioneering followers in the United States. The basic gist is that there are certain signals that a baby makes in advance of having to "go." When parents observe the signals they place the baby on the potty and then signal back to the baby that it's okay to go. For more information on how this works as well as links to resources and books visit Diaper Free Baby, www.diaperfreebaby.org. Good luck!

PERSONAL CARE PRODUCTS

We slather babies and children in numerous personal care products, many of which haven't been rigorously tested for safety. Chapter 3 contains detailed information about the health and environmental impacts of personal care products, but this section outlines the basics for kids, who are especially vulnerable to toxic chemicals.

GREEN

- The easiest and least expensive thing to do is to use fewer products on your child. Cut out unnecessary items. Is bubble bath really necessary? No, especially when you consider the fact that it may cause urinary tract infections, and the synthetic versions are made from petroleum products. Instead of a synthetic wet wipe (which is also a landfill issue and can contain irritating alcohol and fragrances), you might try a plain damp washcloth when you're at home, or use a little mild unscented soap. You can use mild baby soap for hair and body and avoid shampoos for as long as possible. Don't use creams, ointments, and lotions unless your child really needs them.

• Read the labels and avoid the most toxic ingredients (see page 62). When possible, avoid products with fragrances, a mixture of many different chemicals that don't have to be listed on a product's label. They are a common allergen and often have phthalates, a male reproductive toxicant, that's particularly harmful to young boys (see page 71). Other common ingredients in children's personal care products worth avoiding include: parabens; petroleum distillates such as polyethylene glycol (PEG), which are in danger of being contaminated with 1,4-dioxane, a probable human carcinogen; and sodium borate. Avoid baby powder because inhaling it can irritate a baby's airways and some brands contain carcinogenic talc.

GREENER

• Research the products you use and find less toxic alternatives when necessary. Most new parents hardly have time to take a shower, but Environmental Working Group's extensive database, www.cosmeticsdatabase.com, makes doing the research easy. This is especially true when it comes to sunscreen, a necessary but imperfect part of protecting your child's skin from the sun's harmful ultraviolet rays. For more information on the database see page 63, and see page 73 for sunscreen tips.

• Too much fluoride will put kids in danger of having discolored teeth, a condition known as dental fluorosis (see page 68 for more details on fluoride). If your young child doesn't know how to spit properly, you might consider buying a fluoride-free toothpaste until he or she is able to spit it out instead of swallowing it. Talk to you dentist or pediatrician about this.

GREENEST

- Get active in keeping harmful chemicals out of products for babies and children in the first place. See page 81 for resources.

HAIR LICE SOLUTIONS

It's a phone call most parents dread: news from the school nurse that your child has lice. Though lice aren't harmful, they are certainly a major inconvenience. At a moment's notice you have to retrieve your child and come up with a plan to banish the lice and their eggs from your child's head before he or she can return to school. This is not necessarily an easy task. Shampoos and other commercial lice treatments are made from pesticides, some more harmful and/or effective than others—and they kill only the lice, not the eggs, so you have to keep using them. Hopefully, you'll never get that call, but here are some tips on how to make the best of it just in case.

GREEN

- Avoid prescription shampoos with lindane in them. The Food and Drug Administration (FDA) issued a public health advisory saying it should not be prescribed as a first line of defense and that it should be given only with extreme caution to those weighing under 110 pounds (most children). Side effects include dizziness, headache, and seizure. Over-the-counter products such as Rid and Nix are made from pyrethroids (synthetic versions of a naturally occurring pesticide in chrysanthemums) and are safer than lindane, but they may be losing their effectiveness. If you do use pesticide shampoos, then follow the directions carefully and don't leave it on longer than directed. Don't use these products if you are pregnant or nursing. It's also recommended that if your child has allergies, asthma, epilepsy, or other health concerns, you call your pediatrician first.

● GREENER

• Prevention is always a good thing. Teach your child to keep hair pulled back and not to share brushes, combs, or hats with friends. Run a lice comb (see the "Greenest" section) through your child's hair regularly to stay ahead of any infestations and nip them in the bud.

• Take a whole-house approach. You don't need any lice sprays or other products. It's better to avoid them because you're essentially spraying pesticides all over your house. Simply wash bedding, towels, worn clothing, and stuffed animals in hot water and run through the dryer. Vacuum rugs and furniture well.

● GREENEST

• The safest and most effective way to get rid of lice is the most time-consuming method: combing them out manually. This deals with both the lice and the eggs. You can buy a nit comb at your local drugstore or buy the LiceMeister from the National Pediculosis Association, www.headlice.org, where you'll also find information on how to remove lice and answers to many questions. Or ask your school nurse if there are any professional nit pickers in your area—this will cost money, but may ultimately save you time as they are extremely efficient and sometimes do a follow-up check for free.

CRIBS, MATTRESSES, AND SLEEPWEAR

Babies spend much of their time sleeping, so it's important to provide a healthy place for them to snooze. This isn't as easy as it sounds since there are quite a few potentially harmful chemicals that can lurk in cribs, mattresses, and sleepwear. Permanent press sheets may be treated with formaldehyde. Plywood furnishings can release volatile organic compounds (VOCs). Most conventional mattresses are made from a cocktail of petroleum-based products including polyurethane foam, nylon, polyester, and PVC. Mattresses as well as sleepwear are often treated with flame retardants, a class of chemicals designed to slow the spread of fire (see page 168).

GREEN

- If you are buying a new conventional mattress for your child, let it air outside before using.

- Consider purchasing a used crib. Make sure it meets the Consumer Product Safety Commission's guidelines, such as having no more than 2⅜ inches between slats and no cutout designs on the head or foot boards. If it's painted, test for lead (you can find test kits at any hardware store). For more tips visit the Consumer Product Safety Commission's website, www.cpsc.gov.

• Avoid permanent press sheets. Less is more when it comes to bed linens for babies. The Consumer Products Safety Commission recommends that you don't put pillows, quilts, sheepskins, and pillowlike stuffed toys in cribs and suggests dressing the baby in a sleeper instead of using a blanket.

• Nylon and polyester pajamas can be treated with flame retardants. You can buy 100 percent cotton sleepwear, but it must fit snuggly in order to meet federal flammability standards.

GREENER

• Buy organic cotton crib-mattress pads and sheets, wool puddle pads, and organic cotton sleepwear for babies. Conventional cotton consumes huge amounts of synthetic pesticides and fertilizers, which deplete soil and pollute water. You can find the organic products at Our Green House, www.ourgreenhouse.com and Ecobaby Organics, www.ecobaby.com, among other sources.

• Spring for an organic mattress made from unbleached cotton, wool (which has natural fire-retardant properties), and natural rubber foam padding. They are more expensive than conventional mattresses, but it's worth it if you can afford one. One option is to buy a used crib and put your savings toward a good-quality organic mattress. You can find them at Lifekind, www.lifekind.com; Dax Stores, www.daxstores.com; and the Organic Mattress Store, www.theorganicmattressstore.com.

GREENEST

- Look for cribs made from solid wood rather than pressed woods, which can contain formaldehyde and other chemicals you might want to avoid. They're not easy to find and they can be expensive. Pacific Wood makes solid maple cribs that you can buy at www.theorganicmattressstore.com, www.daxstores.com, and www.ourgreenhouse.com. Lifekind, www.lifekind.com, sells a solid wood crib. Q Collection Junior, www.qcollectionjunior.com, sells cribs and other nursery furniture that is made with Forest Stewardship Certified (see pages 118–119) or locally sourced wood. The company uses formaldehyde-free glues and low VOC paints and stains.

TOYS

Toys are an inevitable part of childhood, but some playthings come with risks. While we've long been aware that choking and strangulation are dangers associated with certain toys, it's less well known that what a toy is made of can be a health issue. As any parent knows, it's virtually impossible to keep toys out of children's mouths, so it's important to find the safest toys possible. Many plastic toys are made of PVC, which has added phthalates to increase flexibility and softness. They can leach out over time and are known to cause reproductive problems and other adverse health effects (see page 72 for more information). The European

Union banned the use of some phthalates in toys, and San Francisco is attempting to do the same. PVC production is also bad for the environment (see page 120) and it's not recyclable. Other toys, especially toy jewelry and old painted toys, contain lead, a known neurotoxin that can cause learning and behavioral problems. In 2007, thousands of toys from China were recalled because of lead contamination (see page 103 for more on the dangers of lead).

GREEN

- Choose safer plastics. Lego and Sassy don't use PVC. All of Chicco's hand-to-mouth toys are PVC-free. A few toys, such as dolls, have PVC but not phthalates.

GREENER

- Minimize plastic. Even those that aren't made of PVC still pose problems for the environment because they are made from petroleum, a nonrenewable resource. Choose solid wood toys when possible. It's true that wood contributes to deforestation, but it is renewable, and if it doesn't have toxic finishes, it can be safer and more enduring than plastic. If you can, buy toys made from sustainable wood from Forest Stewardship Council certified forests or reclaimed wood when you can find them (see pages 118–119). Another alternative to plastic is cotton and wool—look for organic when possible. Here are a few options for finding safer toys: Organic Gift Shop, www.organicgiftshop.com; Ecobaby Organics, www.ecobaby.com; and North Star Toys, www.northstartoys.com.

- Buy locally made toys at craft fairs and farmers' markets.

PERSUADING YOUR CHILD'S SCHOOL TO USE SAFER PRODUCTS

Environmental advocate Patti Wood, executive director of Grassroots Environmental Education, spends much of her time working to get schools to stop using pesticides and embrace green cleaning products. Why? Wood points to the fact that we're seeing rising rates of children's asthma, learning disabilities, development disorders, and allergies. "We need to be concerned about indoor air quality because kids today are spending more and more time inside," says Wood. "During the school year, kids learn and play in the same buildings and classrooms day after day, and if there are air-quality issues related to cleaning products and other chemicals this can mean significant exposures." She's met with considerable success so far, having helped many private and public schools make the transition to "ChildSafe" products, which meet a very strict standard that Wood developed for use around children.

Harsh cleaning products are used on a daily basis in most schools. Many common products, for example, contain 2-butoxyethanol, a liver and kidney toxicant absorbed through the skin. Wood offers the following advice to concerned parents looking to make changes in their child's school (for more information and supporting materials visit www.grassrootsinfo.org and look for the ChildSafe School Program):

1. Get a list of cleaning and pest control products that your child's school uses from the principal or building and grounds person and ask

GREENEST

• Buy less. Find safe "toys" around the house such as wooden spoons and pots and pans. Borrow books and tapes from the library. Get together with a group of families in your neighborhood and rotate toys, books, and videos. Children become bored easily, so it's one way to keep things fresh and exciting.

for a Materials Safety Data Sheet (MSDS) for each product used, which will tell you whether there is a health warning or danger associated with the active ingredients in a product (see Chapter 8). Although this information is useful, an MSDS will reveal only acute and immediate effects, not long-term effects, which are the ones that are particularly troubling, according to Wood.

2. Do your own research. Go to *Environmental Health Perspectives*, www.ehponline.org, and search the active ingredient names to find related peer-reviewed scientific studies. For pesticides, go to the Pesticide Action Network's database, www.pesticideinfo.org.

3. Get a list of alternative cleaning products by going to www.grassrootsinfo.org. There are many effective, cost-competitive, and safe products on the market, according to Wood, so there's no reason not to use them. It's up to knowledgeable and concerned parents, though, to encourage their schools to make the transition to safer products.

4. Go back to school armed with your research about the health impacts of the products that the school is using along with the list of alternative products that are safe and work well and ask your school to try them. Providing the names of local distributors and enlisting the help of the parent-school organization and other local environmental agencies can be useful.

Spotlight On: Lead

Lead is a heavy metal and a known neurotoxin. It's associated with behavioral problems, learning disabilities, seizures, and death, and it's especially dangerous for children under six years old because their growing bodies absorb more lead and because their brains and nervous systems are more sensitive to it, according to the EPA. The good news is that the number of children with elevated lead levels in the United States has dropped dramatically.

Kids are exposed by eating soil or peeling paint chips containing lead, breathing in or swallowing lead-contaminated dust, and drinking water with lead in it. Certain kids' products such as toy jewelry or old painted wooden toys can have high amounts of lead.

If you live in a home built before 1978, it might have lead paint. It's generally not a problem if it's in good condition, but if it's cracked or peeling or there are other reasons why you're worried, you can get your home tested. The National Lead Information Center can give you a list of certified lead-based paint professionals to fix any problems that are detected. If you live in an old house and your children play outside in a place where they can easily get dirt on their hands you might want to have your soil tested. Call your local cooperative extension (see page 226). Old pipes can leach lead so water testing is another good idea (see page 48). Inform your pediatrician if you have identified a problem.

For More Information

There are several organizations working to improve children's environmental health. Here's a small sampling of websites you can turn to to learn more and get tips for protecting your family:

Healthy Child, Healthy World, www.healthychild.org, has a wealth of valuable information on its website aimed to educate and show you how to create a healthier home so your child is exposed to fewer harmful environmental toxins. Check out Health eHouse, an interactive virtual house that helps you identify the hazards in your home. You can sign up for a monthly email that outlines age-specific environmental health lessons from pregnancy until your child turns two.

Institute for Children's Environmental Health, www.iceh.org, has fact sheets, practice prevention columns in English and Spanish, the latest children's environmental health news, and links to other resources.

Healthy Schools Network, www.healthyschools.org, has information about how to ensure that your child has a safe school environment.

Environmental Protection Agency, www.epa.gov/children, has an extensive section on its website called "Children's Health Protection," which offers basic information, tips, and resources. The site also provides specific information based on where you live.

The Green Guide, www.thegreenguide.com, has many articles and product reports on its website.

5 HOME BUILDING AND IMPROVEMENT

We all want our homes to be as safe, functional, and comfortable as possible. It makes sense then to use the least hazardous and most efficient building materials available—and this means sourcing supplies that are easier on the environment and less toxic to live with. Whether you're building a new home from the ground up or replacing your kitchen floor, there's a whole spectrum of green options available today.

More and more consumers are taking advantage of these choices as a way to lower utility bills, protect the planet, or improve indoor air quality by reducing toxins. Whatever your motivations, it's getting easier to green up your home thanks to a growing number of architects, builders, and other professionals who are well versed in sustainability. There is also a rapidly expanding array of sustainable and nontoxic building materials on the market. If you are looking to buy a new home, you can even find one rated by the government's Energy Star program (the joint project of the Environmental Protection Agency [EPA] and the Department of Energy designed to promote consumer conservation) or build one that's Leadership in Energy and Environmental Design (LEED) certified by the U.S. Green Building Council (see page 129). The world of green home building is changing fast—even weekly, says Evelyne Michaut, green building advocate at the Natural Resources Defense Council (NRDC).

The flip side to the green building boom is that all the choices can be overwhelming. Home renovating and building is always stressful. For the average person, any home project, let alone a green building project, can be confusing. This chapter will introduce you to the basics and offer resources to obtain more information depending upon your goals and interests. In Chapter 6, you can also find additional information on heating and cooling systems, windows, home appliances, and energy use.

Looking at the future of green building, new homes and renovations are only the tip of the iceberg—and that's good news for all of us. Schools, hospitals, office buildings, and others are starting to incorporate green building principles into their plans. Studies are beginning to show these changes afford multiple benefits to occupants. For example, when offices and schools use more daylight and full-spectrum lighting not only do energy bills decrease, but also the people inside are happier, workers are more productive, and students perform better on tests. Green building can mean more money and more planning up front, but the long-term savings and other advantages are worth it.

Green Building 101

There's no single right way to build green and no perfect green building product to use. As an individual consumer, you need to factor in your priorities, including budget, sustainability, energy use, aesthetics, and comfort. Here's a green building cheat sheet to get you started:

WHY BUILD GREEN?

Most people are motivated by one or more of the following three reasons:

- **Lower utility bills.** It's possible to design your home with strategies and products that conserve energy and water and therefore lower your bills. This is increasingly important to some consumers as energy costs rise.

- **Protect the planet.** Greener homes conserve energy and water. Using less energy means power plants spew out fewer greenhouse gas emissions and other types of air pollution. Water is a finite resource that's in limited supply, so it's also important to save. Less than 1 percent of all the water on the Earth is usable for drinking. It takes energy to treat and transport water, so conserving water makes a positive impact on climate change as well. The building materials and products you use can impact the environment in many ways. For example, some wood products may contribute to deforestation and the polyvinyl chloride (PVC) that's ubiquitous in building products has numerous deleterious impacts on the planet (see page 120).

- **Health concerns.** Greener homes can be healthier to live in. Indoor air can be more polluted than outdoor air; dust, mold, and chemical fumes are associated with allergies, asthma, and other health issues (see page 123). Using products that don't significantly off-gas chemicals can have a positive impact on the air you breathe at home. There are also strategies you can employ to avoid moisture problems that can lead to unhealthy buildup of mold.

WILL IT COST MORE MONEY?

It definitely can be more expensive to build green, but experts say it doesn't necessarily have to be. Many of the materials, such as triple-glaze windows and solar water heaters, are more expensive to buy but may save you money in the long run, especially if energy costs continue to rise. Here are some tips to help you cut your costs:

- You can keep your budget down by bringing in a team of green experts and making all the plans in a methodical way from the beginning of the process, according to Monica Gilchrist of Global Green USA's Green Building Resource Center. Much of green building is in the initial planning, she advises. You'll have more flexibility and better choices if you start from the beginning, but don't be discouraged if you're in the midst of a project and decide to green it up. It is possible to shift gears even simply by purchasing low-flow toilets or energy-efficient appliances.

- Size matters. The simple decision of building a smaller house can save you a significant amount of money even if you're boosting the overall quality of construction, says Alex Wilson, president of BuildingGreen, Inc. He also points out that in most cases, a smaller house is a greener house by definition because it takes fewer materials to build, requires less energy to heat and cool, and affects less land when it's sited.

- Figure out what your priorities are. You'll make different decisions depending upon whether you're primarily motivated by protecting your family's health, saving money on your utility bills, or protecting the planet. There are going to be trade-offs associated with every decision you make, so the clearer you are from the beginning about what you're trying to accomplish the more efficient the process will be. If you're constructing a new home you'll also want to consider where you're building and if it's at all possible choose a location that allows you to use public transportation or walk or bike frequently.

- Find an experienced green architect, designer, contractor, or building store. The U.S. Green Building Council, www.usgbc.org, has a directory of experienced professionals on its website (see page 129 for more information). You can also search for green architects and designers in Co-op America's National Green Pages, www.coopamerica.org, a directory of screened green businesses. If possible, try to find professionals who have some green experience so you're not paying them to learn on the job.

INSULATION

Insulation isn't the most exciting part of a building project, but it's getting more interesting as innovative green products hit the market. Insulation that's well installed can make a big difference in your heating and cooling needs. It's great for your wallet and for the planet, too, since the less energy you use the less greenhouse gas emissions will be emitted from power plants. Standard insulation is made of fiberglass, which is a carcinogen when it becomes airborne, according to Gilchrist of Global Green USA. Today there are several great alternatives on the market. You can use different insulation materials for different parts of your house to offset your costs if need be. For tips on how to insulate and more information see page 143.

GREEN

- If you use fiberglass, then Gilchrist suggests you buy a product that's labeled formaldehyde-free or is certified by The Greenguard Environmental Institute, www.greenguard.org, an Atlanta-based nonprofit that has a certification program for furnishings and building materials that meet its standards for chemical emissions. Johns Manville formaldehyde-free insulation is a widely available brand; go to www.jm.com. Also look for products made with the most post-consumer recycled content.

GREENER

- Blown cellulose—recycled or natural fiber product such as recycled newsprint—is blown in damp so it gets into hard-to-reach places. Gilchrist says it's cost-effective, but in most cases you're going to need to pay someone to install it. Contact the Cellulose Insulation Manufacturers Association, www.cellulose.org, if you can't find it at one of the resources listed in "Green Home Shopping" (page 126) or through one of the organizations listed in "For More Information" (page 128).

• There are now nontoxic spray-foam products that work well, and while they're more expensive than fiberglass they are competitive with other foam products. Try Icynene, www.icynene.com, or BioBased, www.biobased.net, products.

GREENEST

• Your sexiest option is denim, says Gilchrist, which is made from industrial scraps. Cotton insulation, including denim, is more expensive, but you can install it yourself and it works well. Log onto www.bondedlogic.com to find a local provider.

ROOFING

The climate you live in is a huge consideration when picking roofing materials, so this is not an area where you'll find many one-size-fits-all options. There are entire books dedicated to the subject if you're up for it, but in general, you'll want to consider energy efficiency, durability, and your location. Try to find the most durable option that works in your climate so you don't have to replace your roof often. Recycled slate is an incredibly durable and increasingly affordable option that works well anywhere, says Gilchrist. There is also a growing array of recycled rubber roofs that are made to look like natural products. Those who live in the city or nearby suburbs may want to consider the heat island effect—these areas can be up to 10 degrees Fahrenheit hotter than surrounding rural areas—and choose a roofing option that will help cut down on air-conditioning costs and air pollution. For more information on the heat island effect and related topics visit the EPA's website, www.epa.gov/hiri.

GREEN

• The majority of roofs in the United States are dark colored and absorb a considerable amount of heat, which is then released at night, keeping air temperatures high. Simply painting your roof white will help keep your home cooler by reflecting the sun's energy.

GREENER

• Consider an EnergyStar reflective roof, which can lower the surface temperature by up to 100 degrees Fahrenheit, decrease the amount of heat transferred into your home, and reduce peak cooling needs by 10 to 15 percent.

GREENEST

• Photovoltaic shingles and panels are available for those who want to capture the energy of the sun to create electricity in their home. In most states if you install solar panels, excess electricity can be sold back to utility companies through something called "net metering," which means that when the sun is out your electricity meter runs backward, giving you a credit. At night or at other times you can get your electricity from the grid. High demand and a shortage in silicon used in the panels have kept prices too high for the average consumer, according to Wilson of BuildingGreen, Inc. Rebates and other incentives can reduce the price tag some, depending upon where you live. Check the Database of State Incentives for Renewables & Efficiency, www.dsireusa.org, which gives information on state, local, utility, and federal incentives that promote renewable energy and efficiency.

• Living roof systems range from simple to fairly complex and pricey. The general concept is the same: soil and plantings are used over waterproof membranes and specialized green roof components. Proponents name multiple benefits, including reducing the heat island effect by keeping your roof (and your home) cooler; filtering pollution from rainwater and diverting some from sewage systems; and providing a place for birds and other small animals to live. Consider a living roof if you have a roof that's relatively flat and can handle a lot of weight, and money isn't an object. They tend to be more practical for commercial buildings that have low-sloped roofs. For more information visit www.greenroofs.com and www.epa.gov/hiri.

FLOORING AND CARPETING

Some people consider it a luxury to have lush wall-to-wall carpeting. Others choose it as an inexpensive option in places they don't want to install flooring. No matter how you slice it, though, carpeting is not the best choice for your health or the planet. Carpeting fills up with dust and dirt that can aggravate allergies and asthma. Rugs and their backings can also be a major source of volatile organic compounds (VOCs; see page 123). Many are made from petroleum products that contribute to our dependence on foreign oil. It's also not easy to find places that recycle old carpets, so they often end up in landfills, but it's worth a call to your local municipal waste center to find out if there are any programs in your area (see Chapter 12 for resources).

Conventional floors are hardly the epitome of green. There are numerous concerns with many materials. Hardwood floors can contribute to deforestation and off-gas formaldehyde. The stains used to treat hardwood can release toxic fumes into the air. PVC may be cheap and durable, but nothing about it is eco-friendly (see page 120). Toxic adhesives are often used to bond laminate flooring to subflooring. The following suggestions will help you make environment-friendly flooring choices.

GREEN

- Consider alternatives to wall-to-wall carpeting. Use washable area rugs when possible. If you do buy carpeting, the American Lung Association suggests taking the following precautions: ask the retailer to unroll and air out the carpet in a well-ventilated area before delivering, leave during installation and, immediately after, open doors and windows to get more fresh air inside. You can request that the installer follow installation guidelines of the Carpet and Rug Institute, www.carpet-rug.com.

- Use the least toxic stains, sealants, grouts, and glues available. Check the label. You'll want less than 50 grams of VOCs per liter for indoor products, says Gilchrist.

- Look for the Carpet and Rug Institute's Green Label Plus stamp of approval, which you'll see on products that meet standards for emitting low amounts of VOCs.

GREENER

• Carpet tiles are a great way to minimize waste because you just replace tiles as needed and the rest remain intact. The following products are your best bets in terms of eco-friendly manufacture and materials and end-of-life considerations:

Interface's FLOR line, www.interfaceinc.com, is made of low VOC–emitting materials, and the company recycles old tiles into new product.

Shaw's EcoWorx tile, www.shawgreenedge.com, is PVC free and made from recycled fibers. The company will pick up your old tiles for free.

• There are pros and cons to many of the eco-friendly flooring choices available today. Taking into account your goals and your budget, consider the following options: bamboo (without added formaldehyde), cork, recycled tile and stone, natural linoleum, and wood from certified forests (see pages 118–119). A good source for a wide variety of products is the Environmental Home Center (see page 126).

• Use a waterborne polyurethane finish for your wood floor to avoid toxic fumes if it fits in your budget. They wear comparably to solvent-based finishes, according to Wilson of BuildingGreen, Inc.

• RugMark, www.rugmark.org, is a nonprofit dedicated to ending illegal child labor in South Asia's carpet industry. Look for the RugMark label for a guarantee that a carpet or rug is child-labor-free.

WOOD PRODUCTS

Wood is a ubiquitous part of many home improvement projects. It's likely, though, that many of the wood products found inside your home are made from particleboard and medium-density fiberboard (MDF), which usually off-gas formaldehyde (see page 124). MDF is a popular material for cabinets, shelving, and stair treads, among others. Your best bet is to avoid MDF whenever possible. Purchase formaldehyde-free versions when available. Products don't have to be labeled, but most manufacturers who aren't adding formaldehyde to products will say so. PureBond is one company that makes formaldehyde-free plywood. Consider alternatives such as enameled metal, bamboo, wheatboard, or Forest Stewardship Council (FSC) certified solid wood.

The Forest Stewardship Council is a nonprofit that runs an excellent certification program and encourages responsible management of the

GREENEST

- Buy carpets and rugs made from recycled or natural materials such as wool (ask your retailer to make sure any wool products haven't been treated with toxic moth repellants), alpaca, or hemp. Some of these options can be pricey.

PAINT AND WALL COVERINGS

Ever wonder what's behind that new-paint smell? It's the vapors that are released from hazardous chemicals and solvents used, such as formaldehyde, toluene, and xylene, and other known irritants, carcinogens, and neurotoxins. These VOCs have a range of world's forests. (More than half of the earth's original forest cover has been destroyed, according to the NRDC.) The FSC logo guarantees consumers that the wood is from a certified, well-managed forest: one that is not contributing to habitat destruction, water pollution, displacement of indigenous people, or violence against wildlife and people who work in the forest. Not all certified wood is the same. Make sure any products you buy are FSC accredited, which the NRDC calls the only credible forest certification program. You can find products at Home Depot, Lowes, and other retailers. You'll pay a premium, but prices are coming down as demand increases. Visit www.fscus.org for a database that searches manufacturers and distributors.

For more information, go to the Rainforest Alliance website, www.rainforest-alliance.org, which offers valuable information on sustainable wood and forests. Check out the "Smart Guide to Green Building Wood Resources."

health and environmental impacts (see pages 123–124). Luckily, nontoxic paints are widely available and cost competitive. Try AFM Safecoat, which also makes nontoxic seals, adhesives, and stains; other good options are Yolo Colorhouse or Benjamin Moore Eco Spec. Most of the major paint companies have eco-friendly lines that work well, says Gilchrist of Global Green USA.

GREEN

- Avoid oil paints, which contain substantially more VOCs than their latex counterparts.

- Make sure the area you're painting is well ventilated and use a fan. Air out your newly painted house before sleeping in it.

GREENER

- Check paint labels and buy paints with low VOC levels when available. The California Air Resources Board recommends a range of 100 to 150 grams per liter (g/l) or lower.

- Most wallpaper is made from PVC and applied with toxic adhesives, so it's best to avoid it altogether. If you're set on wallpaper, try the vinyl-free versions from Innovations, available at the Environmental Home Center (pages 126–127). JaDecor Natural Wall Covering, www.jadecor.com, is made from cotton, plant fibers, and minerals. Try American Clay, www.americanclay.com, a clay-based natural earth plaster, as an alternative to wallpaper. Other alternative wall coverings include bamboo and cork paneling or sponging with nontoxic paint.

GREENEST

- Seek out paints with no VOCs.

Spotlight On: PVC

It's well known that plastics are not an eco-friendly material, but there are some that are worse than others. Polyvinyl chloride, also known as vinyl or PVC, is considered the most environmentally damaging plastic around. The whole lifecycle of PVC is a problem. The production of it creates and releases dioxin, a known carcinogen that's now a part of our food chain, particularly in fatty foods such as meat and dairy products. Phthalates, which are linked to reproductive and birth defects in animal studies, are added to make it soft and flexible (see page 71). These chemicals can leach out of products and have been found in human bodies. PVC is also difficult to get rid of. It's rarely recycled because there are many additives in it, so it usually ends up in landfills where toxins can leach into nearby groundwater. Incineration isn't a great option either because it just releases more dioxin into the air.

PVC is ubiquitous even though there are alternatives available in many cases. The following products can be made from it: flooring, wallpaper, window frames, blinds, pipes, shower curtains, toys, packaging, plastic wraps, garden hoses, and credit cards.

It's unlikely that you'll be able to completely avoid PVC, but there are certainly measures you can take to minimize your exposure to it.

- Check labels for recycling code 3 (see Chapter 12), which means it's made from PVC, or look for the word "vinyl," and buy alternative products if available. The same goes for packaging. Buy a comparable product with packaging that's PVC-free if you can.

- Your shower curtain can off-gas phthalates for years, so replace it with one that's PVC-free.

- Choose PVC-free building products such as flooring and window frames when possible.

RESOURCES

- The Healthy Building Network, www.healthybuilding.net, has a series of tools to help you identify PVC-products. The GreenSpec database is also a good source (see pages 129–130). See Greenpeace's PVC Alternatives Database, http://archive.greenpeace.org/toxics/pvcdatabase, for more ideas.

- The Vinyl Institute's website, www.vinylinstitute.org, has a directory of companies involved in recycling PVC plastic.

VENTILATION

Good ventilation is essential if you want your home to be filled with healthy air (see page 123). The goal is to bring in enough outdoor air to dilute emissions from pollutants in your house and carry some of those pollutants outside. There are a number of variables to consider when determining the kind of ventilation to install in your home, including whether you have a new tight house or an old leaky home, whether you are building from scratch or retrofitting a system for your existing home, and what the climate is like. Mechanical ventilation is important and should be included in any home that is reasonably well insulated, but generally, newer homes are tighter so ventilation is more important, says Wilson of BuildingGreen, Inc., who also points out that there are a number of ways to do it, from simple to expensive.

GREEN

- Change filters in heating systems. Keep them clean and well maintained.

- Opening a window can be a simple and easy way to introduce fresh air into your home under certain circumstances. There needs to be either a temperature difference between the inside and outside air or some breeze outside, says Wilson.

GREENER

- Install bathroom and kitchen fans that exhaust to the outside, and run them intermittently.

GREENEST

- Whole-house ventilation is the most effective option. There are many ways to accomplish this, from adding a ventilation component onto your central furnace or air-conditioning system to buying an entirely new system that may or may not be integrated with a furnace and air-conditioning system. Your best bet is to find a knowledgeable professional who can advise you on ventilation strategies for your home. Visit the Air Conditioning Contractors of America website, www.acca.org, and search by ZIP code for contractors who specialize in ventilation and indoor air quality.

Breathe Clean: Indoor Air Quality

The air inside your home or office can be more seriously polluted than the outdoor air in even the largest cities, according to the EPA. That's particularly concerning, given that we spend about 90 percent of our time indoors. Aside from having good ventilation, your best bet for maintaining healthier air at home is to prevent as many sources of pollution as possible from entering your home in the first place. Here are some of the most common indoor air pollutants:

Volatile Organic Compounds (VOCs) are organic compounds that evaporate into the air. They can be emitted by many household products such as building products, furniture, paints, varnish, cleaning supplies, pesticides, dry-cleaned clothing, and others, according to the EPA. Health effects vary from eye irritation, headaches, and nausea to liver, kidney, and central nervous system damage. Some are known to cause cancer in animals, and some are suspected or known human carcinogens. The EPA says that we don't know a lot about the health effects from levels commonly found in homes.

Formaldehyde is a chemical that can be found in many products around your home. Building materials, particularly pressed-wood products, are a common source. Other potential sources include cigarette smoke; unvented fuel-burning appliances; and a number of household products including paints, permanent press clothing, antibacterial soaps, beauty products, and others. Exposures to formaldehyde vapors can cause eye, nose, and throat irritation; coughing; skin rashes; headaches; dizziness; nausea; vomiting; and nosebleeds, according to the American Lung Association. It's also considered a probable human carcinogen by the EPA. Buy formaldehyde-free pressed wood products and other building materials when available (see pages 118–119). Some other ways to minimize exposure: avoid permanent press fabrics as well as paints with high levels of VOCs by checking labels.

Molds thrive in warm, damp, and humid conditions. They can cause allergic reactions, wheezing, or other respiratory issues. Prevention is your best bet. The Centers for Disease Control and Prevention (CDC) recommends keeping humidity levels in your house between 40 to 60 percent, using an air conditioner or dehumidifier when needed, and making sure your house is well ventilated. If you do have mold the first thing you should do is determine the source of moisture and eliminate it. Fixing roof or plumbing leaks, repairing roof flashing, taking measures to stop moisture from entering your basement, and adding storm windows so you don't get condensation are some things you might need to do depending on the circumstances, says Wilson of BuildingGreen, Inc. After you dry things out you'll need to clean them up. Try soap and water, commercial products, or a weak bleach solution. The CDC says not to use more than one cup of bleach per gallon of water. Open the windows and wear gloves and something to protect your eyes. Never mix bleach and ammonia. For more information visit www.epa.gov/mold/moldguide.html.

Carbon monoxide can kill you before you're even aware it's in your home, according to the EPA. This is especially problemátic at night while you are sleeping. Install a battery-operated carbon monoxide detector in your home, available at most home-improvement stores. The U.S. Consumer Product Safety Commission, recommends buying models that meet the requirements of the most recent Underwriters Laboratories (UL) Standard 2034 (labeled on the package). Don't forget to change the batteries. The CDC recommends that you replace them when you change the time on your clocks each spring and fall for daylight savings. Put detectors in your bedroom or other places where your family spends a lot of time and where you can hear the alarm. Common symptoms of exposure include headache, dizziness, nausea, fatigue, chest pain, and confusion.

Radon is a naturally occurring gas found in the ground that can accumulate in your basement and rise into your living area. The only way to know if it's in your home is to test for it. Why bother? It's the leading cause of lung cancer in nonsmokers and the second among those who smoke, and is responsible for 20,000 deaths a year, according to the EPA. You can test for it yourself with kits from hardware stores or from the National Safety Council, or call in a professional. Get in touch with your state radon contact by visiting www.epa.gov/iaq/whereyoulive.html and click on your state for testing and remediation resources. The EPA recommends that you address the problem if radon levels are 4 picoCuries per liter (p Ci/L) or higher, but warns that lower levels also pose a risk, especially those in the 2 to 4 p Ci/L range. The average radon level in buildings is 1.3.

GREEN HOME SHOPPING

Green products are popping up everywhere, from traditional retail stores to websites dedicated exclusively to eco-friendly products. Bear in mind that some of the specialized stores can be great sources of information because they are wholly committed to green products.

As of April 2007, **Wal-Mart** (the world's largest retailer) and **Home Depot** (the world's largest home improvement chain and America's second-largest retailer) had both launched major ad campaigns announcing that their stores will be offering consumers a greater range of ecologically friendly products. Wal-Mart is carrying everything from organic baby food to compact fluorescent (CFL) lightbulbs. Home Depot is using the label "Eco Options" on thousands of designated greener items and plans to increase offerings.

Environmental Home Center, www.environmentalhomecenter.com, is a national distributor of green building and household products. You can find a wide range of eco-friendly products from paints to insulation to FSC certified wood online or, if you live near Seattle, at its showroom. The website also offers information on installation, how products were picked and topics like how to go green on a budget. It's also possible for homeowners to email customer service with questions.

Livingreen, www.livingreen.com, has a number of retail stores in California selling products ranging from cleaning supplies to paint to clothing. You can shop for many items on the website.

By the time this book is published there will be many more retailers offering greener home-building products. However, there will probably also be many not so eco-friendly items being advertised as green. When looking to buy an environmentally friendly new product to renovate your home, consider whether or not it has any of the following characteristics: conserves energy and/or water, is salvaged, is made from renewable or recycled materials, can be recycled, will last a long time, is a certified wood product, or is an alternative to a hazardous product.

In some cases, the greenest product may be the one you already own. It takes energy and other natural resources to make and transport new materials and products. Before you buy something new, consider whether you can reuse what you already own to cut down on what gets sent to the landfill. Try to donate old stuff, and if you can't find someone to take it try to recycle (see Chapter 12). You can also buy salvaged products from used building materials stores. The ReUse People's website, www.thereusepeople.org, is a nonprofit dedicated to keeping usable building products out of landfills. You can donate used products or buy them. Habitat for Humanity also takes donations of building materials. The Freecycle Network, www.freecycle.org, and CraigsList, www.craigslist.org, are online communities (with regional links) where you can list items that you are trying to give away.

For More Information

BuildingGreen, Inc., www.buildinggreen.com, is considered the *Consumer Reports* for green building information. Many of the resources are geared toward building professionals, but if you know how to navigate the website you'll find a wealth of accurate, unbiased information that's explained simply and clearly. Consumers can pay a small fee for a week's online access to the entire site including *Environmental Building News* articles and case studies as well as GreenSpec, a database of thousands of products that the editors consider "green" after extensive research. Any architect you're considering for a green renovation or new home should have access to this resource.

Green Building Blocks, www.greenbuildingblocks.com, is geared toward professionals, but some of its tools can also be useful to consumers. Parts of the GreenSpec database are available for free and you can also search for green building pros in your area.

Green Building Resource Center, www.globalgreen.org/gbrc/index.htm, a partnership between Global Green USA and the city of Santa Monica, offers resources both online and in its Santa Monica and New Orleans locations. The centers are stocked with samples of popular eco-friendly materials, publications about green building, and databases listing local products and professionals. The staff provides free advice on green building and design and can connect consumers to experienced green building professionals. If you don't live nearby you can call the center and they'll help you find resources near your home. Online you'll find information on green building as well as links to great local and national resources.

U.S. Green Building Council, www.usgbc.org, is a nonprofit with thousands of members from the building sector seeking to transform the way buildings are created. It runs the Leadership in Energy and Environmental Design (LEED) green rating building system, which was originally designed for commercial buildings but has grown to include a variety of projects including schools, hospitals, homes, and even neighborhoods. Points are awarded for meeting criteria in several different areas including site planning, water and energy management, materials, and indoor air quality. There are four levels of approval: "certified," "silver," "gold," or "platinum." The directory of LEED-accredited professionals is a useful tool for finding architects, engineers, and other building professionals with knowledge about green building (whether or not you are seeking LEED certification). Visit their consumer-oriented website, the Green Home Guide, www.greenhomeguide.org, for extensive residential information and resources.

The Green Guide, www.thegreenguide.com, has numerous product reports and suggestions on a whole range of building products.

You might also find the following two books helpful:

Green Building Products: The GreenSpec Guide to Residential Building Materials (New Society Publishers) by Alex Wilson and

Mark Piepkorn gives the basics on all the varying components in clear, easily understandable language and offers an impressive list of green products in every category you can think of.

Your Green Home: A Guide to Planning a Healthy, Environmentally Friendly New Home (New Society Publishers) by Alex Wilson is a great tool for those who are building from the ground up.

6 ENERGY AND WATER CONSERVATION

Using less energy at home is a win-win proposal. It's a significant way each of us can save money and at the same time have a positive impact on global climate change. The energy used in the average home can be responsible for twice as many greenhouse gases as the average car. Contrary to what many people might think, it's pretty easy to start conserving today. The average family spends about $1,900 a year on utilities, according to EnergyStar, and as much as $600 of that energy is wasted. That means that most of us have plenty of room for improvement.

The average U.S. household emits 22,000 pounds of carbon dioxide a year. According to Bill Prindle, deputy director of the American Council for an Energy-Efficient Economy, a typical U.S. household can use 30 to 40 percent less energy a year over time by employing several strategies, many of which are outlined in this chapter. It's difficult to do all at once, says Prindle, but if you start with the relatively easy things you can use 15 to 20 percent less energy per year, and therefore emit less carbon dioxide, without a significant investment of time or money. His suggestions on where to start and how much carbon dioxide you'll save a year:

- Installing an EnergyStar thermostat (500 pounds)
- Switching to low-flow showerheads (700 pounds)
- Using five compact fluorescent bulbs (300 pounds)
- Sealing up leaks around doors and windows (500 pounds)
- Reducing air-duct leakage (1,600 pounds)

It's becoming increasingly clear that conserving water is important, but most of us don't realize that it's also a great way to use less energy—about 13 percent of home utility bills are dedicated to water heating. Energy is also used to deliver and treat public water supplies. Public water supply and treatment facilities consume vast amounts of electricity, enough to power more than 5 million homes a year, according to the Environmental Protection Agency (EPA). Running your faucet for five minutes uses as much energy as letting a 60-watt lightbulb run for 14 hours, says the EPA.

Generating electric power is highly polluting. Power plants spew emissions that contribute not only to global climate change but also to acid rain and urban smog. They're also a major source of toxic air pollutants such as mercury, which makes its way into animals, fish, and ultimately into our bodies through the foods we eat.

As consumers, many of us now have choices about what kind of electricity we buy—something not everyone is aware of. We can choose for our electricity to be generated by cleaner, renewable sources such as wind or solar without having to make major investments (see below). Buying green power for the average U.S. home for one year saves as much carbon dioxide emissions as planting nearly two acres of trees or taking one car off the road for the same amount of time, according to Worldwatch Institute.

Coal is currently our cheapest, most abundant, *and* most polluting source of energy, and it's not going anywhere soon. In the future, technologies that make it possible to burn coal cleaner may become an important part of the equation. While nuclear power may ultimately become a desirable alternative to coal, the Sierra Club, Natural Resources Defense Council (NRDC), and Environmental Defense concur that at present it poses unacceptable safety, security, and environmental risks. It's also not economically viable without hefty goverment subsidies.

The simplest and most immediate steps we can take to save energy involve basic habit changes—switching off the lights when you leave a room or turning off the faucet while you're brushing your teeth, for example. It's great to keep these in mind, but you don't have to do it all yourself. There are an increasing number of products on the market designed to do the conserving for you, making it easier for you to save energy and water and also to save money, both on your utility and water bills and through tax credits and rebates.

Choosing a Green Energy Program

You don't have to slap solar panels on your roof to tap into the benefits of alternative energy. Renewable energy, which can generate electricity with very low or no amounts of emissions, is available to many consumers who are willing to spend a little more money each month for electricity. Here are your options:

- Many utility companies have "green pricing" programs in which you pay a small premium for the company to use renewable energy or to develop sources of it. Your local area will be fueled by green power, but participating in a program doesn't guarantee that your house is. However, it does help reduce overall fossil fuel consumption, which ultimately benefits everyone and impacts global warming and air pollution.

- In some states you can switch to a different supplier offering green power. If you have a choice, pick a supplier that uses renewable power resources such as solar, wind, low-impact hydroelectric, or geothermal.

- Consider buying renewable energy credits (RECs), also known as "green tags," if your local utility doesn't offer a green pricing program or you're unhappy with your supplier options. Each certificate represents a specific amount of clean power added to the nation's energy grid in place of electricity drawn from conventional sources. By purchasing a tag or certificate, you can help offset global warming pollution created in generating electricity for your home or office.

For More Information

To learn more about your green power options, including renewable energy credits, and to find out where you can buy green power in your state visit the U.S. Department of Energy at www.eere.energy.gov/greenpower/buying/buying_power.shtml.

Power Scorecard, www.powerscorecard.org, rates the environmental impact of different types of electric generation in states where consumers can make choices. At press time, the ratings are available only for residents of California, New Jersey, New York, Pennsylvania, and Texas, but it's worth checking if your state has been added.

Green-e, www.green-e.org, a green power certification program run by the nonprofit Center for Resource Solutions, sets standards for green pricing and ensures that utility companies are delivering on their promise to invest in renewable resources. Your best bet is to look for its seal of approval.

WATER

Water is a finite resource that's both essential to our survival and in short supply. In the United States, water shortages are already an issue for the Western states, but as the population continues to grow, other areas will be affected as well. According to the EPA, every American uses an average of 100 gallons a day—enough to fill 1,600 drinking glasses—so there's plenty of room for improvement! The EPA created its WaterSense program, which labels products and services that meet water efficiency criteria and perform well, to make conservation easier. The program is in its infancy but will certify showerheads, urinals, and other equipment in the future. Saving water will also save you money. The EPA reports the average household spends as much as $500 a year on its water and sewer bill, which, by just making simple changes, could be reduced by an average of $170.

GREEN

• Don't let the water run when brushing your teeth, washing your face, or shaving. The EPA estimates that you can save 8 gallons of water a day or 240 a month by turning off your tap while you brush your teeth in the morning and evening.

• Take shorter showers. Don't fill the tub up all the way when taking baths, and immediately stopper the drain. You can adjust the temperature as you fill the tub. According to the EPA, a five-minute shower uses 10 to 25 gallons of water and it takes 70 gallons to fill a tub.

• Don't let the tap water run to get cold drinking water. Store it in the refrigerator.

• When washing dishes by hand, fill the sink with soapy water instead of letting the tap water run.

• Avoid unnecessary toilet flushing.

• Run dishwashers and washing machines only when full. Remember to adjust load sizes when you're washing clothes.

• Fix leaks and drips. Leaky faucets dripping one drip per second can waste more than 3,000 gallons of water each year, and a leaky toilet can waste about 200 gallons of water every day, according to the EPA.

GREENER

• Buy low-flow showerheads and faucets. See *Consumer Reports* for performance ratings. You don't have to replace entire fixtures. For faucets, you can screw in an aerator. Alex Wilson, president of BuildingGreen, Inc., recommends not going below two gallons per minute for your kitchen faucet, but says a half to one gallon per minute is adequate for your bathroom (it will take longer for hot water to reach your faucet with a lower flow rate). For showers, you'll just need to replace the showerhead. Go for a good quality model, says Wilson. Look for the WaterSense label on faucets and aerators.

• Wash your car by hand with a bucket of water.

• Sweep your sidewalk and driveway instead of hosing it down.

• Don't pour unused water down the sink; use it to water plants or your garden, or give clean, unused water to pets.

• There are several strategies you can employ to conserve water in your garden. See Chapter 10 for suggestions.

● GREENEST

• Install low flush toilets, especially if your toilet was made before 1992. The average American home uses more water for flushing the toilet than showering and could save more than 16,500 gallons of water every year by replacing a traditional toilet with a WaterSense model. You'll also save a considerable amount of energy. If 1 percent of American homes replaced an older toilet with a high-efficiency model, the power saved would be enough to supply more than 43,000 households with electricity for one month, says the EPA. Look for the WaterSense label as a guarantee that you're purchasing a high-performing, water-efficient model. See *Consumer Reports* for performance ratings. Recycle your old toilet.

- Don't let the water run when taking showers. Get wet, turn off water while you're soaping up, and then turn the water on to rinse off.

For more information on water conservation check out:

EPA WaterSense Program, www.epa.gov/watersense. You'll find basic information on water conservation strategies, water-saving product information, and a quiz to determine how much you know about water efficiency.

H_2OUSE: Water Saver Home, www.h2ouse.net, developed by the California Urban Water Conservation Council. This site offers a virtual tour to show you water-saving opportunities in every area of your home. The Water Budget Calculator helps you find out how much water you're using.

WATER HEATING

Water heating accounts for around 13 percent of your utility bill. The most obvious things you can do are to conserve water when possible and prevent heat from escaping your system. See page 135 for water saving tips.

GREEN

- Set the thermostat on your water heater to 130 degrees F, suggests Alex Wilson, president of BuildingGreen, Inc. You may see recommendations for lower settings, which can save energy, but

Wilson says that it could actually increase your operating costs if your dishwasher uses its booster heater to raise the water temperature (it depends on what your energy sources are for each type of heat). He also cautions that it's possible for the bacteria that causes Legionnaires' disease, a type of pneumonia, to survive in a tank set at 120 degrees F.

● GREENER

• Insulate your hot water heater. You can buy water heater "blankets" at most hardware and home improvement stores.

• The U.S. Department of Energy (DOE) recommends draining a quart of water from your tank every three months to remove sediment; this will help it run more efficiently.

● GREENEST

• Insulate the pipes connected to the water heater. You can do this yourself fairly easily with readily available foam insulation sleeves, says Wilson.

• When it's time to replace your water heater, buy an energy efficient model. Use the EnergyStar Home Advisor, www.energystar.gov/homeadviser, to find the best options for where you live.

• Consider alternative heating methods such as tankless or solar water heaters. Both are more expensive options but can save energy. In the case of solar it depends on your climate and the cost of the fuels being displaced, according to Wilson. The Solar

CONDUCTING AN ENERGY ASSESSMENT

A home energy audit will help you determine the places where you are leaking the most energy. There are several levels of commitment you can make to this process, from conducting your own inspection to hiring someone to carry out the assessment for you.

CONDUCT YOUR OWN ENERGY AUDIT

It's not going to be as comprehensive as a professional assessment, but you'll get some benefit and it won't cost you any money. There are plenty of places on the Internet that can help you through this process:

The EnergyStar Home Energy Yardstick, **www.energystar.gov, checks your home's energy use by comparing six months of your utility bills with those of other similar homes. This isn't an actual energy assessment, but it will let you know how well you are doing without much effort.**

The DOE's Office of Energy Efficiency and Renewable Energy (EERE) **offers many resources for consumers. To read about how to conduct your own energy audit or to get information on how to prepare for a professional energy audit visit www.eere.energy.gov/consumer. Click on "Your Home" and then click on "Energy Audits."**

Rating and Certification Corporation and the Florida Solar Energy Center offer ratings of products. The Database of State Incentives for Renewables & Efficiency, www.dsireusa.org, can tell you if you qualify for any tax credits or rebates.

The Lawrence Berkeley National Laboratory's Home Energy Saver, http://hes.lbl.gov, will assess your home's energy use and suggest ways to make improvements. Once you decide on an improvement, it offers many tools to help make it happen.

CALL IN A PROFESSIONAL

Ask your local utility if they offer free or discounted energy audits. If not, consider hiring someone yourself. An energy rater will come into your home with special equipment to identify areas where you can make cost-effective improvements in energy efficiency. Some might even calculate return on investment for you. The best place to find raters is through one of the following two services:

Residential Energy Services Network (RESNET). **Visit** www.natresnet.org to access the nonprofit's state-by-state directory of certified raters who have committed to following strict standards.

California Home Energy Efficiency Rating Services (CHEERS). California residents can log on to www.cheers.org to find independent contractors that have been trained and certified.

HEATING AND COOLING

Heating and cooling account for about half of every American home utility bill and produce combined atmospheric emissions of more than 150 million tons of carbon dioxide a year, according to the Department of Energy. The good news is that there are plenty of ways to reduce your energy use in this area, ranging from easy and free to more complicated and costly. Here are the basics:

1. Use less heat and air-conditioning when possible.

2. Prevent warmed or cooled air from escaping.

3. Use the most energy-efficient equipment possible and maintain it well.

GREEN

- Set your thermostat lower in the winter and higher in the summer. Experts usually suggest keeping your home around 68 degrees in the winter and 78 in the summer. When you are away from your house or sleeping, the U.S. Green Building Council recommends adjusting the thermostat to 62 degrees or lower in the winter. On average, you'll save about 121 pounds of carbon dioxide a year for each degree you adjust your thermostat, according to Prindle. Depending on where you are starting from, there may be room for you to turn it up or down even more and the savings can really add up.

- Rather than turning up the thermostat when it is cold outside, wear warmer clothing and slippers.

GREENER

- Install a programmable thermostat to make it easier for you to adjust temperatures when you are sleeping or when you're not home. An EnergyStar model can save you $150 a year in energy costs (usually paying for itself within a year).

• Keep your air-conditioning and heating systems properly maintained by changing air filters and keeping air conditioner coils clean. EnergyStar recommends a yearly checkup.

• The cumulative gaps around the windows and doors in an average American house are the equivalent of a three-by-three-foot hole in the wall, according to the NRDC. Caulk and weather-strip to seal off air leaks. Stop air from escaping under doors with "sweeps" attached to the bottom. The EERE Consumer's Guide to Energy Efficiency and Renewable Energy, www.eere.energy.gov/consumer, offers extensive information on the different types of weather stripping and caulking available along with installation instructions.

• Install a ceiling fan to improve heat and cool-air circulation.

• Fireplaces can be a significant source of heat loss because the warmed air from your house escapes up your chimney. If you never use your fireplace then plug and seal the chimney flue. Otherwise, keep your fireplace damper closed unless there is a fire so that warm air can't escape. For more tips on how to make your fireplace more eco-friendly see the EERE's "ENERGY SAVER$ Tips on Saving Energy and Money at Home," www.eere.energy.gov/consumer.

● GREENEST

• Older homes tend to have higher heating and cooling costs because they aren't properly insulated. For extensive information and ideas on insulation visit the EERE's website, www.eere.energy.gov/consumer. Click on "Your Home" and then on

"Insulation and Air Sealing." The Department of Energy's Insulation Fact Sheet is another great resource, www.ornl.gov/sci/roof+walls/insulation/ins_01.htm. Some greener insulation materials are Icynene, BioBased, and industrial denim scraps. See Chapter 5 for more information on insulation.

• When it's time to replace your heating or cooling system go for an EnergyStar model, which can save you up to 20 percent on utility bills if it's installed correctly. When buying a new furnace look at the Annual Fuel Utilization Efficiency (AFUE) ratings. The higher the better. The national minimum is 78 percent, but some EnergyStar models exceed 90 percent, according to the EERE. When shopping for an air conditioner, look for models with a high Seasonal Energy Efficiency Ratio (SEER). The EERE says the minimum is 13 for central air conditioners.

• Size is important when it comes to room air conditioners, and bigger is not always better. How much cooling capacity you'll need (measured in British thermal units, or BTUs, per minute) is determined by the square footage you're looking to cool. If a unit's too big for the room it's trying to cool, it will perform less efficiently than one that's designed for the space. Visit www.energystar.gov for a chart that maps this out for you as well as other important buying information.

• If you're building a new home or doing a major renovation consider incorporating passive solar design, such as placing larger insulated windows on south-facing walls, to heat and cool your house. If your architect doesn't have experience with this, ask him or her to find a consultant to work with.

WINDOWS, DOORS, AND SKYLIGHTS

Window technology has come a long way since the days of single-paned models. New energy-efficient windows help prevent energy loss and lower your heating and cooling bills. If installing new widows is not in your budget and you want to improve your current windows, there are plenty of other options.

GREEN

- Keep shades up in the winter and down in the summer.
- In the winter keep south-facing windows clean to let in more warming sunlight.
- During the winter use a heavy-duty self-adhesive clear plastic sheeting to seal the inside of your windows.

GREENER

- Storm windows are a great option for those who live in rentals and those who have a limited budget. Adding interior storm windows reduces the air movement in and out of existing windows. There are a whole range of options from bare minimum and cheap to more complicated and expensive. If you own your own home, at a certain price point you might want to consider whether it is a better investment to put your money into new windows. See www.eere.energy.gov/consumer for detailed information on storm window options.
- The EERE says carefully selected window treatments and

coverings from shades to mesh screens to awnings can reduce heat loss in winter and increase natural cooling in summer. See www.eere.energy.gov/consumer for specific tips.

GREENEST

• Consider upgrading single-pane windows. You can get all kinds of benefits, from energy efficiency to noise reduction. There are several measurements and ratings you should take into account when buying windows. These are the most common:

The **U-factor** measures a window's insulation ability. The lower the U-factor the more energy efficient the window is. Ideal U-factors depend on where you live.

A low **Solar Heat Gain Coefficiency (SHGC)** means a product is good at blocking the sun's heat and can reduce your cooling costs in the summer. For homes with overheating problems or with high air-conditioning bills, the NRDC suggests looking for a SHGC of .35 or lower. You'll want to take several factors into account, such as climate and housing site, when looking at SHGC information. For more information visit www.eere.energy.gov/consumer.

The **EnergyStar** label means that windows, doors, and skylights meet guidelines based on U-factor and SHGC. For specific climate recommendations visit www.energystar.gov.

If you want to do more, the **National Fenestration Rating Council**'s Certified Products Directory is a great resource for those looking to buy energy-efficient windows, doors, or skylights. The certification is based on many measurements. Just go to the website, www.nfrc.org, to search the extensive database or look for the council's stamp of approval on products.

LIGHTING

About 11 percent of your energy bill is dedicated to lighting, but using new technologies can reduce lighting energy use in your home by 50 to 75 percent, according to the EERE. This is a relatively easy and inexpensive place to make a big difference. What can you do? In a nutshell, buy energy-efficient lightbulbs, turn out the lights when you're not using them, and buy products that will help you do the conserving. Here's how:

GREEN

• Buy just one compact fluorescent lightbulb (CFL). If every household in the United States replaced one regular lightbulb with a CFL it would reduce pollution equivalent to taking 1 million cars off the road or lighting 2.5 million homes for one year (see pages 148–149).

• Get into the habit of turning out incandescent lights, which are inefficient and produce a lot of heat, whenever you leave a room. For CFLs, the EERE recommends leaving them on if you'll be back within 15 minutes (5 minutes for places with very high electricity costs). The reason is not a factor of how much energy it takes to start up. Turning any lightbulb on and off reduces the operating life. CFLs are more sensitive to this, and since they

COMPACT FLUORESCENT LIGHTS

One CFL bulb prevents more than 450 pounds of carbon dioxide emissions from a power plant over the course its lifetime, uses at least two-thirds less energy than incandescent bulbs, and lasts up to 10 times longer. You'll save $30 or more over the life of the bulb. The light quality has improved, but if you are skeptical, try replacing the bulb in your closet, garage, or basement and see what you think.

- Check out Environmental Defense's lightbulb guide at www.environmentaldefense.org to find the best choices for you. The lighting industry is currently working on a consistent way to categorize and market CFLs around color, according to EnergyStar spokesperson Maria Vargas, but there is no standard currently in place across all retailers and manufac-

are more expensive to buy it's more cost-effective to leave them on for a little longer than you would an incandescent.

- Use task lighting when possible instead of lighting up an entire room.

GREENER

- Buy three CFLs to use in your house. If every U.S. household did that it would be the equivalent of taking 3.5 million cars off the road for one year.

- Buy dimmers to reduce wattage of bulbs.

- Install motion sensors to automatically turn on lights when needed and off when no one is around. Photo sensors prevent outdoor lights on motion sensors from operating during daylight.

turers. Typically, it is best to look for bulbs that are labeled either "soft white" or "warm white," as those are common terms used by manufacturers to correlating the bulb's color to that of an incandescent. Labels such as "cool white" and "daylight" fall within a cooler, crisper color range, less similar to that of an incandescent bulb. EnergyStar fluorescents are tested for quality and longevity.

- CFLs contain a tiny bit of mercury so dispose of them with other household hazardous waste. Visit http://earth911.org or www.epa.gov/bulbrecyling to find local recycling options. If you have no other options and your state permits you to put used or broken CFLs in the garbage, EnergyStar recommends sealing them in two plastic bags before disposing, and don't ever put them in an incinerator.

● GREENEST

- Replace a significant amount of incandescent bulbs with CFLs and buy EnergyStar-rated lighting fixtures, which are more energy efficient than standard models. Buy a CFL for friends and family.

- Light-emitting diode (LED) bulbs, which use little energy, are much more expensive than CFLs, but the prices are coming down and the quality is improving, according to Wilson of BuildingGreen, Inc. They're definitely something to keep an eye on. One of the big benefits over CFLs is that they have no mercury, says Wilson.

- Turn out the lights at work. Work with your office manager to have someone turn out lights at the end of the day, and switch off lights you see on in conference rooms and other public places when no one is using them.

APPLIANCES

Buying new energy-efficient appliances is the best way to save energy in this case, but there are plenty of things you can do to make the most of what you already have. About 7 percent of your utility bill goes toward powering your refrigerator and another 9 percent is spent on dishwashing, laundry, and cooking appliances. When buying new appliances consider both the purchase price and the amount of money it will cost to operate over time. EnergyStar has calculators for each appliance on its website to help you determine how much money you'll save.

DECODING THE LABELS

EnergyGuide. Established by the Federal Trade Commission, this is the yellow and black label you'll see on most home appliances. It provides estimates of a product's energy consumption and compares its energy efficiency to similar models.

EnergyStar. EnergyStar products meet strict energy-efficiency criteria established by the EPA and the Department of Energy. Appliances earning that stamp of approval use 10 to 50 percent less energy and water than standard models.

GREEN

- Cover pots on the stove to avoid using excess heat and wasting energy. Preheat the oven only for as long as necessary, and make sure the seal on your oven is tight.

- Use a microwave or a toaster oven for cooking smaller dishes.

- Set your refrigerator to between 35 and 40 degrees Fahrenheit and your freezer to 0 to 5 degrees. Use the power-save switch if your fridge has one and make sure the doors are sealed tightly, suggests the NRDC. Vacuum your refrigerator coil to maintain efficiency.

- Unplug small appliances like blenders and toaster ovens when you aren't using them. The power cord alone draws energy even when the appliance isn't in use. Unplugging large appliances that you don't use very often, such as a second refrigerator in a garage, can save you around $10 per month, according to the NRDC.

GREENER

- Turn off the dishwasher drying cycle and air-dry or towel-dry dishes when you're not in a rush. Load bigger items on the outside and smaller on the inside of your dishwasher. Wash full loads and use shorter cycles when possible. Use a prerinse instead of hand washing if necessary.

- Rinse your clothing in cold water and try to wash in cold water when you can. Use the moisture-sensor option on your dryer if you have it because it will automatically shut off the machine when clothes are dry. It saves energy and your clothes! Cleaning the lint filter after every load improves air circulation.

GREENEST

- When shopping for new appliances, buy the most energy-efficient models available. Your best guarantee of that is the EnergyStar label. Here's what it guarantees:

Washing machines use 40 percent less energy than standard models and 18 to 25 gallons of water per load compared to 40 for conventional machines. EnergyStar doesn't label clothes dryers, but try to buy one with a moisture-sensor setting.

Dishwashers use at least 41 percent less energy than federal minimum standards and use significantly less water.

Refrigerators/freezers use half as much energy as those made before 1993 and 15 percent less than current federal standards. Things to keep in mind when shopping: top freezers use 10 to 25 percent less energy than side-by-side models; automatic ice makers and through-door dispensers increase energy use by up to 20 percent. In general, the larger the refrigerator, the more energy it consumes.

For more info and buying tips visit www.energystar.gov.

HOME OFFICE AND ELECTRONICS

We're using more electronics and home office equipment than ever, and that means more energy use overall. Luckily energy-efficiency advances are being made in this area all the time. As with most products, EnergyStar is the gold standard and the easiest way for you to know that the items you are buying meet strict criteria. But even if you're not in the market for new equipment, you can save energy by following these tips:

GREEN

- Unplug chargers for cell phones, personal digital assistants (PDAs), digital cameras, and other devices when you aren't using them because they draw energy even when they aren't charging anything.

- Turn off your computer monitor if you're not using it for more than 20 minutes and both your computer and monitor if you're away from your desk for more than two hours, suggests the EERE.

- Set up the power-down feature on your desktop or laptop through your operating system software. It puts the computer in a slower power mode that uses less electricity after a certain period of inactivity.

GREENER

- Plug home electronics, such as TVs and DVD players, into power strips; turn the power strips off when you go to bed or aren't using the equipment for long periods of time. You can also do this with printers, fax machines, and other peripherals. They still use several watts of power when in standby mode. It's interesting to note that Americans spend more cumulative energy to power

DVD players when turned off then when in use. In fact, 40 percent of all electricity used to power home electronics is consumed while the products are turned off, according to EnergyStar. Across the United States, this equals the output of 17 power plants!

● GREENEST

• Do a personal electronics audit: determine which are really necessary. This could mean trying to get more life out of existing electronic gadgets before purchasing new ones. Do you really need a new computer or can you add more memory and hang onto your current one for a while longer? How many televisions or DVD players do you need? The fewer products you have plugged in, the better. There's also the growing problem of what to do with the mountains of electronic castaways. See Chapter 12 for more information on this.

• When you do need to buy new electronics or office equipment buy energy-efficient models. Overall, EnergyStar office equipment uses 60 percent less energy than standard models by employing special power-management features. For example, an EnergyStar computer in sleep mode uses 80 percent less energy than when on full power. Another buying tip: laptops use much less energy than desktops so choose one if you can.

FOR MORE INFORMATION

There is a wealth of information available online to help you save energy at home. Your best bet is to visit some of the following government sites where you can find countless tips:

Department of Energy's Office of Energy Efficiency and Renewable Energy (EERE), www.eere.energy.gov. Just Click on "Consumers" for a range of information and resources. The site features a section on different calculators you can use to help you evaluate your home's energy use and calculate savings you can achieve with improvements. The "ENERGY SAVER$ Tips on Saving Energy and Money at Home" is particularly useful.

EnergyStar, www.energystar.gov, is a joint program of the EPA and DOE to help consumers save money and to protect the environment. EnergyStar products meet strict energy-efficiency requirements set by the EPA and DOE. You can find the label on everything from battery chargers and DVD players to windows and furnaces. Check the website before buying any new products such as appliances, electronics, office equipment, and so on. The EnergyStar Home Advisor is a tool that gives customized recommendations for improving energy efficiency based on where you live and the types of fuel used to heat and cool your home. The website offers extensive information and tools for saving energy even when you're not in the market for new products. It also offers information on federal tax credits for energy efficiency.

You might also find the following book helpful:

Consumer Guide to Home Energy Savings, 9th edition (New Society Publishers, 2007) by Jennifer Thorne Amann, Alex Wilson, and Katie Ackerly, is a comprehensive and detailed guide to saving energy and money at home.

7 APPAREL AND FURNISHINGS

There is a growing awareness that what we wear and how we furnish our homes can impact our health and the planet's, and affect the workers who toil long hours to make these products for us. Conventionally grown cotton, for example, is a huge eco-offender—it consumes enormous amounts of synthetic pesticides and fertilizers that deplete soil and pollute water. Fabric and upholstery dyes are made from heavy metals and other toxic chemicals; the dyeing process uses vast amounts of water and is highly polluting. Furniture that's made from wood not culled from sustainably managed forests contributes to deforestation.

Luckily, there are more choices than ever for conscious consumers. Of course, you don't need to go out and buy eco-friendly products to start being green, but for those times when you do need new things you'll find some interesting options. As for clothing, according to Leslie Hoffman, executive director of Earth Pledge, fabric and textile options have burgeoned over the past couple of years and quality has improved. But she cautions, "They aren't ubiquitous yet. It's not like you can go to Macy's and say, Now

I'm going on my sustainable shopping spree." The same could be said for greener furniture. Much of the innovation has been occurring at the high end, but that's slowly changing. Ikea and Crate & Barrel, for example, are making laudable efforts on the sustainable furniture front. Wal-Mart and Target now sell organic cotton.

If you're willing to seek it out, you can find hip clothing made from organic cotton and other sustainable materials such as bamboo and interesting furniture made from sustainably harvested or salvaged wood. As with most other green products, there are no perfect solutions. Everything takes energy to produce and transport no matter how pure the raw ingredients are. A good example is bamboo. It is a sturdy renewable plant that doesn't require the use of pesticides. However, critics point out that it usually has to be shipped all the way from China, and processing it into fabric is polluting. The processing of Tencel is cleaner than that for producing rayon, but both fabrics are made from wood pulp. It's a matter of trade-offs and what issues are most important to you.

It can also be hard to know exactly what you're paying for, but that's going to slowly change as efforts continue in both the apparel and furniture industries to create universal sustainability standards and as certification systems mature. For now, it's best to find products that are certified by a third party when available or that make specific sustainability claims such as "made from salvaged wood" as opposed to vague general terms such as "eco-friendly."

APPAREL

The trend toward cheap, disposable clothing is definitely not sustainable, but interesting earth-friendly apparel has arrived—if you know where to look. Big, boxy hemp clothing is hardly the norm anymore when it comes to eco-fashion. Organic cotton is becoming more widely available, as are a number of more environmentally friendly materials such as bamboo and organic linen and wool. It's relatively easy to find jeans and T-shirts made from organic cotton or hemp.

Sustainable clothing does usually cost more money, but it's getting easier to find affordable options, especially as mainstream retailers and manufacturers take part. Wal-Mart is a major seller of organic cotton garments in America. Levi's has a line of organic denim with some modestly priced offerings. American Apparel sells organic cotton T-shirts that are affordable and widely available. Simple Shoes uses recycled rubber in its products and recently launched its Green Toe collection of shoes made from renewable materials like jute, hemp, cork, and bamboo. Timberland strives to consider its impact on the environment from energy use to the sustainable materials it incorporates into its products, packaging, and stores. Nike is blending organic cotton into some of its products. Some Whole Foods Markets sell many of the organic clothing brands mentioned in this chapter and offer vegan shoes and gifts.

As of press time, the only label that you'll see that's consistent and meaningful is the "organic cotton" label. It's a guarantee that cotton was grown without the use of synthetic chemicals or genetically modified seed. You can trust that label right now, according to Ronnie Cummins, of the Organic Consumers Association. However, it's not a guarantee that low-impact processing or dyes were used. In the future there will be a label that certifies that a product was not only sourced sustainably but also processed, dyed, and transported in the most nontoxic manner possible under the Global Organic Textile Standards. For now, you'll have to do your own sleuthing.

GREEN

- Wash your clothes less often when you can. The actual maintenance of your clothes (washing, drying, and ironing) has more of an impact on the environment than the creation and distribution of a garment. According to "Well Dressed?," a report from researchers at Cambridge University, 60 percent of the carbon emissions generated by a cotton T-shirt come from the energy required to wash and dry it.

- Instead of buying something new for an important event such as a job interview or formal occasion, raid your friends' closets.

GREENER

- Buy secondhand clothing.

- Buy fewer but more durable pieces of clothing.

- Repair clothes: sew buttons back on or hire a professional to refresh old items.

- If you're drawn to a piece of clothing that makes sustainability claims, then try to buy it. It's a great way to support those companies and spread the word, says Hoffman, who suggests finding a few pieces that fit into your wardrobe even if you have to spend a little extra money and then wearing them to death. Every little bit helps. Each T-shirt made from 100 percent organic cotton saves one-third of a pound of synthetic agricultural products from being used, according to the Sustainable Cotton Project.

- Check out Bag Borrow or Steal, www.bagborroworsteal.com, where you can borrow handbags and jewelry for as long as you want for a monthly fee depending upon which collection you borrow from. When you're bored, just order up something else and send the old one back so someone else can use it.

GREENEST

- Actively seek out sustainably produced clothing and choose it whenever it's an option.

- When clothes shopping, ask store owners or managers to stock organic and sustainable options.

- Shop at flea markets, street fairs, and farmers' markets for clothes made by local artisans.

- Don't throw out clothes that are still wearable. Instead, find places to donate your old castaways or organize a clothing swap. Invite a bunch of friends to bring over all their unwanted clothing and pick up someone else's castaways. If you're remotely crafty and have a little extra time on your hands consider going to a Swap-O-Rama-Rama event, www.swaporamarama.com. It's a communitywide clothing swap that also offers do-it-yourself workshops where local artists show you how to transform your newfound stuff into unique items. They offer sewing machines for you to use; materials for sewing, embroidering, knitting, and repairing your finds; and silk-screen and iron-on stations (where you can access Photoshop, design a decal, print it out, and iron it on).

- Get active. See pages 174–175 for ways to support broader change.

For more information and resources check out the following websites:

Organic Exchange, www.organicexchange.org, is a nonprofit dedicated to increasing the production and use of organically grown fibers such as cotton. You can search for organic cotton apparel, home furnishings, and personal care products by product type or brand.

Co-op America, www.coopamerica.org, has a National Green Pages section that includes listings for companies the organization screens and approves. Search for green clothing, furnishings, and other items by state. You'll also find extensive information on sweatshops and how to avoid products made in them.

Green People Directory, www.greenpeople.org, has a comprehensive clothing and furnishings section. You can search by ZIP code or state to find your local options.

The following retailers offer wide selections of eco-friendly wares:

Gaiam, www.gaiam.com, is the best place for one-stop green Internet shopping. You can find sustainable apparel, furnishings, bedding, cleaning products, lightbulbs, recycled toilet paper, natural-rubber yoga mats, toothbrushes, and razors made from recyclable plastic, and many other products. It's a good place to check out no matter what you're looking for.

VivaTerra, www.vivaterra.com, doesn't have nearly the quantity of choices that's available on Gaiam, but you can find good-quality apparel, bedding, furnishings, gardening supplies, and other products. It's a great place to shop for gifts.

Eco-Chic: Sustainable Designers

The greenest clothes may be those that you own already, but even the most hard-core environmentalist needs to go on an occasional shopping spree. You'll feel better about buying these products:

Anna Cohen, www.annacohen.com, aims to create a sustainable line of "Italian street couture" from her company's headquarters in Portland, Oregon, and offers a diverse line of products from trench coats to bikinis. The designer is trying to incorporate sustainability into the whole life cycle of her products from raw materials to disposal, but is realistic about what she can accomplish right now. As of printing time, Cohen says her business is 75 percent sustainable.

Deborah Lindquist, www.deborahlindquist.com, is a high-end Los Angeles–based designer who dresses the stars. She uses recycled cashmere, vintage silk scarves, hemp blends, organic cotton, and wool to make everything from wedding dresses to dog sweaters.

Edun, www.edunonline.com, is the socially conscious fashion company in which designer Rogan Gregory has teamed up with Ali Hewson and Bono. Edun aims to create sustainable employment in Africa and other developing areas and also incorporates organic materials such as cotton into some of its designs.

Linda Loudermilk, www.lindaloudermilk.com, uses self-sustaining plants to make her highly original and high-end fashion pieces and denim collection.

Loomstate, www.loomstate.org, is Rogan Gregory's line of fashionable organic denim, available online, at select boutiques, and at Barney's.

Patagonia, www.patagonia.com, is a pioneer when it comes to sustainability; it uses organic cotton and wool, and makes recycled polyester from postconsumer recycled plastic soda bottles and other materials for its rugged outdoor clothing line. So far, the company has saved 86 million soda bottles that would otherwise be considered trash. Patagonia also offers a recycling program for some used clothing. See Chapter 12.

Stewart+Brown, www.stewartbrown.com, sells hip clothing made from sustainable materials such as organic cotton, hemp, Tencel, and Mongolian cashmere. Its line of creative, affordable tote bags is made from surplus organic cotton canvas. You can buy from retailers or directly on the company's website.

Boutiques dedicated to selling sustainable wares are popping up in cities across the country. Most major cities have at least one store: Juniper in Seattle, Envi in Boston, Kaight or Gomi in New York City. Check out their websites, too. Portland, Oregon's The Green Loop, http://thegreenloop.com, boasts an extensive online selection of stylish green clothing from the likes of Loomstate, Edun, Stewart+Brown, and many others. It's a great place to browse and get a sense of the breadth of sustainable fashion options. For more retailers see the Lazy Environmentalist's Directory of Eco-Fashion Retailers, www.lazyenvironmentalist.com.

LEATHER OR SYNTHETIC?

It's ultimately a personal choice based on your values. The desire to not cause animals to suffer is a major reason why vegans shun any animal product, whether it's a steak dinner or a pair of leather shoes. In terms of environmental impact, you can make good arguments either way. The tanning process, which uses chromium and other chemicals, is highly toxic. (Look for manufacturers that say they use vegetable tanning or employ sophisticated water cleansing, recommends Hoffman of Earth Pledge.) On the other hand, the chemicals, waste, and energy involved in making synthetic shoes and other accessories also take a toll on the environment. It's really hard to know what the "right" thing for the environment is. So your best bet is to buy shoes and bags that are well made and that you love enough to wear for a long time.

For those who want to eschew leather altogether there are now more hip choices than ever. Beyond Skin, www.beyondskin.co.uk; Charmoné Shoes, www.charmoneshoes.com; and Stella McCartney, www.stellamccartney.com, make products that are animal free. MooShoes, www.mooshoes.com, based in New York, has extensive online offerings for animal-free belts, shoes, bags, and other products. Pangea, www.veganstore.com, is a source for all things animal free, from vitamins to books.

JEWELRY

Diamonds may be a girl's best friend, but they can also be the source of bloody conflicts in war-torn African villages. Mining for gold disrupts ecosystems, produces large amounts of waste, and can seriously pollute water with heavy metals such as mercury, arsenic, and lead. There's no need to shun jewelry entirely, though.

GIVING BACK WHEN YOU BUY

Shopping may not be the most environmentally friendly activity on the planet, but there is a way that you can support your favorite charity while ordering from select retailers such as Target, Gap, Amazon, Staples, and Gaiam. The best news: it won't cost you an extra cent. Just log onto Maatiam, www.maatiam.com, and click on the retailer you want to buy from. The retailer pays a commission to Free Pledge, which then gives a percentage of your purchase to the charity of your choice. There are plenty of environmental organizations to choose from. iGive.com has a similar program.

GREEN

- Buy from retailers that are willing to give you information and documentation about where a piece comes from.

GREENER

- Buy fewer but better quality pieces that won't go out of style quickly.

- Buy recycled metals when available. Try www.greenkarat.com.

GREENEST

- Buy vintage or antique jewelry exclusively.

MATTRESSES, BEDDING, AND TOWELS

You spend more than a quarter of your lifetime in bed, so it's not a bad idea to do what you can to assure that where you sleep is as healthy and comfortable as possible. Many mattresses are made with multiple chemicals such as polyurethane, synthetic fabrics, chemical fire retardants, toxic dyes, formaldehyde, and stain-resistant chemicals that can off-gas over time and may lead to allergic reactions and other health problems, according to Greenguard Environmental Institute. Linens are frequently made from conventional cotton and polyester, which is made from petroleum. They're often bleached white with chlorine, which spews toxic chemicals such as carcinogenic dioxins into the air that can ultimately land in our food chain. The harsh chemicals used to dye fabrics can pollute water, and some linens are treated with formaldehyde to make them permanent press. Some towels have added antimicrobials, such as the controversial triclosan (see page 181). Organic mattresses are still very expensive, but there's an ever-increasing selection of affordable bedding and towels made from sustainable fabrics such as organic cotton and bamboo. The following suggestions will help you make greener choices:

GREEN

- Choose cotton and wool linens over polyester, and avoid permanent press and triclosan.

GREENER

- Buy linens made from sustainable fabrics, such as organic cotton and bamboo and low-impact dyes. You can find relatively inexpensive options at Target. Under the Canopy, www.underthecanopy.com, is a great source for affordable sheets, towels, and clothing. Pure Grow wool blankets are pesticide free. If you're looking for high-end sheets and towels check out Ana Sova Luxury Organics, www.annasova.com.

● GREENEST

- Next time you're in the market for a new mattress consider going organic. Organic mattresses are definitely more expensive, but prices will come down as demand increases. Look for products made from natural latex, organic cotton, and wool. Mattresses from Lifekind, www.lifekind.com, are certified by Greenguard Environmental Institute. Other sources include North Star Beds, www.northstarbed.com; the Organic Mattress Store, www.theorganicmattressstore.com; Good Night Naturals, www.goodnightnaturals.com; and EcoChoices Eco Bedroom, www.ecobedroom.com.

Spotlight On: Flame Retardants

Flame retardants are a group of chemicals that inhibit the start and slow down the spread of fire. They're used in a wide range of products including furniture, mattresses, textiles, plastics, and cars, as well as many others. According to the EPA, there is growing evidence that people are being exposed to some brominated flame retardants, also known as polybrominated diphenyl ethers (PBDEs), which are persistent in the environment. Studies have found traces of these chemicals in samples of human blood, breast milk, and fish. The EPA says that there is evidence that these chemicals may cause thyroid and neurodevelopmental toxicity.

Two of the most concerning commercial mixtures of these chemicals, PentaBDE and OctaPBDE, have been phased out, but they're still present in many of the products that consumers already own. There's been growing concern about a third commercial mixture of PBDEs called Deca, which has been banned in Sweden, Washington State, and Maine so far. Although it is great that some of these chemicals are being phased out, there are still very strict flammability standards that manufacturers have to meet and many of the replacement chemicals have not been tested, says Sarah Janssen, MD, PhD, MPH, a science fellow at the Natural Resources Defense Council.

Some ways to cut down on flame-retardant use that Janssen suggests include moving away from petroleum-based materials and toward those that are more naturally flame resistant such as wool, cotton, hemp, flax, and sisal; changing the way products are designed; and revising flammability standards.

There's not a whole lot you can do as a consumer, but you can avoid items made from petroleum-based products when affordable alternatives are available. Vacuuming regularly with a high-efficiency particulate air (HEPA) filter or wet mopping will minimize dust exposure. No one knows the exact route of exposure, but PBDEs are present in household dust.

For more information visit Clean Production Action at www.cleanproduction.org, a nonprofit committed to eliminating toxins from product and production. Its Safer Products Project page, which you can access from the home page, offers extensive information about flame retardants and information on which companies are taking initiatives to find safer alternatives.

FURNITURE

The list is long when it comes to environmental degradation and health impacts associated with making furniture and shipping it across the world. Enormous amounts of energy are used in mining for materials, manufacture, and transportation. Trees are cut down to make wood furniture, contributing to deforestation and climate change. Formaldehyde—common in glues, finishes, and plywood—flame retardants, and other chemicals can pollute indoor air and contaminate household dust. There are solutions to all of these issues, but it's difficult to find any one piece of furniture that doesn't have any of these problems, so you'll have to choose the issue most important to you and make your purchase decisions accordingly.

The eco-friendly furniture market is in its infancy, and the term itself has no clear definition. Some characteristics to look for: wood from well-managed forests; furnishings produced with the least toxic finishes and glues; items made from reclaimed, recycled, or renewable materials; and furniture that can be recycled at the end of its life. How do you know what the real deal is? For now, the best thing you can do is look for stickers on items to indicate if they've been certified by any of the following independent parties:

Forest Stewardship Council (FSC), www.fscus.org. The nonprofit puts its stamp of approval on wood or furniture that was harvested from well-managed forests.

Greenguard Environmental Institute, www.greenguard.org. The Atlanta-based nonprofit has a certification program for furnishings and building materials that meet its standards for acceptable chemical emissions.

MBDC Design Firm, www.mbdc.com. The firm was founded by William McDonough and Michael Braungart, co-authors of *Cradle to Cradle: Remaking the Way We Make Things* (North Point Press, 2002), a book that calls for a complete industry transformation. Cradle to Cradle Certification ranks products based on a number of criteria, including their use of environmentally safe and healthy materials, use of materials that can be reutilized, compliance with certain standards of social responsibility, and others. Products are rated as Silver, Gold, Platinum, or as a Technical/Biological Nutrient. Herman Miller, www.hermanmiller.com, and Steel Case, www.steelcase.com, are two manufacturers with goods that have earned the Cradle to Cradle stamp of approval.

The **Sustainable Furniture Council**, www.sustainablefurniturecouncil.com. This relatively new organization is working to create a broad-based certification system for furniture that will ultimately include a tiered label on products in furniture stores. For now, you can go to its website to view its member list and find out about the educational events it periodically hosts nationwide. Manufacturers commit to sustainability practices and continued improvement and agree to have third-party assessment. It's a good place to get a sense of which manufacturers are making an effort to create eco-friendly furniture. Some members include Room & Board, Vermont Woods Studio, Lee Industries, ABC Carpet & Home, South Cone, and Century Furniture.

GREEN

• Buy the best quality, most durable furniture you can afford. If you spend a little more upfront and plan on making repairs when necessary, then you'll probably save money over the long run and avoid buying replacement products in the future.

• Buy secondhand furniture.

• Don't throw out old furniture. Give it to a friend, sell it, or donate it. Try eBay or CraigsList if you want to make some extra cash, or you can give it away through Freecycle Network, www.freecycle.org. See Chapter 12 for more resources on donating household items.

GREENER

• Buy wood products from FSC certified forests and those that are reclaimed. Also look for products with water-based finishes and less toxic glues. This can be tough to figure out. Monica Gilchrist of Global Green USA suggests contacting the manufacturer and asking them about the kinds of finishes they use and what's in them.

• Ask lots of questions when you're purchasing furniture, suggests Susan Inglis, executive director of the Sustainable Furniture Council. Some questions to ask: What is the product made of? Where is it made? What finishes are used? What kinds of adhesives are used? "It's the consumer asking the sales person that is going to get the question trickling up the line," says Inglis. Eventually, manufacturers will get the picture that consumers care about these issues.

● GREENEST

- Buying local furniture is about the greenest thing you can do because you're not dealing with all the shipping, says Gilchrist. An added benefit: you're supporting a small industry. Look in your local yellow pages for furniture makers in your area or search Co-op America National Green Pages, www.coopamerica.org.

Buying Green Furniture

Most of the offerings available today are high-end and pricey, but that's likely to change as consumer demand helps bring down prices and companies like Crate & Barrel add eco-friendly components to their furniture lines. Here's a small sampling of what's available:

DESIGNERS

Q Collection, www.qcollection.com, is a high-end furniture line that's made from sustainably harvested wood and low-impact fabrics. Its furniture is free of formaldehyde, polyurethane, and PBDEs.

Furnature, www.furnature.com, is a specialty furniture line that's free of chemicals like formaldehyde, foam, and vinyl, and made with sustainable fabrics such as organic cotton.

RETAILERS

ABC Carpet & Home, www.abchome.com, is headed by Paulette Cole, a CEO with a strong commitment to sustainability. Inside the eclectic store and on its website you'll find recycled and reclaimed pieces, as well as upholstered furniture made to order with choices of sustainable fabric such as organic cotton, hemp, wool, and jute, and with FSC certified or salvaged wood and nontoxic fillings. You can also buy products to clean and maintain your furniture such as organic furniture polish and alcohol-free stain remover.

Ikea, www.ikea.com, is a good source for inexpensive products from a company that cares about the environment and is working to create sustainable products. The company says it considers raw materials, manufacturing, product use, and end of life when designing furniture, and also says it follows the precautionary principle and considers the impact of potentially hazardous substances. They are working with the World Wildlife Foundation on forestry initiatives and are aiming to source all of their wood from verified, well-managed forests.

Vivavi, www.vivavi.com, has modern eco-friendly furniture and home furnishings for every room in your house on its website.

For more information, Co-op America's Woodwise Program, www.coopamerica.org, has tips on buying wood products.

Get Active

The **Organic Consumers Association**'s Clothes for a Change Campaign, www.organicconsumers.org/clothes seeks to raise

CANDLES

Candles can do wonders for your home's atmosphere, but they're not so great for your indoor air quality. They're typically made from petroleum-based paraffin that can emit fine particulate matter (candle soot) into the air, which can trigger allergies and asthma. Some people are allergic to scented candles, whether the source is synthetic or essential oils-based. Wicks can be made with metal cores that can emit lead. Look for soy- and vegetable-based candles, which burn cleaner, and that have all-cotton wicks. Your greenest option is to buy unscented beeswax candles that have organic cotton wicks. Better yet, buy at your local farmers' market to cut down on transportation miles and support your local economy. Read the label to make sure paraffin isn't mixed in. You'll find a good selection of soy and beeswax candles at Green Feet, www.greenfeet.com, and Bluecorn Naturals, www.beeswaxcandles.com.

awareness about the negative health and environmental impacts of conventionally grown and genetically modified cotton as well as the exploitation that occurs in sweatshops. It calls for retailers and manufacturers to stop using genetically engineered cotton and to start blending in organic cotton into garments and to adopt fair labor policies.

SweatShop Watch, www.sweatshopwatch.org, is a coalition of organizations dedicated to eliminating the exploitation of workers that occurs in sweatshops. The focus is on California garment workers, but action alerts also deal with national and global conditions.

8 CLEANING

The psychology of cleaning has certainly changed since the days when our grandmothers used elbow grease and a few basic ingredients to get their homes spic-and-span. After World War II, chemical companies began marketing a whole new generation of cleaning products for everything from freshening air to cleaning carpets to polishing metals. We now have an arsenal of cleaning supplies under the sink; many of us simply rely on the same products we grew up with without questioning whether we need to use so many or such strong cleaners.

Cleaning is supposed to make our homes healthy, but in our frenzy to banish dirt, dust, mold, and germs we may be doing more harm than good. The sheer number of products is completely unnecessary, and we know very little about the effects of combining all of these chemicals, says Patti Wood, executive director of Grassroots Environmental Education. Many conventional cleaning products are made from petroleum, a nonrenewable resource, which takes its toll on the planet. In terms of human health, they contain some of the most hazardous chemicals that most of us encounter on a daily basis. The toxic residues remain on our surfaces and clothing. What's more, many of the chemicals that are in those products cheerfully lining supermarket shelves haven't been tested properly for household use. We know their acute effects—reactions that occur as a result of short-term exposure, such as watery eyes or skin irritation—but scientists are only now beginning to uncover what happens when we are exposed day in and day out to persistent low-level doses.

Some of the chemicals found in cleaning products can pollute indoor air, which, according to the Environmental Protection Agency (EPA), can be more contaminated than outdoor air (see page 123). Research has shown that many of the toxic chemicals in cleaning products can cause a range of health problems, from eye, skin, and respiratory irritations and allergies to more serious issues such as nervous system and reproductive disorders, and in some cases cancer, says Wood. Young children, she notes, are particularly vulnerable because they crawl on the floor and touch surfaces where chemicals have been used and then put their hands in their mouths. These substances can interfere with their developing bodies, and pound for pound, children take in more contaminants than adults. If ingested, some cleaning products can be poisonous; swallowing cleaning products is one of the most common reasons for emergency calls concerning children under the age of six, according to the American Association of Poison Control Centers.

Depending upon how your residential waste is handled, when you wash these chemicals down the drain they can make their way into groundwater (which is a major source of drinking water) or wind up in streams, rivers, and ultimately in oceans. Many ingredients are harmful to plants and marine life.

The bottom line is, you don't need to blitz your bathroom—or any room in your house—with toxic chemicals for it to be "clean." There are plenty of affordable products currently on the market that work well and won't harm you or the environment. Some are common household items such as white vinegar or baking soda that you probably already have in your cupboard, and others are products formulated specifically for cleaning. If you are shopping for new products, the brands Seventh Generation and Ecover have extensive lines of cleaning products that are affordable, effective, and widely available at Whole Foods, supermarkets, and health food stores. Drugstore.com has a great selection of green cleaning products including a well-respected brand called Biokleen. Mrs. Meyers is another brand that is growing in popularity, but it has strong fragrances, which are natural but still may aggravate sensitive people with allergies and asthma. You might want to try a couple of brands to find which work best for you. Like any cleaners though, even green products must be kept out of the reach of children.

GENERAL HOUSEHOLD

If we simply cut down on the number of products we use, we can save money and protect our health. Another way to reduce the need for less toxic cleaning products is to clean up as we go in order to prevent our homes from getting too dirty. Here are some other tips to help you maintain a clean and healthy home without using too many harsh products:

GERM-FREE—WITHOUT ANTIBACTERIAL SOAP AND DISINFECTANTS

Disinfectants are regulated by the EPA because they are considered pesticides. While effective at killing micro-organisms (both bacteria and viruses) on surfaces like toilet seats and countertops, it's not clear that we need to be using pesticides to clean our homes or wash our hands under normal circumstances. Despite our excessive phobia about germs, humans don't require a completely antiseptic living environment. If you live with someone who is immune compromised or has other serious health concerns you should talk to your doctor. For anyone else, though, just cleaning thoroughly and often with regular soap is enough to do the trick. It's worth remembering that surfaces don't stay disinfected indefinitely anyway, so it's not possible to have a completely sterile home. It also may not be preferable. Experts hypothesize that our overly clean living environments and relative lack of serious early childhood diseases may be contributing to the rise of asthma and allergies because if developing immune systems aren't exposed to bacteria they may not develop normally. Grassroots Environmental Education recom-

GREEN

- Remove shoes before entering your home.
- Put mats outside and inside of your door to trap incoming dirt.
- Open windows for airing rather than using a commercial air freshener, which may contain synthetic fragrances that can aggravate asthma and allergies. In 2007, the Natural Resources Defense Council tested 14 brands of common household air fresheners and found phthalates in 12 of them. The hormone disrupting chemicals, which have been linked with reproductive problems, were even found in products marketed as "all

mends products containing tea tree, thyme, or eucalyptus oils as well as grapefruit seed extract as household disinfectants for those who are hooked on Clorox.

There's been a proliferation of household products with germ-killing ingredients in everything from hand soap to clothing to pens. It's hard to find a liquid soap these days without triclosan, a pesticide that kills bacteria (but not the viruses most often associated with colds and flu). Studies have not shown that triclosan is any more effective at removing germs than good old-fashioned soap and water, and there are concerns that it may promote antibiotic-resistant bacteria. It's also a suspected endocrine disruptor and has shown up in human bodies and breast milk as well as in streams. The Danish EPA has recommended that consumers avoid products containing triclosan. In the United States, the jury is out on triclosan, but experts suggest washing with just plain soap and water. Not very exciting, but effective. Stephen Ashkin, president of green cleaning consulting firm the Ashkin Group, makes a great point: while it is important to clean germs off our hands, we don't necessarily need to kill them. It actually doesn't matter to our health if they go down the drain alive!

natural" and "unscented." Phthalates were not listed on the labels or packaging. For more information, including brand names, see "Clearing the Air—Hidden Hazards of Air Fresheners," on the NRDC's website, www.nrdc.org.

- Clean up spills when they are new and wet as opposed to a dry stain, suggests Ashkin.

GREENER

- Find the source of an odor and fix it rather than mask it.

- Some furniture and metal polishes contain solvents, which

are very dangerous if swallowed. Try plain olive or walnut oil to polish furniture, suggests Wood of Grassroots Environmental Education. Look for alternative metal polishes that don't carry the "Danger" warning.

• Many house plants can improve indoor air quality by absorbing contaminants. Leaves, roots, and soil bacteria all work to trap toxic vapors. Some suggestions: Spider plants (chlorophytum) and golden pathos (scindapsus). For more ideas go to retired NASA scientist Dr. B. C. Wolverton's website, www.wolvertonenvironmental.com.

● GREENEST

• You don't necessarily have to use your own elbow grease to get your home spic-and-span without harsh chemicals. Eco-cleaning services are popping up nationwide, so check your local yellow pages to find one nearby. Before signing up ask which cleaning products they use. If they make their own or use a brand you've never heard of, ask to see a label or a Materials Safety Data Sheet (MSDS), required for all chemicals and pesticides by the Occupational Safety and Health Administration. It's a fact sheet that lists active ingredients and may include some inerts. The sheet also includes some health, first aid, storage, and disposal information, but you'll want to do your own research since the manufacturer is the source. If there isn't an eco-friendly service near you, see if a conventional service is open to using products you provide. Here's a small sampling of green cleaning services around the country:

Ecoclean Services, ecocleanservices.com, in San Diego, California

Organic Cleaning, www.organiccleaning.net, in Hampton Bays, New York

The Green Mop, www.thegreenmop.com, in Arlington, Virginia

ZENhome Cleaning, www.zenhomecleaning.com, based in New York City

Green and Clean: Safe Alternatives from Your Pantry

Making your own cleaners can be less expensive and healthier for you and the environment, but many of us barely have time to make dinner let alone create cleaning solutions that may not always work well. The growing array of eco-friendly products available also makes it unnecessary to mix your own cleaners if you're able to spend some extra money. But for those who want a little bit of a homemade feel without too much effort, there are a few pantry staples that you can reach for. No complicated recipes necessary.

Baking soda. Has many uses. Keep a box in your refrigerator or freezer to absorb odors or use it on your carpet. It also makes a great scouring powder. A little baking soda on a damp sponge or rag can clean sinks, bathtubs, kitchen counters, and more. Visit the Arm & Hammer website, www.armandhammer.com, for more tips.

White distilled vinegar. Helps kill germs, and mixed with water, it's commonly used to clean floors and windows. You might want to add a little dish soap for windows.

Liquid Soap. Use for all sorts of things. Patti Wood recommends castile soap because it is made from vegetable oils and doesn't contain harsh petroleum products or their contaminants. Mix it with baking soda for a super scouring powder, suggests Philip Dickey, formerly a staff scientist at the Washington Toxics Coalition, a Seattle-based nonprofit that aims to eliminate toxic pollution by educating consumers and advocating policies.

If you want to try out some more complicated recipes, check out the following sources. Some may not work as well as others so you'll have to let trial and error be your guide.

- Care 2, www.care2.com
- The following books by Annie Berthold Bond, an expert on toxic-free living: *Better Basics for the Home: Simple Solutions for Less Toxic Living* (Three Rivers Press, 1999) or *Home Enlightenment: Practical, Earth-Friendly Advice for Creating a Nurturing, Healthy, Toxin-Free Home and Lifestyle* (Rodale, 2005)
- *The Green Guide,* www.thegreenguide.com (has extensive product reports on cleaning and laundry products)

KITCHEN

The three most dangerous cleaning products in the average home are drain, oven, and acid-based toilet bowl cleaners, according to Dickey, so you're contending with two out of three of them in the kitchen. Drain and oven cleaners are considered corrosive and can cause severe burns both externally and internally if swallowed. Luckily, you can find safer alternatives to oven and drain cleaners.

Automatic dishwashing detergents can also be harmful. Many contain phosphates, which can pollute water and harm wildlife. Chlorine, a lung and eye irritant, is also found in automatic dishwasher detergents, and Wood says the steam coming out of your dishwasher can pollute your indoor air. Cleaned dishes may also contain some of these chemicals.

● GREEN

• Safe food-handling techniques can go a long way toward reducing your need for harsh chemicals around the kitchen. Wash your hands with soap and water if you handle raw meat or poultry.

• Prevent drain clogs by using a trap or screen to keep food scraps out, and don't pour cooking grease down the drain. Use a plunger if a drain becomes clogged or try pouring boiling water down to clean it out. If that doesn't work buy an enzyme-based drain cleaner that doesn't use caustic chemicals. Enzyme-based products will probably be labeled as such and the label will not include a danger signal word, says Dickey.

• Line the oven with foil to make clean up easier, and wipe up any spills immediately.

● GREENER

• Use an automatic dishwashing powder or liquid that is phosphate and chlorine free. Many are labeled as such. *Consumer*

Reports rates automatic dishwashing detergents and also notes if they are phosphate or chlorine free (visit www.greenerchoices.org for free access to their Cleaners Buying Guide). Ecover's tablets and Biokleen powder, which claim to be both phosphate and chlorine free, did fairly well and were among the top 10 performers in the category.

- Buy oven cleaners that do not have the "caustic" label on them. Easy-Off makes a noncaustic version.

- Most conventional liquid dish soap is made from petroleum, a nonrenewable resource. Try choosing a product with a plant-based surfactant, such as coconut or corn oil, if ingredients are listed.

● GREENEST

- You can make your own cleaners with common ingredients such as baking soda. Check out the "General Household" section on page 179 for ideas.

Chemistry 101: Decoding Cleaning Product Labels

Manufacturers of cleaning products are not required to list their ingredients on labels if they are considered trade secrets. This makes it difficult to determine what harmful chemicals some of them contain. However, if you look closely enough at a label you will find some clues about toxicity because the government requires toxic products to be labeled as such. Signal words can help you decipher just how toxic a product is. Products that aren't considered toxic by the federal government do not have a signal word, but that doesn't always mean that they are free of hazardous ingredients. In many cases, the amount of toxic chemicals used are considered too low to be of concern by the government, according to Dickey (formerly of the Washington Toxics Coalition). It's wise to stay away from cleaners that carry a "Danger" or "Poison" warning because they are typically the most hazardous. "Caution" and "Warning" signal a medium short-term hazard. You'll find more information about the specifics of the danger next to the signal word. Unfortunately, there aren't any meaningful labels for cleaning products right now. Here are a few that you'll see most often:

Biodegradable. The label is not a guarantee because the claim is not based on specific standards and there is no verification process. It's more useful when a product gives a specific timeframe for how long it will take to break down.

Non-Toxic. This label isn't meaningful because there is no official definition of what standards have to be met for a product to be considered nontoxic, and there isn't a third-party certification.

Organic. Cleaning products aren't regulated, but some of their ingredients can be.

For more information, see www.greenerchoices.org/eco-labels/eco-home.cfm.

Consumer Reports' Greener Choices has ratings of some green cleaning products on its website, www.greenerchoices.org. You can see which products claim to not have certain ingredients and how well they clean. You can also search the National Library of Medicine's Household Products Database, www.householdproducts.nlm.nih.gov. It's a guide for consumers that provides information on potential health effects of common household products. It lists ingredients and health effects and provides links to other government websites to get more information. You can search by category, manufacturer, product, ingredient, chemical, or health effects.

BATHROOM

Mold, mildew, and bacteria thrive in damp, warm environments, so bathrooms are a perfect breeding ground. However, you don't have to rely on the "big guns" to clean your bathroom. As for the toilet bowl, acid-based toilet cleaners are among the most toxic in your household because they are corrosives and can cause severe internal and external burns. You can find safer alternatives to clean your bathroom.

Be especially careful when using multiple products because sometimes dangerous gases can form. This can happen in any room, but more of these products tend to be used together in the bathroom. Mixing chlorine bleach with ammonia, for example, will produce lung-irritating chloramine gas. Mixing chlorine bleach with an acid-based product like a toilet bowl cleaner may release chlorine gas. Chlorine bleach, which on its own can irritate your eyes and lungs, is often found in mildew-stain removers and some bath and toilet cleaners, according to Dickey. Ammonia, which is also a strong lung irritant, is marketed on its own and in some glass, bathroom-surface, and floor cleaners.

GREEN

- Try cleaning your toilet bowl without a specific toilet bowl cleaner by using a nontoxic scouring product such as Bon Ami, which is inexpensive and widely available.

- Try to prevent mold from forming so you won't need to rely on cleaning products regularly. Fix leaks and wipe up wet surfaces and shower curtains right away. Also deal with any mold immediately rather than waiting for it to build up.

- If you don't have good ventilation in your bathroom, open the window after a steamy shower or bath to prevent mold from growing.

GREENER

- Buy less-toxic bathroom and glass cleaners, such as those offered by Seventh Generation, Ecover, or other brands. If a product doesn't list its ingredients you won't know if what you are buying is any safer than conventional products. However, as more companies list ingredients voluntarily it will be easier to get a sense of what you are buying. Dickey and other experts suggest not buying cleaning products unless ingredients are listed. In addition to ammonia, some glass cleaners contain 2-butoxyethanol, which has been shown to harm the central nervous system, kidneys, and liver in rats.

• If you must use a toilet bowl cleaner buy one that's not corrosive. Look for products without the signal word "Danger."

GREENEST

• Consider adding an exhaust fan in the bathroom if mold and mildew are a problem and you don't have a window to open. If you have a fan already, make sure it's not clogged with dust.

CLEANING EQUIPMENT

If you want to keep your home both spic-and-span and free of hazardous chemicals, it's also important to consider the tools you use to tidy up. In a nutshell: use good quality reusable materials whenever possible to avoid unnecessary waste.

GREEN

• Don't use throwaway wipes. Use rags or good-quality microfiber towels to cut down on unnecessary waste. Better yet, cut up old T-shirts and towels, which will save you money and reduce waste. Use old newspapers to clean your windows. It sounds wacky, but it works. Simply crinkle up a piece of newspaper and wipe away. Just make sure you wash the ink off your hands afterward so you won't stain your clothing or other fabrics. Microfiber towels suck up dirt and bacteria with just water, and they are washable. The brand Method makes towels for different cleaning needs.

• Buy pure cellulose sponges without antimicrobial treatments. Using antimicrobial tools and products may do more harm than good by helping create antibiotic-resistant bacteria. Try your local hardware store if you can't find them at the supermarket. Williams-Sonoma's Pop-Up sponges don't have antimicrobials and come in packs of 6 or 12, which also cuts down on excess packaging. Run sponges through a dishwasher cycle or place them in boiling water to sterilize. Replace them when they begin to smell.

GREENER

• It's best to minimize using paper towels for cleaning, but if you must, use towels that are made of recycled paper; the exception is for cleaning glass and windows because recycled paper towels don't tend to be as absorbent and break apart easily.

GREENEST

• The next time you buy a vacuum, consider one with a high-efficiency particulate air (HEPA) filter. Vacuums with HEPA filters prevent dust from escaping as you clean. It will cost you more money, but the benefits may be worth it, especially if someone in your family suffers from asthma or allergies. The Carpet and Rug Institute has a searchable list of Green Label–approved vacuums on its website, www.carpet-rug.org, or look for its CRI Green Label on packaging to ensure that strict standards on soil removal, dust containment, and carpet appearance have been met. You might also want to check out *Consumer Reports'* Vacuum Cleaner Buying Guide available at its green website, www.greenerchoices.org.

LAUNDRY

There is something very satisfying about a basket of clean, fresh clothing, especially when it's achieved without harsh chemicals. It's increasingly easy to get that kind of satisfaction these days thanks to a wide variety of effective laundry products that clean well without harming your health or the environment. Conventional laundry products typically contain a cocktail of chemicals such as diethanolamine (DEA) and triethanolamine (TEA) designed to destroy dirt, make your clothes brighter, remove stains, and soften your fabrics, but can cause health problems from skin and lung irritation to endocrine disruption and neurological problems. Chlorine bleach (sodium hypochlorite) is a popular way of whitening clothes, towels, and bed linens, but it's a powerful lung and eye irritant.

These chemicals get washed down the drain and can contaminate waterways. A 2002 U.S. Geological Survey found detergent metabolites in 69 percent of the streams it tested across the country. Washing your clothes is also an energy-intensive process, but there are plenty of opportunities for conserving (see Chapters 5 and 6 for additional advice on reducing energy use).

GREEN

- Use cold water for all rinse cycles instead of hot or warm to save energy. The U.S. Department of Energy estimates that 90 percent of the energy used for washing clothes goes to heating water.

- Regularly clean out your dryer's lint filter to maximize energy efficiency.

• Try using less laundry detergent, especially in front-loading machines. Your clothes will get just as clean and will be less likely to have detergent residues built up on them.

• Reduce the volume of your laundry by making sure clothing is really in need of a wash before tossing it into the hamper.

GREENER

• Buy in bulk and use a concentrated detergent to cut down on packaging and trips to the grocery store in your car.

• Buy green laundry detergents without nonylphenol ethoxylates (NPEs), which are known to break down into endocrine disrupters. This should be fairly easy to do because the EPA recognizes these compounds as pollutants and is encouraging manufacturers to voluntarily phase out their use. Many conventional products no longer have these chemicals or won't in the near future. Switch to chlorine-free bleach made from hydrogen peroxide or sodium percarbonate.

• If your machine has a separate temperature control for the rinse cycle and you're already using cold water to rinse your clothes, consider limiting the use of hot and warm water for the wash cycle as well.

• Line-dry clothes when possible (this is better for certain fabrics as well).

• Spot clean items when possible rather than tossing them into the machine.

• Look for products with specific claims, such as "phosphate free" or "chlorine free," rather than general claims such as "natural."

- Decide where you stand on fragrances and determine what they are made of. Many greener products use plant oils, which are generally okay for the environment, but can aggravate allergies and asthma. Synthetic perfumes use toxic-dispersing agents known as phthalates, which are endocrine disruptors so it's best to avoid them.

- Skip the dryer sheets and fabric softeners when you can, or choose an option from an alternative brand such as Seventh Generation. The conventional varieties contain petroleum-based fragrances and other potentially toxic chemicals.

GREENEST

- Always line-dry clothing.
- Use cold water for all washing to save energy.

DRY CLEANING

Dry cleaning is the most popular way to clean sensitive fabrics, but it's not so healthy for humans or the planet. The main problem is that the solvent used by most dry cleaners—perchlorethylene or "perc," boasts a long list of health effects such as headaches, dizziness, liver and kidney damage, and is considered a probable human carcinogen by the EPA. Perc also pollutes the air, ground, and water so most of us are exposed to it, but the EPA says the amounts are usually small enough to not harm the average person's health.

It's a different story for those who work in the industry or who live in or near buildings with perc dry-cleaners. The U.S. Department of Labor recognizes that dry-cleaning workers are at risk of a developing a range of health problems, and the National Institute for Occupational Safety and Health reports that perc is a "potential occupational carcinogen." On a positive note, perc appears to be on its way out thanks in part to the EPA's efforts at imposing stricter regulations and the availability of alternative methods for cleaning sensitive fabrics. The EPA is also phasing out perc dry cleaners in residential buildings.

The EPA recommends the following processes as environmentally preferable to traditional solvents:

Wet cleaning. Uses water and nontoxic soaps to clean clothes. It's not toxic and it doesn't harm the environment, but it may not be the best bet for everything you dry clean, especially an item of clothing like a fitted wool suit. This method did not perform well in some tests by *Consumer Reports*. It's best used for items that you would consider hand washing at home such as silk or linen. The quality of wet cleaning depends on where you go. Make sure you go to someone experienced and ask them if they think wet cleaning will work on the garments you want to clean. One important caveat: if you wet-clean an item and it gets ruined the manufacturer is not responsible for it.

Carbon dioxide dry cleaning. Uses liquid carbon dioxide to clean clothes in high-pressure machines. Hangers Cleaners, www.hangerskc.com, has a nationwide chain, or visit www.findco2.com to find a cleaner near you. This method performed the best in a *Consumer Reports* test, even higher than traditional dry cleaning.

Silicone dry cleaning. Liquid silicone and detergent are used to clean fabrics. More information is needed on this process. *Consumer Reports* found this worked well, but the jury is still out on what the impact on human health is. One study by Occidental College found that silicone D5 causes cancer in rats, and there are concerns about potential liver toxicity. The chain GreenEarth cleaners use this process. At press time, silicone dry cleaning was not considered environmentally preferable by the EPA.

Here are some ways to reduce exposure to dry cleaning chemicals, and how to rely less on dry cleaning in general:

GREEN

- Air out your clothes after they've been dry-cleaned. Take dry-cleaned clothes out of bags and air them outside before bringing them into your home to remove as much perc as possible. If you are picking up dry cleaning by car, drive home with your windows open if possible.

- Don't get your clothes cleaned in a place that smells of chemicals. The odor may mean that solvents are being improperly used or processed, according to the EPA.

GREENER

- Ask your dry cleaner if he or she uses wet cleaning and if so, whether it is appropriate for some of your items. Try it on a few items and see how it goes.

- Look for a cleaner that uses the carbon dioxide method to

clean. Silicone isn't yet recommended by the EPA, so it's your call on whether you want to try it while more testing is being done.

• Bring your own garment bag to cut down on unnecessary waste.

GREENEST

• Buy fewer clothes that require dry cleaning if you don't have access to a new nontoxic method of cleaning.

• If there aren't any options nearby ask your local cleaner to consider using a non-perc method.

• Hand wash as many items as possible. Some washing machines now have a hand-wash cycle.

Get Active

If the government required ingredients lists on cleaning products it would help consumers make safe and healthy choices. It would also be a benefit if hazardous chemicals were better regulated. Get involved with a group working to establish better labeling laws or to ensure that hazardous chemicals are not allowed in household products. You'll find suggestions for specific product groups such as pesticides in designated chapters. You can find a group locally or contact one of the following organizations for national advocacy and lobbying (see page 81 for information on getting active in your state):

Washington Toxics Coalition, www.watoxics.org, based in Washington state, is known nationally for its work on consumer products issues.

Environmental Working Group, www.ewg.org, is a nonprofit research and advocacy organization.

Pollution in People, www.pollutioninpeople.org, is a study of toxic chemicals found in the bodies of 10 Washingtonians.

9 PEST CONTROL

Mice, roaches, fleas, you name it—indoor pests are definitely a nuisance and often a health concern. They carry diseases, trigger allergies and asthma, and are just plain bothersome, so there's no question they need to be banished from your home. How they are eradicated, though, is critical. Many of the chemicals we immediately reach for when dealing with household bugs and rodents come with their own sets of health problems. Pesticide residues can stick around for a long time. Moreover, they aren't necessarily the best defense because they don't get to the root of the problem and pests keep returning. Still, according to the Environmental Protection Agency (EPA), an estimated 45 million pounds of pesticides are used annually in homes and gardens in the United States, with sales totaling more than $2 billion each year.

A 2005 Centers for Disease Control and Prevention (CDC) report of chemicals in blood and urine found that 90 percent of all people in the United States have a mixture of up to 43 pesticides in their bodies. Many of these chemicals have been linked to health problems such as birth defects, neurological problems, cancer, and reproductive health complications for both men and women. It's not just the active ingredients, which are labeled on the product, that you need to be concerned about. Many inert ingredients, considered trade secrets, are not listed even though they can make up the majority of a product. These chemicals, typically designed to make the product easier to use or more potent, are not intended to kill pests, but some of them can be hazardous to human health as well as the environment.

Children are more vulnerable to pesticides because their bodies are still developing. They tend to get their biggest dose of pesticides from crawling on the floor where most of these chemicals accumulate and then putting their fingers in their mouths. A 2000 University of Southern California study published in the journal *Cancer* reported that children with non-Hodgkin's lymphoma were more than seven times more likely than healthy children to have grown up in a home where pesticides were sprayed, and were three times more likely to live in a home treated regularly by a professional exterminator.

Pregnant women should also be careful; according to a study published by the journal *Environmental Health Perspectives* in 2001, more than 75 percent of 230 women in New York City had common household insecticides in their blood and the chemicals were also found in their babies' umbilical cord blood. The study found that more than 95 percent of the infants in the study had insecticide residues in their first bowel movement. A Mount Sinai Hospital study linked household insecticide residues in umbilical cord blood to lower birth weight and length, and reduced head circumference. Of course, whether or not you have any ill health effects from pesticide exposure depends on several factors including the level and duration of exposure, other chemical exposures, and genetic predisposition.

Pesticide application, especially outdoors, can wreak havoc on the environment as well. Rainwater can wash the chemicals down storm drains, which empty into creeks or bays. A U.S. Geological Survey study carried out between 1992 and 2001 reported that over 80 percent of urban streams and over 50 percent of agricultural streams nationwide contained at least one pesticide in levels that may adversely affect aquatic life. One or more pesticides were also found in 96 percent of fish, 100 percent of surface water, and 33 percent of major aquifers.

If all this information makes you feel as if you won't be able to deal with the pesky critters that make everyone squirm, don't panic. When it comes to pest control, prevention is your best defense; you won't have pests if they can't get into your home or if there's nothing for them to eat or drink. Throughout this chapter you'll find information on what kinds of measures you can take so that you won't attract pests in the first place. There are also natural ways to deal with pests that really do work and in most cases are worth trying before you resort to using chemicals. If they don't do the trick, then you might try some of the least toxic chemicals before moving on to the big guns. How you apply chemicals is also crucial. Try to stay away from indiscriminate spraying all over your house. Instead, use more targeted approaches such as applying a gel into out-of-the-way cracks and crevices or using baits. There may be times when you need outside help dealing with pests. A growing number of professionals employ safer control and extermination methods.

IPM: Getting to the Root of the Problem

Integrated Pest Management (IPM) is a step-by-step method based on preventing, monitoring, and controlling pest problems in order to eliminate or drastically reduce the use of pesticides. Although it may ultimately lead to using pesticides in certain cases, it doesn't always, says Jonathan Kaplan, senior policy specialist at the Natural Resources Defense Council (NRDC). You start out by correcting conditions that lead to pest problems, such as sealing cracks or holes that bugs or mice can crawl into or eliminating food and water sources such as crumbs or leaky faucets. Pesticides are used as a last resort after everything else has been tried, and the least toxic materials are always tried first and applied in limited ways to minimize exposure to nontarget animals and people.

There are a number of compelling reasons to try IPM when you have a problem with insects or rodents. It's better for your health, the environment, and ultimately, your pocketbook, plus it works better because you are eliminating the problem rather than continually treating it. An EPA-sponsored study published in 2006 by the journal *Environmental Health Perspectives* showed cockroach infestations decreased substantially in New York City households that employed IPM but not in the homes that used conventional controls such as regular spraying. IPM reduced pest complaints by 89 percent and pesticide use by 93 percent in government buildings over 10 years. Multiple studies show that the cost of IPM is equal to or lower than that for conventional pest control.

If you can't seem to lick an infestation by yourself with IPM, you can call in a professional. It's not always easy to find a responsible practitioner, but that is slowly changing as databases and certification programs are springing up. You can also look in the yellow pages to see if any local providers advertise "ecological" methods. No matter how you find a provider, it's always good to ask lots of questions. Ultimately, you want someone who tries to understand your problem and wants to find the source and deal with it instead of just coming in and spraying everywhere. The more information you can give about the problem, the better. It's also important to mention if any pregnant women, young children, or pets live in the house.

WHAT TO ASK BEFORE HIRING A PROFESSIONAL

1. **How are you going to deal with my pest problem?** If pesticides are immediately suggested, ask if there are any nonchemical strategies available. Pest control professionals should be able to demonstrate that they have thought through nonchemical strategies.

2. **What chemicals are you going to use?** Ask for the names of the products and active ingredients or ask to see a Materials Safety Data Sheet (MSDS). Read the next section to find out how to research chemicals. If it turns out that spraying is your only option, then discuss where it's really necessary. It's best to avoid spraying everywhere if possible. You only want to target the pest.

3. **Do you plan to spray outside?** Try to avoid this if possible to prevent water contamination.

HOW TO RESEARCH CHEMICALS

1. The best way to find out which chemicals you are dealing with is to ask the practitioner for a label or Material Safety Data Sheet (MSDS). If you are buying a product from a store try downloading an MSDS from the manufacturer's website or call and ask for one to be sent to you. For more information, check out

"How to Read a Material Safety Data Sheet" on the American Lung Association's website, www.lungusa.org.

2. Once you know which chemicals you are dealing with you can go to Pesticide Action Network's Pesticides Database, www.pesticideinfo.org, to look up health effects and to see if your pesticides fall into a high-risk category.

3. You can also search for product information on the National Library of Medicine's Household Products Database, www.householdproducts.nlm.nih.gov, a guide for consumers that provides information on the potential health effects of common household products (see page 187 for additional information).

AVAILABLE RESOURCES FOR IPM

- Green Shield Certified, www.greenshieldcertified.org, is the first national IPM certification program in the country. The program is operated by the IPM Institute of North America, a nonprofit organization that has received awards from the EPA. Supported by the NRDC and other environmental organizations, this program certifies structural pest control service providers who meet its stringent prevention-based standards.

- Safety Source's Beyond Pesticides database, www.beyondpesticides.org/safetysource, lists practitioners who took a survey to indicate that they use the least toxic practices and materials. There's no guarantee that you'll get toxic-free treatment, so you'll have to ask lots of questions. The list is a good place to start if there aren't any certified providers in your area. Click on "Find a Service Provider" then "Search by State" for local listings.

GENERAL PEST CONTROL

A number of tactics can help prevent both rodent and insect infestations. We'll move on to specific actions for individual species in later sections, but here are some general tips:

GREEN

- Keep food in containers with tight-fitting lids. Put garbage in cans with lids and take it outside often.
- Thoroughly clean food-prep areas and used dishes and wipe them dry immediately. If you can't get to dishes immediately submerge them in soapy water until you have time to clean and dry. Sweep up crumbs on floors and counters. When cleaning your kitchen, also focus on areas where grease accumulates and don't forget under refrigerators, sinks, stoves, and vents.
- Remove pet food and water dishes at night or place them in pans of soapy water.
- Eliminate any standing water throughout your home.

GREENER

- Vacuum with a high-efficiency particulate air (HEPA) filter to remove crumbs and dust. See page 191 for more information on HEPA filters.
- Fix dripping faucets and other leaks.

GREENEST

- Weather-strip around doors and windows. Repair holes in screens. Seal around electrical socket covers and areas adjacent to pipe entry points. Place screens behind any heating or cooling vents and caulk around the edges of the screen. It's a lot of work, but once you do all of this you can keep out a lot of pests, says Kay Rumsey, librarian at the Northwest Coalition for Alternatives to Pesticides.

COCKROACHES

Roaches travel in some nasty places so you don't want them crawling around on your kitchen counters. Not only are they repulsive and disgusting, but they also trigger allergies and asthma, contaminate food, and carry disease-causing bacteria. Roaches prefer warm, moist places and tend to hide in cracks and crevices during the day. They travel in groups and feed at night on water and food scraps. They're not picky when it comes to food; they'll even eat such unlikely items as wallpaper paste, envelope glue, and soap.

The most common way of dealing with roaches is spraying pesticides, which then deposit on surfaces in your home such as kitchen counters and rugs, where children play. This isn't the most effective approach given that roach eggs are not killed by pesticide sprays and roaches are becoming resistant to many synthetic chemicals. Because sprays don't address the cause of the problem, roaches will always come back. However, you can control cockroaches without employing an arsenal of toxic poisons.

The simplest approach is starvation: they'll move out if they can't find enough food and water.

GREEN

- Damp, dirty mops attract roaches, so clean and dry them thoroughly.

- Avoid clutter. Roaches can hide in stacks of old newspapers and magazines, piles of paper bags, rags, and boxes.

- Boric acid is a natural alternative to conventional pesticides that is very effective at killing roaches, but is poisonous. A 2004 report by the EPA linked it to a decrease in male fertility. Boric acid is moderately toxic, says scientist Philip Dickey, formerly of the Washington Toxics Coalition, but one benefit is that it doesn't evaporate or move into the air. Apply it only in cracks and crevices where humans can't go, and use eye protection, a dust mask, and gloves when applying. It works slowly so it will take a little while to see results, but they should be significant. Studies show that this is equal to or more effective than pesticides and roaches aren't resistant to it. If it remains dry and undisturbed it can be effective for a long time. You can also look for products with boric acid as a main ingredient.

- Silica aerogel and diatomaceous earth are also less toxic options. They kill by abrading or absorbing the waxy layer on the cockroach's body that prevents water loss. Apply in a thin layer under and behind appliances and cabinets in cracks and around holes. Silica gel damages lungs when inhaled in lab studies, so wear a dust mask when applying. Be aware that some silica gel products and diatomaceous products have added insecticides.

GREENER

- Bait stations are effective and environmentally sound choices. Baits are filled with insecticides that are confined to a small area rather than being dispersed everywhere. They don't attract roaches, so place near hiding spaces.

GREENEST

- Seal cracks with paint or latex or silicone caulk. Before sealing, vacuum out the crack to remove food, fecal material, or egg cases that may be present, and wash the area.

CLOTHING MOTHS

How aggravating is it to put on your favorite sweater and discover that moths have feasted on it? It's actually the larvae that do the chewing. They're small and hard to see, often hiding in cracks and crevices. They can forgo food for long periods of time, but when they eat, their diet can be quite varied. Larvae typically munch on animal fibers such as wool and furs, but acrylic, silk, polyester, and cotton can be damaged as they cut through the fibers in order to eat the dirt and stains on a fabric. They'll eat clothing, blankets, rugs, and upholstery. Prevention is your best bet when it comes to moths. If you have a moth infestation you may need to call a professional for help.

Mothballs are a common but unhealthy way to repel the pests. The strong odor they emit comes from naphthalene and/or paradichlorobenzene, toxic chemicals that are considered neurotoxins and are associated with health effects ranging from eye, nose, throat, and skin irritation to headaches, nausea, and dizziness. Paradichlorobenzene is also an allergen and is a suspected carcinogen, and naphthalene can damage red blood cells and the liver. Sometimes moth control products may smell like cedar or lavender but still contain toxic chemicals, so check product labels, suggests Dickey. You can get exposed to chemicals from inhaling, touching, or swallowing them. Wash or dry-clean clothes that smell like mothballs because you can be exposed to chemicals through your skin if you wear them.

● GREEN

- Inspect used clothing or furniture carefully before purchasing, and clean them before bringing them home.
- Get rid of unused wool such as sweaters, blankets, yarn, and others.
- Dry cleaning or washing in hot water kills moths at all stages of development.

● GREENER

- Wash sweaters before packing them away, and store them in airtight containers such as cedar chests or bags that have been sealed with tape to keep moths out.

- High heat and freezing can kill moths. Running infested items through a clothes dryer is an effective way to kill moths.
- Put inexpensive cardboard traps in your closet. They use natural insect attractants called pheromones to lure moths inside where they are caught on sticky surfaces.

GREENEST

- Prevention goes a long way. Keep your clothes and furniture clean. Vacuum regularly; clean closets and behind baseboards and cracks in floors. Clean closet shelves frequently.

PANTRY MOTHS

If you see small moths with reddish brown wings flying around your kitchen, chances are they are Indian meal moths. By the time you see them, their larvae are contaminating some of your food with their bodies and by-products. Larvae are fond of a number of foods such as flour, cereal, rice, pasta, dried fruits, nuts, chocolate, candy, and dry pet food. You'll most often find them in food that's been opened or in new food with damaged packaging. There are plenty of measures you can take to prevent and solve the problem, but if your infestation is bad and you aren't making progress, you may want to call in a professional.

GREEN

- As soon as you see moths in your kitchen or pantry you should immediately find the food source and get it out of your house. It's a good idea to check all likely foods for damage. Look for worms or flossy insect webbings. Get rid of any questionable food.

- Don't buy food in damaged packages.

GREENER

- Store infrequently used food in the freezer or refrigerator to prevent infestation.

- Use pheromone traps after you've dealt with an infestation. Moths are attracted to the scent of the sex chemicals produced and get stuck on the sticky side of the trap.

GREENEST

- Work on preventing problems from occurring in the first place. Regularly clean pantry shelves. Vacuum cracks and use soap and water on shelves.

ANTS

It's discouraging to see a line of ants marching across the kitchen floor. Spraying may be a common way to get rid of nuisance ants, but it's certainly not the most effective strategy because it doesn't get to the root of the problem. No matter how much spraying you do, more ants will make their way back into your home. It's hard to totally eradicate ants, but you can banish most of them if you take the steps that follow.

Carpenter ants are a different story because they can do damage to your house. They are usually about a quarter- to a a half-inch long and are either red and black or just plain black. Don't panic if you see one because it takes two to four years for a colony to grow to several hundred workers, according to the Northwest Coalition for Alternatives to Pesticides (NCAP). In general, you'll want to take the steps below that apply to preventing ants from entering your house. If they have penetrated, you'll probably want to call in a professional to find and eradicate the primary nest. If you decide to tackle it by yourself, check out the NCAP carpenter ant management fact sheet at www.pesticide.org/carpenterants.html for tips on how to find and remove nests.

● GREEN

- Follow the steps suggested in general pest control.

● GREENER

- Caulk or seal any cracks or holes that give outdoor ants a way to get inside your house.
- Mix a teaspoon of liquid soap and water in a quart size spray bottle, suggests the NCAP, and spray areas where the ants are active to destroy the chemical trails left by worker ants.
- Repair leaks and replace rotten wood around the house or deck.
- Use baits in closed cases instead of sprays if you decide you need to use pesticides.

GREENEST

- Trim branches of shrubs and trees so that they don't touch the house because ants can crawl from branches directly into your home.

- If all of your preventative efforts fail, try to locate and destroy the colony. The NCAP suggests following a trail of ants until they disappear or placing syrup or honey on cardboard or wax paper squares along ant trails. A thick trail of ants leading from the syrup can lead you to the nest. You can destroy outdoor nests by pouring a lot of boiling water directly into the nest. Indoor nests, which are likely to be in warm, moist places such as in walls, under floors, or near hot water heaters, can be vacuumed up with a HEPA filter. Adding a little cornstarch to the bag will help suffocate ants. Dispose of the bag immediately.

TERMITES

You need to know what kind of termite you're dealing with in order to treat the problem effectively. If you find you have termites, your best bet is to call in an expert to assess and treat the situation immediately since termites can seriously damage your house. If possible, try to find an IPM provider who will work with you to avoid the most toxic chemicals. The University of California has extensive information if you want to learn more about the different types of termites and treatment options, www.ipm.ucdavis.edu.

FLEAS

Dogs may be man's best friend, but the accompanying fleas definitely aren't. The relentless biters are more than just a nuisance: they transmit tapeworms and several human pathogens, and may cause allergies in both animals and humans, according to Dickey, the former staff scientist at Washington Toxics. Unfortunately, they are hard to get rid of because you are often dealing with two problems: fleas on your pet and fleas in your house. You really need to tackle both effectively and at the same time to make any real progress. Plus, if your pet goes outdoors, then fleas will inevitably make their way onto its body again. To make matters even more complicated, fleas have four stages of life—eggs, larvae, pupae, and adults—and different methods work for different stages. Once you master the problem, good maintenance and controls are essential.

Traditional methods such as flea collars, insecticidal powders and shampoos, and aerosol bombs contain very potent chemicals. Children who pet dogs and cats may pick up the chemicals on their hands and then put their hands in their mouths. Studies have shown that people with brain tumors were twice as likely to have grown up in a home where flea and tick products were used. The risk increased tenfold when the products were applied as a spray or fogger, according to a 1997 study published in *Environmental Health Perspectives*. They're not so great for your pets either, which can be poisoned by treatments.

If your pet has fleas, start with nonchemical solutions. If stronger controls are needed, use the least toxic options first. As soon as the symptoms recede, discontinue chemicals. Definitely stay away from foggers and other delivery devices that spray chemicals over your entire home.

GREEN

- Vacuum floors often. It's very effective at eliminating adult fleas. They can escape from the vacuum bag, so seal it inside a plastic trash bag to keep fleas from escaping and throw it away, or fasten a plastic bag over the end of the vacuum cleaner hose until you vacuum again.

- Wash your pet's bedding and any throw rugs in hot water regularly because they are common places for flea eggs to develop and hatch.

- Shampoo your pet. Try regular soap before using insecticides, and never let children apply insecticide shampoo if you do resort to using it.

GREENER

- Steam-clean and/or shampoo rugs and upholstery.

- Try insect growth regulators, chemicals that stop the growth of young fleas so they never reach adulthood and therefore can't reproduce. The EPA says the active ingredients are not expected to harm human health when used properly.

- Ask your vet to prescribe a gel that can be applied to a small spot on the pet's skin or a substance that can be safely ingested by your pet that is toxic or repellant to insects.

• If you have to use an insecticide then spot treat small outdoor areas with insecticidal soap, such as patios or decks where pets spend a lot of time.

GREENEST

• Mow lawns where pets spend most of their time as frequently as you can. Fleas and ticks thrive in longer grass.

• Apply beneficial nematodes to your lawn to control flea larvae in the summer or fall. You can find them at gardening supply stores (see Chapter 10 for sources).

• Use a flea comb regularly to remove fleas without pesticides. Comb outside and drown fleas in a container of soapy water or in the bathtub and then rinse pests down the drain.

• If fleas are really bad then limit your pet's access to certain areas of your home, or in extreme cases, have your pet stay solely indoors or outdoors until you have a handle on the problem.

BEDBUGS

There's been a resurgence of bedbugs recently. These nasty blood-sucking creatures are turning up in dorm rooms, fancy hotels, and hospitals as well as in homes. For the most part, they aren't harmful to your health since they aren't known to transmit disease, but people can have unpleasant allergic reactions to their saliva, and in severe cases children and the elderly can develop anemia, according to Cornell University's Cooperative Extension.

Bedbugs feed on human blood at night when you are sleeping and then hide in crevices during the day. Your best bet is preventing them from entering your home.

GREEN

- Move your bed away from the wall, and make sure that there isn't a blanket or bed linen touching the floor. This will make it harder for bedbugs to crawl into your bed.

- When travelling, check your hotel room for signs of bedbugs. Look for blood stains and fecal spots on pillows or linens, check out the mattress seams, and look behind the headboard for the bugs themselves.

- Wash your bed linens in hot water and throw them in a hot dryer to kill bedbugs.

- If you have a severe infestation it might make sense to call in a pro to apply chemicals. Try the least toxic options first, such as silica gel dusts in walls and other inaccessible places. This causes bedbugs to lose water and die. Many of these products also contain pyrethrins, which can cause skin and respiratory irritation in people as well as trigger allergies. Call your local cooperative extension office for other ideas.

GREENER

- Vacuum with a HEPA filter thoroughly every day to deal with an infestation. You'll need to cover a lot of ground: both sides and seams of mattress, furniture, baseboards, and so on. To kill the bedbugs place the bag in the freezer for at least 24 hours before disposing of it.

GREENEST

- For severe infestations it may make sense to replace your mattress or whatever the bedbugs have embedded themselves in, but remember to keep cleaning and take the preventative measures above so they don't reinfest your new mattress.

RODENTS

Since rodents can carry some serious diseases, it's important to keep them out of your home environment. If you do find mice or rats roaming around your home or yard you'll need to act fast because they reproduce rapidly. Mice can live almost anywhere, and they'll eat almost anything. It can be difficult to detect an infestation because they are usually more active at night. They also spend most of their time behind or underneath objects, and they usually travel along walls or other structures, which gives them cover. Small black droppings in food cupboards, drawers, or even the stove are a dead giveaway.

Some rodents carry hantavirus pulmonary syndrome, a potentially fatal disease. It is spread when humans breathe in dust contaminated by droppings, urine, or saliva from an infected rodent, or when people handle contaminated items and then touch their nose or mouth. For information and pictures of rodents that are potential carriers along with suggestions for cleaning rodent-infested areas and other tips, go to the CDC website, www.cdc.gov/ncidod/diseases/hanta/hps/noframes/FAQ.htm. Call your local health department to find out what to do with dead rodents and for any special cleaning instructions. Never touch a dead rodent with bare hands.

● GREEN

- Follow all the steps in general pest control.

● GREENER

- Try traps before poison. There are many varieties on the market so pick what feels most comfortable for you. Place traps where rodents are active, but out of reach of children and pets, and move them around if you aren't catching mice. You'll have better luck if you place triggers facing walls, and you may even want to try putting out the traps with bait but not set for a few nights so mice and rats get comfortable with them. Dickey, formerly of Washington Toxics, recommends using gloves when setting traps so rodents don't get scared away by human scent.

- If you do decide to use poison baits, keep them away from children and pets. Bear in mind that poisoned animals can die inside the walls of your house, creating a horrible stench.

● GREENEST

- Your best bet is to keep rodents out of your house in the first place. Seal up gaps and openings that are larger than a quarter inch. A mouse can fit through a hole the size of a pencil eraser, according to a University of California fact sheet. They can jump high, run up sides of buildings, and cross cables and wires. Repair broken windows, doors, and screens.

• Eliminate places where mice and rats can find shelter both inside and directly outside of your home. Remove blackberries, ivy, and other brush near your house.

Spotlight On: Pesticides

Pesticides are not all created equally. They target different pests and work in different ways. The information below will give you the basics on how to distinguish them from one another.

WHAT THEY KILL

Herbicides: weeds and other plants

Insecticides: insects and arthropods

Rodenticides: mice and other rodents

CATEGORIES OF PESTICIDES

Organochlorine Pesticides. Most have been banned in the United States, such as DDT, dieldrin, and chlordane. However, they persist in the environment and in our bodies. Lindane is still being used in shampoos to treat head lice.

Organophosphate Pesticides. These affect the nervous system by disrupting an enzyme that regulates a neurotransmitter called acetylcholine, according to the EPA. Many residential uses have been phased out in the United States. However, you might have some chemicals that have been banned for home use lying around. Chlorpyrifos (also listed as Dursban) were banned at the end of 2000. It became illegal to sell Diazinon to consumers at the end of 2004. The EPA says some organophosphates are very poisonous, but they are usually not persistent in the environment.

Pyrethroid Pesticides. These are the synthetic version of the naturally occurring pesticide found in chrysanthemums. Pyrethroids can be used in pet sprays, household insecticides, and lice shampoos. The CDC says they are less hazardous to health than older insecticides. The agency reports that exposure to large amounts of pyrethroids can cause dizziness, headaches, nausea, convulsions, or loss of consciousness.

Carbamate Pesticides. The EPA says they affect the nervous system by disrupting an enzyme that regulates a neurotransmitter called acetylcholine, but says the effects are usually reversible.

For More Information

The following organizations have excellent resources for those looking for more information on individual pests and pesticides, or seeking ways to enact change. The suggestions throughout the chapter were adapted from fact sheets from the following sources as well as interviews with some of their representatives and other experts. For more information on individual pests the best place to start is with the fact sheets:

Beyond Pesticides, www.beyondpesticides.org. Offers updates on the latest news regarding pesticides and has numerous fact sheets.

Northwest Coalition for Alternatives to Pesticides, www.pesticide.org. Offers extensive fact sheets on numerous pests and pesticides. Also lists guidelines on researching health effects of pesticides on the Web and has excellent links. Search this website to discover all of NCAP's resources, or for specific questions that you can't find answers to contact the organization at 541-344-5044 or info@pesticide.org.

Pesticide Action Network North America, www.panna.org. Features pesticide database, several reports on pesticide use, and offers resources to get active on pesticide reform.

University of California–Irvine IPM Program, www.ipm.ucdavis.edu. Provides loads of information on integrated pest management and offers strategies for dealing with a range of different pests.

Washington Toxics Coalition, www.watoxics.org. Offers many fact sheets with excellent tips on how to get rid of pests reasonably and responsibly, both inside and outside. It has great resources for getting toxics out of all areas of your home, not just pesticides.

10 BACKYARD AND GARDEN

Our backyards and gardens can be a great source of pleasure for the entire family. We spend a lot of time in them during the relaxed months of summer, and they are the setting for many happy memories—evening barbeques, games of catch, naps on hammocks. Ironically, though, the greenest part of your home can be one of the least environmentally friendly. The classic American yard consumes vast amounts of pesticides, drinks hundreds of gallons of water, and creates a mountain of waste. Part of being "green" is realizing our impact on the world around us, and as with most other things, what you do in your outdoor space has larger implications: yard waste is the second largest component of solid waste in the United States, says the Environmental Protection Agency (EPA); pesticides leach down into groundwater or rain washes them out into creeks and streams; and it's already well known that water is in short supply and only going to become scarcer. Many pesticides are hazardous to human health, linked to everything from Parkinson's to infertility to some cancers. Do we really want our children rolling around on chemical-laden grass or tracking chemicals inside on the bottom of their shoes?

Luckily, there are many ways to be kinder to your own little patch of nature and protect your family's health at the same time. An added bonus: many of the strategies outlined in this chapter can ultimately end up saving you time and money. Of course, it's going to take time to learn and make transitions to sustainable ways of creating and maintaining outdoor space, but once you're up and running, the maintenance will be easier, especially if you make changes to your lawn. There may be times when the use of a chemical seems like the only choice, but if you pause to consider alternatives before grabbing a can of chemicals, it will make a big difference. In most cases, there is a better solution. As with most other things, if you can prevent problems or catch them early you won't have to go to extreme measures to fix them.

Entire books are dedicated to gardening and lawn care. This chapter will give you the basics for starting down the organic gardening path and offer you a smattering of what's available. If you want to learn more, there are plenty of resources listed to help you with the technicalities.

GARDEN

For some of us, there's nothing more satisfying than tinkering in the garden for hours on end. But your hobby shouldn't compromise your health or the planet's, and it doesn't have to. Your garden can be perfectly lovely without the use of harsh chemicals. In fact, natural methods are generally more effective over the long run—pests can develop resistance to pesticides, for example, and if you don't overwater your plants they will develop deeper roots that will serve them well during droughts. Your ultimate goal is to provide your plants with healthy soil to grow in, soil that's well balanced and teeming with nutrients. If you can do that, you'll see many benefits: weeds and pests will be less of an issue, and you won't need to force-feed your plants with Miracle-Gro because they'll already be healthy and strong. There are all sorts of exciting things happening on the sustainable gardening front right now, such as the movement toward using native plants, new low-watering planting plans, and more.

GREEN

- Avoid using synthetic pesticides. If you've tried all the strategies outlined in this chapter and feel you must use chemicals, then do your homework to make sure you try the least toxic options first (see page 220). The Pesticide Action Network's database, www.pesticideinfo.org, is an excellent resource for learning a specific pesticide's potential health impacts and whether it is considered high risk. You can search by product ingredients or product names. If you have a specific pest in your garden, target it using a "selective" pesticide rather than a "broad-spectrum" pesticide. Read the label of any product you buy and pay attention to toxicity warnings like "Caution," "Warning," and "Danger" (see page 186).

- Save water. There are plenty of strategies throughout this chapter that you can use to save water, such as building your soil with compost, covering with mulch to reduce evaporation, and choosing xeric (low water) plants. If you aren't able to take those steps just yet, try these simple and inexpensive water-saving strategies: water in the cool of the morning to avoid evaporation; check hoses for leaks; make sure sprinklers are watering plants and not pavement; buy a rain barrel with a spigot to catch water from your gutter and use it to water your plants. The EPA says using soaker hoses or drip irrigation on flower beds can save 50 percent or more compared with sprinklers. For more tips see www.h2ouse.org.

• Garden with your kids. This is a great way to spend quality time with them. They'll also learn basic science and develop a connection with the outdoors—an awareness that will hopefully translate into a love for the planet. The Brooklyn Botanic Garden, www.bbg.org, has a Children's Gardening section on its website that includes books and pamphlets with activity ideas for different age groups.

● GREENER

• Get your soil tested so you know if you need additives to enrich it. A good soil test can tell you how much nitrogen, phosphorous, potassium, and lime your soil has. Contact your local cooperative extension to get your soil tested. Every state has one and in addition to helping you test your soil, it can be a great resource for local advice. If you're worried about toxins in your soil, a concern if kids play in dirt, then you can ask your extension to test for heavy metals, pesticides, and other contaminants as well. You can find your extension by clicking on the map at www.csrees.usda.gov/Extension. You can also buy soil-testing kits at a garden supply store, but these only test for pH levels.

• Invest in good tools that will last you a long time, and take good care of them by removing soil and oiling wood handles and metal parts. Buy garden equipment made from recycled content such as hand tools made with recycled plastic or garden hoses made from old tires. Check out the offerings at Gardener's Supply, www.gardeners.com.

• Use hoes, rakes, shovels, and other manual garden tools instead of gas- or electric-powered ones to prevent air pollution and save fossil fuels.

GREENEST

• Practice companion planting. Plan your garden so that you have pest-repellant plants next to susceptible plants. Planting mint, garlic, chives, or coriander near more vulnerable plants will keep aphids away, for example. You can find more information at many of the resources listed throughout this chapter and at www.companionplanting.net.

• Consider introducing some native plants, the ultimate low-maintenance plants. Native plants have adapted to local conditions over thousands of years and can survive without much help. They don't require much irrigation or fertilization and are naturally resistant to pests and disease. Other benefits: they won't become invasive and overrun your garden, and they may enrich the soil because their root systems help rainfall permeate the soil, reducing erosion and runoff. You can buy native plants at most gardens and nurseries, or try www.nearlynativenursery.com, a great source for finding the best plants for your particular growing conditions.

• Redefine your definition of beauty. Allow plants that would grow naturally to flourish. If you live in a climate that is hospitable to one plant, do not inhibit its growth to support an exotic import.

- Xeriscaping is a technique that involves designing gardens and lawns by incorporating the natural landscape. Xeriscape gardens are designed to reduce water usage and soil erosion, lower maintenance costs, and preserve natural resources. For more information visit your local cooperative extension's website. High Country Gardens, www.highcountrygardens.com, has a great catalogue.

- Landscaping choices can help reduce your energy use. For example, planting trees strategically to provide shade can offset cooling costs, and shrubs and vines can insulate your home. For more information on how you can use landscaping to help save energy, see the U.S. Department of Energy brochure *A Consumer's Guide to Energy Efficiency and Renewable Energy* at www.eere.energy.gov/consumer.

- Grow your own organic food. You can't get more local than that! Seeds of Change, www.seedsofchange.com, has a wide range of USDA Certified Organic seeds to choose from.

Organic Gardening 101

The best way to avoid harsh chemicals in your garden is to prevent pests and other problems from occurring in the first place, and the secret to this is in the soil. A healthy soil biology will contain beneficial bacteria, fungi, and other living organisms that are essential for healthy plant growth and disease resistance, says Patti Wood, executive director at Grassroots Environmental Education.

A simple soil test will give you basic information about what nutrients or amendments you need to add (see page 226). Mulching stabilizes soil temperature, prevents weeds, feeds the soil, and helps conserve water. You can mulch with leaves, aged wood chips, compost, or other organic matter. Select pest-resistant plants. Pull weeds before they seed and spread. Rotate annuals to minimize their susceptibility to pests and disease.

When you do have problems, trade in chemical pesticides for botanical and biological controls. Other methods: introduce some beneficial insects, such as ladybugs to control aphids and praying mantises for help with grubs, beetles, leafhoppers, and caterpillars. The EPA says only 5 to 15 percent of the bugs in your yard are pests. The rest can help control pests.

Talk to your local nursery about finding solutions to your specific problems. *Organic Gardening* magazine, www.organicgardening.com, is a great source of general information. The EPA's GreenScapes program, www.epa.gov/greenscapes, offers environmentally friendly landscape ideas (click on "GreenScapes for Homeowners"). You can find alternative products at the following websites as well as valuable information and resources: Gardens Alive, www.gardensalive.com; Peaceful Valley, www.groworganic.com; Planet Natural, www.planetnatural.com; and Arbico, www.arbico-organics.com.

LAWN CARE

Americans take great pride in perfectly manicured green lawns. Billions of dollars are spent every year caring for them. Hundreds of thousands of gallons of water are used for irrigation. A surprising and chilling fact is that more pesticides are applied to lawns per acre than farmers put on their fields! According to the EPA, surveys show higher concentrations of some pesticides, particularly insecticides, in urban streams than agricultural streams. It turns out that lawns aren't so green after all.

Don't despair. You can still have an attractive lawn without using harsh chemicals. And if you're willing to modify your definition of the ideal lawn, there are even more possibilities. Below are some general tips, but if you want more specific advice on non-toxic lawn care visit www.grassrootsinfo.org, www.safelawns.org, and Cornell University's lawn care website, www.gardening.cornell.edu/lawn.

GREEN

- If you use pesticides on your lawn remove shoes when you enter your home.

- Mow high. Keep grass at about 3 to 3.5 inches long to foster deep, drought-resistant roots and to shade out unwanted weeds. Leave clippings where they fall and allow them to decompose and become nutrients for your lawn. This will not only save you time and money, but it will also keep some yard waste from going to the landfill. Keep mower blades sharp; a dull blade will tear grass and make it more susceptible to disease.

- Water thoroughly but less often. Lawns need about one inch of water a week, including rain, to stay healthy and encourage deep roots. You can use a rain gauge or tuna cans to measure. Remember that early morning is best for watering.

• If you use a lawn service, find one that's organic. Grassroots Environmental Education has a list of landscapers that have completed their two-day EPA award-winning intensive training course in organic turf maintenance. Click on "Find a Landscaper" at www.ghlp.org. The Northeast Organic Farming Association has a list of accredited organic landscapers at www.organiclandcare.net. Safelawns.org has a list of questions that you can ask lawn contractors to determine how natural their methods are.

GREENER

• Healthy soil is essential for lawns. Healthy soil, with a thriving community of microbes and a good amount of organic matter, will produce turf that is naturally resistant to drought, weeds, and insects, says Wood of Grassroots Environmental Education. Get your soil tested so you know what nutrients it needs (see page 226). Spread a thin, protective layer of organic fertilizer or compost over your lawn each spring and fall.

• If you want to entertain outdoors or have kids run around in the yard, you might want a large lawn, but how much lawn area do you really need? Consider planting a smaller section of turf lawn and use ground cover and other creative options to fill in extra space.

• Reseed every fall. A thick turf is great protection against weeds.

• Rethink your position on weeds: is it really important to get every dandelion out? If so, dig them out by hand. Organic corn-gluten products can also help with weeds.

• Banish pesticides. "There is really no reason to use pesticides in a lawn environment," says Wood. "Pesticides will kill not only the target organisms but also the beneficial ones which are there to help us grow things." Studies at Cornell University showed that lawns treated with chemicals are more susceptible to infestations of pests because all of the beneficial microbes have been compromised. Depending upon what you're trying to deal with, beneficial nematodes or milk spore powder might help. Compost or compost tea can help with fungal diseases. You'll need to identify the problem and do some homework to find out the least toxic, most effective solution for a particular problem. Visit the websites listed throughout this section or your local cooperative extension. You can also ask your local gardening store to help you diagnose problems.

• Choose native grasses, those that are adapted to your local area. See your local cooperative extension to find out which grasses are most suitable to your growing climate.

• Reduce the use of power equipment. Power mowers consume 580 million gallons of gas every year. Electric mowers can be more expensive, but they produce less pollution and cost less to operate. Reel push mowers are the greenest option yet, but they work only on flat lawns. It's important, though, that you buy the best mower for your lawn based on calculations of size and grade. See *Consumer Reports* for extensive information and ratings.

GREENEST

- Spread the word and get active by joining forces with the National Coalition for Pesticide-Free Lawns, www.beyondpesticides.org/pesticidefreelawns. Order a Pesticide-Free Zone sign and post it on your lawn to raise awareness, sign the Declaration on the Use of Tóxic Lawn Chemicals, and consider getting involved with your local chapter. You'll also find a wealth of information and resources to help you green your lawn.
- Consider alternatives to traditional lawns. Plant meadow and prairie grass, for example, which are resilient and require less care.

COMPOSTING

Composting is an all-around win-win. It's a great way to turn organic waste into healthy food for your plants. It keeps yard and food waste, which make up about a quarter of the U.S. waste stream, out of landfills. It's a much richer food for your plants than chemical fertilizers, which deplete soil. Adding compost to your soil also provides it with loads of nutrients and improves pH levels. If you use compost, your soil will be able to hold more moisture, making it less prone to erosion, and you won't have to water as often. But before you go out and buy a composting bin, you definitely need to know what you're getting yourself into. Composting can be hard work and it requires a big commitment, but if you're able to do it, it can be immensely satisfying.

BUG OFF: SAFEST REPELLANTS

If you spend much time outdoors, you're bound to run into mosquitoes and/or deer ticks, two very unpleasant pests that can carry serious diseases such as dengue fever, West Nile virus, and Lyme disease. The insect repellant DEET is considered the most effective defense against these pests. The EPA says the pesticide is safe when consumers follow label directions. However, some consumers have been wary of using DEET because of cases of adverse health effects such as skin rashes and neurological problems such as seizures.

If you do use DEET, follow directions carefully, especially when applying to children. The EPA suggests that you also take the following precautions: don't apply over cuts, wounds, or irritated skin; use just enough repellant to cover exposed skin and/or clothing; don't use under clothing; do not apply to hands or near mouths of young children; and wash treated skin with soap and water when you get inside. The American Academy of Pediatrics says not to use DEET on children younger than two months. The CDC does not recommend using products that combine sunscreen and DEET because it's harder to control how much DEET you're getting, especially since it's advised that you apply sunscreen frequently and use DEET with more caution. The amount of DEET in a given product varies, with greater amounts last-

GREEN

- If you don't have the time or the space to make it, then buy commercial compost. Ask your local garden center for sources or get a list of suppliers from your local cooperative extensive office. TerraCycle, www.terracycle.net, is a nationally available brand that does the hard work for you with a minimal impact on the environment. Its fertilizer—worm waste—is packaged in used 20-ounce plastic bottles that the company collects from

ing longer. Use the least amount you can for the amount of time you'll be outdoors.

Cautious consumers may also have some other effective options to choose from. The CDC has declared two less toxic alternatives to be just as effective as DEET—plant-based oil of eucalyptus and picaridin, a chemical repellant. *Consumer Reports* tested products with these ingredients and found some of them to be as effective as those containing DEET. Repel Plant Based Eucalyptus was the best of the DEET-free products the magazine tested. Cutter Advanced Sport, with picaridin, had good results as well. Botanicals, such as soybean and geranium oils, another commonly touted nontoxic solution, did not fare well in the *Consumer Reports* tests. Wearing long pants and sleeves as well as mosquito-net clothing is a good way to cut down on repellant use.

Prevention is always the best defense. When you're at the park or on a hike there's not much you can do, but in your backyard you can take some simple measures to prevent mosquitoes. Check your backyard for any sources of still water, where mosquitoes congregate. Most are obvious, but others, such as improperly slanted gutters and empty bird feeders, can be easily overlooked.

consumers and companies. You can find it in mainstream outlets such as Home Depot, Wal-Mart, and Target. Visit the company's website to find out how you can donate your used bottles.

• If you can't compost, you may be able to donate your yard waste to a community composting program. Contact your local solid waste authority to find out if anyone collects compostable materials in your area.

GREENER

• Start a compost pile for yard waste. During setup place large branches in the pile to aid in air circulation. Many experts suggest choosing a shady spot. Simply add what you can to the pile and allow it to sit. Shredding materials first will help them decay faster. Keep the pile moist by hosing it down if it gets too dry, and turn it every couple of weeks.

GREENEST

• Actively compost yard and food scraps. You can choose to use a bin or an open pile. Plenty of eco-friendly sites sell compost bins, such as www.planetnatural.com or www.cleanairgardening.com, as well as the resources listed earlier in this chapter. *Consumer Reports* has ratings. You can also make one yourself by drilling half-inch diameter holes into the bottom and sides of a metal garbage can. Place moist, carbon-rich browns (dried leaves, wood chips) at the bottom of your bin. Then add food scraps, burying them in the browns to disguise their scent from pests. Almost all organic materials can be added to your compost, but keep in mind that you need a balance of carbon-rich materials to provide energy for the microbes and nitrogen-rich materials for protein (grass clippings, kitchen scraps) to aid in decomposition. Too much carbon will cause the pile to break down too slowly; too much nitrogen will cause your compost pile to smell. You can store scraps in a Ziploc bag in the freezer and dump when full if you don't want to run outside every time you have something to ditch. You'll ultimately have to find your way through trial and error, but if you do want to give it a try, do your homework first. There are plenty of books on the subject, or visit www.composting101.com or your favorite gardening source.

DO COMPOST

Browns	Greens
Untreated wood shavings	Grass clippings
Shredded newspaper	Vegetable waste
Cardboard rolls (and other shredded cardboard)	Fruit scraps
Dead leaves	Coffee grounds
Branches	Dead houseplants (not diseased)
Twigs	
Pine Needles	

DON'T TRY TO COMPOST

Meat
Fish
Dairy products
Lard or grease (can attract rodents)
Diseased plants
Cat, dog, pig, reptile, and bird droppings (might be diseased)
Chicken, cow, and horse manure

• It's harder to compost in the city, but it's not impossible. If you're adventurous and not squeamish about worms, you might want to consider vermicomposting, also known as "worm composting." You purchase or make a bin (which can be stored wherever you like), line it with moist shredded newspaper, add redworms and food scraps, and you're all set. The worms eat and digest the food scraps. After a few months, their feces or castings accumulate and resemble black dirt that can be added to soil and then used as a fertilizer. The benefits: you'll cut down on food scraps going to the landfill and create a nutritious food for your plants. For more information on vermicomposting and resources for buying redworms and other supplies visit Earth Worm Digest, www.wormdigest.org, or Mary Apelhof's website, www.wormwoman.com; Apelhof is an author and expert on worm composting.

- Get active. If your community doesn't have a curbside collection for compostable materials, try to get one started.

CUT FLOWERS

Wouldn't it be nice to have a sustainably grown flower garden to enjoy year-round? It's just not possible in many parts of the country. So, is the next best thing a vase of gorgeous flowers? Not exactly. While receiving an unexpected bouquet can certainly brighten your day, fresh-cut flowers are a bit of an eco-nightmare. Most of the flowers sold in U.S. markets are grown overseas in developing countries where they're produced in huge, poorly vented greenhouses. To reach us, they're shipped thousands of miles, belching fossil fuels along the way. Workers are exposed to terrible poisons because ungodly amounts of pesticides and herbicides are sprayed onto flowers, says Ronnie Cummins, national director of the Organic Consumers Association. Learning about the origins of conventional bouquets is more than enough to kill the romance surrounding them. Luckily, sustainable flower options are sprouting up nationwide.

GREEN

- If you buy conventional flowers, wear gloves when arranging them to protect against pesticide residues, and place the flowers in a well-ventilated area.

GREENER

- Buy organic flowers. Look for the USDA Certified Organic label; if you can't find them in your neighborhood order some from a national source, such as Organic Bouquet, www.organicbouquet.com, or Diamond Organics, www.diamondorganics.com.
- Buy local flowers to cut down on fossil-fuel use. Look for them at your local farmers' market or visit www.localharvest.org to find a grower in your area.
- If you're giving flowers as a gift, give a potted plant instead, or buy your loved one organic flower bulbs.
- Bring in greens from your yard—branches, leaves, and seed pods—instead of buying flowers to decorate your home; you can add a few flowers to the greens for color.

GREENEST

- Ask local shopkeepers where their flowers came from, and tell them that you'd be happier to buy if they could provide local and/or organic sources.

- Grow your own organic flowers, either in an outdoor garden or indoors with pots.

FURNITURE, DECKS, AND PLAY STRUCTURES

Until a few years ago, the pressure-treated wood commonly used to build children's play sets, decks, and picnic tables was treated with an arsenic-based preservative to protect it from rot and pests. The preservative, called chromium copper arsenate (CCA), contains inorganic arsenic, a known carcinogen linked to skin, bladder, and lung cancers. Exposure to high amounts of CCA over a short period of time can result in nausea and vomiting. It can leach into the soil and onto hands where it can be absorbed through skin or ingested when hands are put into mouths. It's been phased out, but many homes still have decks and others structures made out of it.

Plastic patio furniture can withstand bad weather, but it's not the most eco-friendly outdoor furniture option given that it's made from fossil fuels. Outdoor furniture covers are most often made from polyvinyl chloride (PVC). Its production involves the use and release of extremely toxic chemicals, and it can leach some of the chemicals used to make it flexible. Furthermore, it's not widely recyclable. When incinerated, it releases dangerous hydrogen chloride gas and dioxin.

There are many ways to deal with these issues from fixing what you have to buying more sustainable products.

GREEN

- Find out if there is arsenic in your deck, children's play equipment, or other sources of pressure-treated wood. Inexpensive test kits are available from the Healthy Building Network, www.healthybuilding.net. Samples are analyzed by an independent lab that's been certified by the EPA.

- If you find arsenic, then seal it at least once a year with a waterproof sealant such as polyurethane or an oil-based penetrating sealer to reduce the amount of arsenic that can leach out. The Environmental Working Group recommends sealing at least every six months.

GREENER

- If you can't replace all of your wood, then try to replace the boards in high-traffic areas or places that are touched frequently, such as handrails.

- Look for patio furniture made from sustainable materials such as naturally rot-resistant wood and recycled plastic lumber. You won't need PVC-based covers. If you do find you need to buy a separate cover then look for PVC-free versions available at www.ecomall.com.

● GREENEST

- Replace all wood containing arsenic. Some options: cedar and redwood are naturally rot resistant. Looking for FSC certified sustainably harvested wood is your best bet if you can find it and afford it. Recycled plastic lumber can be used for decking. Ammoniacal copper quaternary (ACQ) and copper boron azole (CBA) are nonarsenic-containing alternatives that can be used to treat wood. Ask your lumberyard what's been used to treat any wood you buy.

11 TRANSPORTATION

It's no secret that transportation is a major contributor to global warming pollution and that carbon and other emissions from vehicles (including cars, trucks, buses, planes, and ships) also make our air dirty and unhealthy to breathe. In the United States transportation is the second largest source of greenhouse gases behind coal power plants used to generate electricity. Americans burn billions of gallons of gas and oil each year in order to get around, much of it imported from politically unstable foreign countries. Since most of us depend on cars to get to work, school, supermarkets, and everywhere else we need to go, it can seem like there isn't a lot we can really do on a personal level to impact the situation.

It's true that dramatically changing the transportation landscape is too big for any individual to tackle completely—especially when many Americans live in areas where they have no choice but to travel long distances just to accomplish the basics of daily living. Looking at the big picture, major changes will require the government to step in and work with manufacturers to produce more efficient cars that go a lot further on a tank of fuel. We need to develop cleaner fuels with which to fill those cars up and to create communities where we don't necessarily have to drive everywhere; where there are sidewalks for walking, lanes for biking, and public transportation that's efficient and easy to get to. That said, there is plenty you can do in the meantime to help, from small changes to significant investments. Since global warming pollution is a problem with such serious potential consequences, every little bit counts.

You have the most control over your own car, so that's the place to start. Which car you drive, how you maintain and drive it, and how much you drive it can have a significant impact on climate change. The Sierra Club says that switching from driving an average car to a 13 miles-per-gallon (mpg) sport utility vehicle (SUV) for one year would waste more energy than if you left your refrigerator door open for six years! In a nutshell: drive the most fuel efficient car that you can and try to drive less when possible.

We hear a lot about hybrids, but that doesn't necessarily mean that you have to go out and buy one to make a difference. Hybrids aren't, incidentally, always your most fuel-efficient choice. Greenpeace executive director John Passacantando makes an excellent point: if you have to drop out of the carpool because you traded in your minivan for a Prius, then you're not helping the environment since you're putting another car on the road. And driving less doesn't necessarily mean that you have to make radical changes. It can be as simple as carpooling when it's convenient or thinking twice about getting behind the wheel when you may not have to. Can that errand wait until next week when you will be driving by the shopping center anyway? With a little forethought, you can find the solutions that work for you.

Efforts are underway to make those solutions easier to find. The Leadership in Energy and Environmental Design (LEED) Green Building Rating System is the gold standard for certifying green buildings. Now, its originator, the U.S. Green Building Council, along with other environmental groups, aims to go a step further and certify eco-friendly neighborhood development. The idea is to promote new developments and community revitalization efforts that utilize "smart growth" strategies such as making it safe and practical for residents to walk or bike. These new communities are likely to be beneficial for our health as well as the environment since car-dependent urban sprawl contributes not only to pollution but also to the U.S. obesity epidemic by reducing physical activity. Getting out of your car is good for the planet and good for your body.

Climate Change 101

WHAT EXACTLY IS GLOBAL WARMING?

Light waves from the sun heat up the planet and then get reflected back into outer space as infrared waves. Our atmosphere naturally traps a portion of the infrared, keeping the earth warm enough for us to live here. What's happening now, though, is that rising levels of greenhouse gases (see next question) are causing more heat to be trapped in the atmosphere, and that, in turn, makes our planet heat up. There is still debate among scientists about some of the details of global warming, but there is a consensus that it is occurring and that humans are largely responsible.

WHAT ARE GREENHOUSE GASES AND WHERE DO THEY COME FROM?

Carbon dioxide is the most prevalent greenhouse gas, but there are others such as methane and nitrous oxide, which are not as prevalent but are more potent. We add significant amounts of greenhouse gases to the atmosphere by burning fossil fuels such as oil, natural gas, and coal in our cars, homes, factories, and power plants. Tree loss—whether caused by human action such as cutting or harvesting, or by natural disasters such as forest fires—is also a significant contributor to global warming because the carbon dioxide that would otherwise be absorbed by the trees is released back into the atmosphere.

WHAT ARE THE CONSEQUENCES OF CLIMATE CHANGE?

If we continue spewing greenhouse gases at current rates we'll see the earth's temperature continue to rise. This could lead to more record-breaking temperatures; warming oceans, which will cause more severe storms; melting ice areas and disappearing glaciers, which can lead to rising sea levels; and record numbers of forest fires, which will cause even more carbon dioxide to be released into the air. Habitat loss is already adversely affecting polar bears and penguins. In coming years, the health as well as social and economic consequences for humans will rise as we see more severe heat waves, drought, and famine due to climate change.

HOW CAN WE SOLVE GLOBAL WARMING?

The most important step governments, businesses, and individuals can take right now is to reduce carbon emissions in order to slow global warming.

WHAT CAN GOVERNMENTS AND BUSINESSES DO?

America is a top global warming polluter so clearly there is a lot of room for improvement. Some solutions include building cleaner engines that go further on a gallon of gas; developing renewable energy (see Chapter 6); figuring out how to use coal, an abundant resource in the United States, without spewing carbon dioxide into the atmosphere; and creating mandatory restrictions on carbon emissions. Some advocates even call for a carbon tax.

WHAT CAN CONSUMERS DO?

Conserving energy is one of the most effective ways we can have an impact on climate change. There are also several indirect ways we can help, such as buying local food and other products that don't have to travel long distances to reach us, buying products with less packaging or buying fewer products in general, recycling, and composting. Throughout the book there are countless suggestions on how to conserve energy. Getting politically active is also a powerful way to enact change since industry and government need to take the lead on this issue (see page 261 for suggestions).

For more information visit www.realclimate.org, a website by climate scientists that aims to explain the science to the public.

CARS

If you aren't in the market for a new car, there are plenty of easy steps you can take to maximize the fuel efficiency of your current vehicle. If you are buying a new car, consider buying the most fuel-efficient model in the category that meets your needs. If you need an SUV, for example, buy the one that gets the most miles per gallon and has the lowest emissions ratings. In general, smaller cars get better fuel economy than larger rides. Even one or two miles per gallon can make a big difference over time since the amount of carbon dioxide spewed is directly related to how much fuel is burned, according to Dan Becker, former director of Sierra Club Global Warming Program. It's a pretty simple equation: the less fuel you burn, the fewer emissions you create. If you need a big car, minivans and crossover SUVs tend to be more fuel efficient than standard SUVs. But you really have to look at the fuel economy and emissions stats and compare them to similar cars to find your best options. Hybrids are known for being among the most fuel-efficient cars currently on the market, but that's not always the case. See page 253 for more info.

Flex-fuel vehicles run on both regular gas and alternative fuels such as E85 (85 percent ethanol and 15 percent conventional gas). Many people already own these cars and have no idea that they can fill up with alternative fuels. When buying a new conventional car ask the dealer if it's flex-fuel so that if quality biofuels become widely available you'll know if you're eligible to use them. Right now, there aren't too many places to fill up (see page 252 for more on alternative fuels).

Diesel cars are efficient, durable, and reliable, and in the future they may play a part in solving the climate problem because they can reduce greenhouse gas emissions by 20 to 30 percent. But don't rush out and buy one just yet. They are also responsible for a good deal of unhealthy air pollution. Emissions from diesel are loaded with tiny soot particles that can trigger asthma attacks and lead to heart disease, bronchitis, cancer, and emphysema. Roughly

25,000 premature deaths are caused by diesel pollution every year, according to Rich Kassel, director of the Natural Resource Defense Council's (NRDC) clean vehicles and fuels project. Thanks to new regulations, car manufacturers are making cleaner diesel engines; starting in 2008, some new diesel cars should be clean enough to pass emissions tests in all 50 states. By 2010, most of the car companies should have diesel cars that meet the pollution standards of all 50 states. Diesel technology is definitely one to keep an eye on in the future, especially if you do a lot of highway driving.

No matter which kind of car you drive, here are some things you can do:

GREEN

- Drive the speed limit or below because the faster you drive, the more gas you use. Driving at 65 mph instead of 55 mph increases fuel consumption by 20 percent. Driving at 75 mph, rather than 65 mph, increases fuel consumption by another 25 percent, according the Federal Trade Commission.

- Roll up your windows when you are on the highway. It increases the aerodynamics of a vehicle so you burn less fuel.

- Air-conditioning is a big energy hog, so turn it down whenever possible. (But when you're on the highway, using the air-conditioning will conserve more fuel than opening your windows)

- Bundle errands together.

- Don't idle your engine.

GREENER

• Take good care of your car and get regular tune-ups to maximize energy efficiency. Change your oil every three months or 3,000 miles and use the recommended grade of motor oil.

• Keeping your tires inflated to the recommended level reduces rolling resistance and improves your car's fuel economy.

• When buying a new car, buy the most fuel-efficient car in the class you need. Go to www.fueleconomy.gov for the government's latest stats.

GREENEST

• What should you do with an old diesel car, which can emit 60 percent more pollution than a new one? "Buy a new car," says the NRDC's Kassel. "I hate to be that blunt about it, but there's no way to make that old dirty diesel significantly cleaner."

• Drive less: take public transportation, ride your bike, and walk when you can.

• Consider car sharing if you live in an urban area or don't use a car much. You'll save money and drive less. Here's how it works: you sign up for membership and order a car when you need it. Just pick it up from a nearby parking space and drop it off when you're done. It's cheaper and easier than renting a car, although for weekend getaways and other longer outings it's not ideal. Car sharing is credited with taking cars off the road and reducing pollution and traffic. Some employ hybrids and other fuel-efficient cars to really maximize environmental benefits.

Zipcar, www.zipcar.com, and Flexcar, www.flexcar.com, have national networks, but many car-sharing options are springing up locally as well. In the Bay Area, try City CarShare, www.city carshare.org; in the Twin Cities, try HourCar, www.hourcar.org.

• Rent a hybrid or biodiesel car when you're traveling. For now the options are limited, but that is likely to change. You can rent a hybrid from EV Rental Cars, www.evrental.com, if you're in California or Arizona. Bio-Beetle, www.bio-beetle.com, offers rentals that fill up on biodiesel.

• Take an eco-friendly limo or car service. These taxi companies allow you to take a hybrid to the airport or to get around town. At press time this option was available in New York (OZOcar, www.ozocar.com) and Boston and San Francisco (PlanetTran, www.planettran.com).

• Carpool when you can. You can use the Internet for connecting to potential car-mates. Go to www.crideshare.com to find someone to carpool with or find a cross-country companion. At www.goloco.org you can create your own lists of friends and coworkers or have access to a wider community. Your local department of transportation office may have a hotline that helps riders who want to carpool find each other. At www.nuride.com you can rack up rewards points for sharing a ride that can be redeemed for gift cards to retailers or restaurants and tickets to shows.

• Use greener roadside assistance. There's a greener alternative to the American Automobile Association (AAA) for those who like the services but are unhappy with AAA's questionable environmental record. You can buy reliable national roadside

BIOFUELS

Biofuels are any fuels that come from plant materials. The way they work is that the sugars in plants are converted into fuel that can power vehicles. Biofuels have the potential to significantly reduce global warming emissions and overall air pollution since they tend to burn cleaner. They also diminish our reliance on foreign oil and could ultimately benefit American farmers. However, not all biofuels are created equal: what they are made from as well as how they are produced can vary widely and have tremendous impact on whether or not they benefit the environment. That's why some environmental groups support certification so consumers will know, on balance, if what they are buying makes a positive impact. There's still a long way to go before biofuels reach their maximum potential, and the government needs to significantly support their development, but here's what available now:

Ethanol: You can fill up your tank with ethanol (E85) if you own a flexible-fuel car—one that can run on gasoline or ethanol. The problem is that ethanol is not widely available—only about 1 percent of stations nationwide carry E85, and they're mainly located in the Midwest. Today's ethanol is made from corn, which is not an ideal source. There is much debate about whether using corn-based ethanol actually saves energy since corn takes a substantial amount of energy to grow and process into fuel. A

assistance plans for your car or your bike from an established network of towing companies, book eco-friendly trips, get discounts on hybrid and biodiesel rental cars, and buy insurance from Better World Club. The company donates 1 percent of its sales to environmental clean-up and advocacy, and if you book a flight through the club or buy its car insurance, the company will buy a carbon offset on your behalf, which is used to fund local projects. Go to www.betterworldclub.com for more info.

University of California–Berkeley study published in 2006 says ethanol can reduce gasoline use per gallon by 95 percent, but at this point only reduces emissions by 13 percent. The real hope is that the production of ethanol from corn, which is abundant in the United States, will lead to technological advances that make it possible to create ethanol out of cellulosic materials, such as switchgrass and woody plants. Using these sources has the potential to significantly reduce greenhouse gas emissions, says the Natural Resource Defense Council's vehicles policy director Roland Hwang.

Biodiesel: Biodiesel fuel is a plant-based, renewable alternative to petro-diesel and can be used in most diesel engines. You can even make your own at home with used cooking oil from a restaurant if you don't live near one of the few gas stations that supply it. It produces fewer greenhouse gas emissions and less particulate matter and soot than does regular diesel. Biodiesel is great if you can get it from waste material, but it's definitely not going to cure climate change or eliminate our need for foreign oil on its own, as only a tiny percentage of our oil is being displaced by biodiesel. To find alternative fuel stations near you go to http://afdcmap2.nrel.gov/locator.

Spotlight On: Hybrid Cars

A hybrid is a car that gets its power from a gas engine and an electric motor. Today's hybrids look and operate like standard cars so you don't have to worry about plugging them in, but that will change as more fuel-efficient plug-in models hit the market. For now, the batteries that power the electric motor are recharged by the gas engine or when you step on the brakes. Most hybrids use less gas and emit less pollution than standard cars, but it's important to remember that they aren't all created equally.

Some manufacturers sacrifice maximum fuel efficiency to make their cars more powerful. These types of cars are known as "muscle" hybrids and get only slightly better fuel economy than your average conventional car—not a great benefit to you or the planet, especially when you consider the extra financial investment you're making. A true hybrid can get a 40 to 80 percent improvement in fuel economy, according to Patricia Monahan, deputy director of the Union of Concerned Scientists' Clean Vehicle Program—that adds up to big pollution and money savings. Some conventional cars are marketed as hybrids but really have only a beefed-up alternator that allows the engine to turn off when you come to a stop. This doesn't capture that saved energy the way true hybrids do. As with conventional cars, your best bet is to look at the fuel-economy ratings. If you aren't getting that much better fuel efficiency than the standard version of the same car, then you aren't doing much for the environment, says the NRDC's Hwang. Shop smart by comparing fuel-economy ratings and pollution scores.

In general, hybrids do cost more than conventional cars; the amount varies depending on the model and whether or not tax rebates are available (see the Internal Revenue Service's website at www.irs.gov and search for "hybrid deduction" to learn about rebates for a model you're considering). However, according to an IntelliChoice.com study, hybrids save their owners more money over five years than other vehicles in their peer groups thanks in part to lower fuel costs, better than expected resale values, and no significant differences in repairs and maintenance. So far, batteries haven't needed to be replaced before the end of a car's lifetime, and most major manufacturers are saying that shouldn't be a problem. On average, purchasing a hybrid will cost about $3,000 more than buying a standard car, but it really depends on the car you're buying. Any investment you make will get paid back even sooner if gas prices rise. There's also big savings that you can't measure in dollars and cents—less pollution and dependence on foreign oil. Today's hybrids are not the ultimate solution, but they are one of the better options currently available for those who need to buy a new car right now and have the extra cash to lay out for the most fuel-efficient versions. The next evolution of hybrids are going to be plug-in, where you have the option of charging up the battery by plugging into the electricity grid or allowing the battery to be charged by the engine. They'll have bigger battery packs (which, by the way, are going to require toxic disposal for any type of hybrid) and will be more efficient and cost less to operate.

Do your homework before buying to make sure you are buying a true hybrid, which maximizes fuel economy. The following resources are good places to get more information: www.epa.gov/greenvehicle, www.fueleconomy.gov, www.hybridcenter.org, www.hybrid.com, and www.greenercars.org. The Auto Green Center at Yahoo!, http://autos.yahoo.com/green_center, offers an easy way to see what kind of an environmental impact a car has. Developed in conjunction with the organization Environmental Defense, it provides ratings of 1 to 100; the higher the rating, the greener the car. The rating is based on a number of factors including the car's gas usage, air pollution production, greenhouse gas emissions, and even pollution from manufacturing the vehicle.

As with conventional cars, how you drive is important, too, so follow the driving tips in the car section on page 249. Hybrids are more sensitive to how you drive than conventional vehicles, especially in stop-and-go conditions. Don't put the pedal to the metal when accelerating so that the electric motor can power you. Coasting when it's safe is very advantageous in any vehicle, but it's even more so in a hybrid because it recharges the battery, says Becker.

DIESEL SCHOOL BUSES

Riding the school bus may be the most convenient way for children to get to school, but if your child is riding on an old diesel bus, it's not the healthiest. In fact, studies say the air is cleaner outside of a bus than inside of it. An NRDC study in Los Angeles found that diesel levels inside the buses they tested were four times higher than the levels in the cars just ahead of the bus.

It's especially concerning because, as the EPA points out, children are more susceptible to air pollution than are healthy adults because their respiratory systems are still developing and they have a faster breathing rate. Tiny particulate matter can pass through the nose and throat and lodge deep into the lungs, aggravating conditions such as asthma and bronchitis. Diesel particulates can also cause lung damage and premature death and is classified as a likely carcinogen by the EPA.

The health risks from diesel exhaust are related to the number of years a child rides on the bus, according to the NRDC, which does not recommend that you pull your child off the bus, but says if your child's asthma is getting aggravated you may want to consider other transportation options. In general, following some of these guidelines will help reduce your child's exposure to polluted school bus air:

• GREEN

• Open windows when weather permits and have children who spend the most time on the bus sit toward the front. The NRDC found that levels of diesel inside the bus were highest when windows were closed and that polluted air accumulates in the back of the bus.

• Check out the Union of Concerned Scientists' School Bus Pollution Report Card at www.ucsusa.org to find out how your state fares in controlling pollution from school buses, and the NRDC's report on diesel school buses at www.nrdc.org for more information.

• GREENER

• Idling school buses can pollute the air in and around buses, which can make its way into nearby schools. Ask your child's school to establish anti-idling rules and to minimize the time that children spend outside waiting around the bus. Visit www.epa.gov/cleanschoolbus for other ideas on reducing idling.

• GREENEST

• Get active! New school buses are significantly cleaner, but diesel engines last a long time and many old ones are still in operation. Work with your child's school district to get cleaner buses. Buses that can't be replaced can be retrofitted with cleaner technology. It's best to replace the worst offenders; buses manufactured before 1990 are estimated to emit more than 60 times the pollution than those meeting 2007 standards. The Union of

Concerned Scientists has extensive resources and ideas on their website for protecting your child and getting active. Visit their website at www.ucsusa.org. The EPA also has resources available and ideas on funding cleaner technology and engine maintenance suggestions that can positively impact emissions; go to www.epa.gov/cleanschoolbus.

Healthwatch: Outdoor Air Pollution

Nearly half of Americans live in areas where they are exposed to unhealthy levels of air pollution, according to the "American Lung Association State of the Air: 2007" report, an annual report that ranks cities and counties most polluted by ozone and particle pollution. **Particulate pollution** (also known as **soot**) is the most dangerous and deadly of the widespread outdoor air pollutants, according to the American Lung Association. The most common sources are power plants and diesel trucks, buses, and heavy equipment. Ground level **ozone** (also known as **smog**) is another pollutant. It is formed when the vapors emitted from burning fuel mix with sunlight, so it usually peaks in the summer months

It's well known that outdoor air pollution can aggravate asthma and other respiratory illnesses, but there are other serious health issues associated with it for both adults and children, who are particularly vulnerable. Children's lungs are still growing, they breathe faster, they're more active, and they spend more time outdoors, according to Patrick Kinney, an associate professor at Columbia University's Mailman School of Public Health. Outdoor air pollution may also be connected to the development of asthma, although more research needs to be done to confirm this. Studies also link it to increased severity of asthma attacks, preterm labor, and infant deaths. According to the American Lung Association, additional risks for adults include increased numbers of heart attacks and increased risk of dying from lung cancer and respiratory and cardiovascular disease.

Research is beginning to show that living near busy roadways is particularly unhealthy, especially where young children are concerned. The American Lung Association report says air pollution may prevent children's lungs from developing fully, which could affect how well they breathe for the rest of their lives. A 2007 University of Southern California study concluded that living near freeways has adverse affects on children's lung development.

What you can do:

- Visit http://airnow.gov to find out daily air-quality levels in your area. On high-pollution days avoid exercising outdoors and limit the amount of time your child plays outside. Staying in an air-conditioned space is protective against ozone pollution. In general, try not to exercise in high-traffic areas.
- Get active. Visit the American Lung Association's website, www.lungusa.org, for ways that you can make a difference on a federal level. If you want to get involved in cleaning up the air in your community, call your local American Lung Association office at 800-586-4872.

For information about the quality of your local air see the latest American Lung Association State of the Air report at www.lungusa.org.

AIRPLANES

According to the Sierra Club, a round-trip transatlantic flight for a family of four creates as much greenhouse gas emissions as driving for a year. Airplanes are not the most energy-efficient way to travel, but at the moment they're by far the most convenient option when it comes to traveling long distances, especially across oceans. Finding alternatives to plane travel can be a challenge in today's world, but here are some eco-smart travel suggestions to consider the next time you need to take off:

GREEN

- For a shorter trip, such as from Washington, DC, to New York, take the train. It's a much more efficient and cleaner way to travel, and it takes about the same amount of time door-to-door, says Becker, former director of Sierra Club Global Warming Program.

GREENER

- Buy a good carbon offset (see page 262).

GREENEST

- You can save up emissions for a trip, just as you would save money to go on vacation, suggests Becker (who adds he'd rather make personal changes than pay someone else who says they are going to do things that can't necessarily be verified—as is the case when buying carbon offsets). His suggestions: Buy three compact fluorescent lightbulbs (CFLs); don't drive to places where you can walk or take public transportation, or carpool for the month before air travel; take mass transit once you get to your destination. What if you're already doing everything you can do? Then buy those three CFLs for a friend or sign someone up for a year's membership to Zipcar. If you think creatively, there are all sorts of ways you can reduce your "carbon footprint" (see "Carbon Offsets," page 262).

- Fly less. Think twice about hopping on a plane and try to find ways to cut down on trips. For instance, rather than going on three plane getaways a year, consider taking one longer vacation.

Get Active

Global warming is the most pressing environmental problem we face today. Many environmental organizations have action centers for you to visit to sign petitions and urge elected officials to start making positive changes. The following lists highlight some of the major players. Find the one that you like best and visit regularly or sign up for e-newsletters or take action alerts:

ORGANIZATION WEBSITES

Environmental Defense, www.environmentaldefense.org

Natural Resources Defense Council, www.nrdc.org

Sierra Club, www.toowarm.org

CARBON OFFSETS

We all leave a "carbon footprint" on the planet, meaning each of us creates a certain amount of carbon dioxide any time we drive, fly, or use electricity over the course of our lifetime. Global warming pollution, largely carbon dioxide, is produced when we burn fossil fuels to create electricity or power our vehicles. We even contribute indirectly by buying goods and services that are produced by using energy from fossil fuels. There's ultimately no way to live in the modern world and be completely "carbon neutral" (which happened to be *The New Oxford American Dictionary* Word of the Year in 2006), but now a growing number of organizations are offering programs that help you cancel out your footprint by investing in carbon offsets.

The idea is that when you buy an offset, your money goes to reducing or preventing the accumulation of global warming pollution. You can calculate your emissions and buy enough offsets to cancel out or reduce your footprint. When you buy an offset you are essentially investing in projects that support renewable energy development such as solar or wind, increase energy efficiency, capture carbon dioxide emissions, or even plant trees. You can buy offsets to cancel out emissions from virtually any energy-using activity, from driving a car or traveling by air to running your household or hosting an event such as a wedding.

Sound too good to be true? Maybe. Critics argue that offsets merely allow people to keep using too much energy without feeling guilty about it. They also contend that because it's a voluntary market and there are no standards it's hard for consumers to know exactly what types of projects they are investing in. For example, the emissions savings might not be measured properly or may be counted more than once. There are also questions about whether these programs even help the planet. The value of planting trees is questionable, for instance, because it takes a long time for trees to grow and nobody knows exactly how much carbon dioxide they absorb. There's also no guarantee that the trees won't be cut down before they have matured enough to potentially benefit the environment.

The bottom line: the most effective thing you can do is reduce your personal energy use. For tips on how to do that follow some of the suggestions outlined in Chapter 6 and in this chapter. If you've done the best you can and you still want to do more, especially when you have to fly, then buy a quality offset. Make sure it is verified by a third party. Efforts are underway to create industry standards and a rating system, but until then, you can ask questions such as these: Just what is my money going toward? How much of it goes to the project and how much goes to the company selling it? In the case of non-profits, you can ask how they are distributing their income. Is this a new project that wouldn't be happening without my contribution and others like it?

Or you can let the experts do the work for you:

- For a list of carbon offset programs that are vetted by Environmental Defense, go to www.fightglobalwarming.com.
- In late 2006 two studies examining different offset providers were published. If you are considering buying offsets and have some extra time on your hands you might want to check them out. Interestingly, there were a few overlaps in recommendations. Both reports found NativeEnergy, www.nativeenergy.com; My Climate, www.my-climate.com; and German-based Atmosfair, www.atmosfair.de, to offer the highest-quality programs at the time. Follow these links to read the studies:

  Clean Air-Cool Planet, www.cleanair-coolplanet.org: "A Consumer's Guide to Retail Carbon Offset Providers"

  Tufts Climate Change Initiative, www.tufts.edu/tie/tci: "Voluntary Offsets for Air Travel Carbon Emissions"

FOR MORE INFORMATION

Earth Day Network has a popular quiz designed by a European economist that allows you to quickly assess your impact on the environment. Just go to www.earthday.net and click on "Ecological Footprint." You'll answer a series of questions about what you eat, where you live, and how you get around. The Ecological Footprint then calculates how many planets it would take to sustain your lifestyle if everyone lived as you do. You'll also find out how you compare to the average person in the country you live in.

Union of Concerned Scientists, www.ucsusa.org

Clean Air—Cool Planet, www.cleanair-coolplanet.org

OTHER STEPS TO TAKE

- Join activist Laurie David's Virtual March on Washington to demand that our leaders freeze and reduce carbon emissions now. To sign up, visit www.stopglobalwarming.org.

- Contact your senators and representatives directly. You can find contact information at www.senate.gov and www.house.gov. You can keep tabs on their environmental track record through the League of Conservation Voters, www.lcv.org.

- The United Nation's Kyoto Protocol is an international agreement to curb global warming emissions that the United States hasn't ratified. However, hundreds of U.S. mayors have pledged to meet or exceed the Kyoto reduction targets in their local communities. Find out if your city has pledged to meet Kyoto Protocol emissions targets; if not, contact your mayor's office and ask that he or she join other cities who've pledged to cut emissions.

- The companion website to the movie *An Inconvenient Truth*, www.climatecrisis.net, offers ways for consumers to take action. It also helps you assess your personal impact by letting you calculate how much carbon dioxide you produce each year.

- Earth Day Network, www.earthday.net, has Take Action alerts on climate change that you can take advantage of from the comfort of your home. If you're willing to venture out a bit, going to an Earth Day event is a great way to get active to protect the planet. Every April 22 thousands of events take place throughout the world aimed at promoting environmental awareness for issues large and small, local and global. Search Earth Day Network's database to find one nearby. If you're feeling particularly ambitious you can organize your own event using the nonprofit's Earth Day in a Box kit, which contains everything you need, including a detailed organizer's guide, flyers, and other support materials.

12 THE 3Rs: REDUCE, REUSE, RECYCLE

Waste, like taxes and death, is an unavoidable part of life. As it turns out, humans create quite a bit of it—4.6 pounds per person per day, according to the Environmental Protection Agency (EPA)—and there aren't any ideal ways to dispose of it. Not only do landfills take up land that could be otherwise used, but they also can leach pollutants into groundwater and emit methane (a greenhouse gas more than 20 times more powerful than carbon dioxide). Burning garbage in incinerators creates air pollution, and you still have to deal with the ash.

Some environmental advocates are calling on manufacturers to consider the entire life cycle of products from manufacture through disposal and to create products that don't necessarily need to be dumped at the end of their lives but instead can be composted or made into other products with a minimum of waste. Architect William McDonough is a pioneer in this movement and has coined the phrase "cradle to cradle." To learn more about McDonough's efforts and programs visit www.mcdonough .com or check out the book he wrote with coauthor Michael

Braungart: *Cradle to Cradle: Remaking the Way We Make Things* (Farrar, Straus and Giroux, 2002). Ultimately, we will have to rethink the way we manufacture things to sustain our planet in the long term, but for now, there are many steps you can take to manage waste more responsibly.

"Reduce, Reuse Recycle," also known as the "3Rs," is the cornerstone of environmental philosophy for good reason. We've all heard it before, but that's just because it's so important. Besides, most of us can do a much better job with just a little forethought and some creativity. We've gotten better at recycling paper, cans, and bottles (although there's still room for improvement in that arena). Beyond the obvious, though, there are so many other relatively painless ways that we can make a difference. While the concept of the 3Rs has been around for ages, there are plenty of fresh ways to incorporate these principles into your life thanks to the Internet's ability to put you in touch with a larger community and connect you to endless resources.

In general, before you chuck something in the garbage, determine whether it might be useful to someone else, be suitable for recycling, or require special disposal. We often throw items such as batteries into the trash because we don't know what else to do with them. However, batteries, motor oil, tires, printer cartridges, floppy discs, video tapes, CDs and cases, pharmaceuticals, and other tricky items *can* be disposed of properly with only a small amount of research. More basics are outlined in this chapter.

If you are trying to determine how to pass along or safely dispose of an item, the best place to start is Earth 911, http://earth911.org. Just type in your ZIP code for a listing of local resources. You can also call 1-800-CLEANUP. The National Recycling Coalition website, www.nrc-recycle.org, has links to state government waste departments on its consumer page that will provide info on standard trash removal, recycling, and hazardous waste disposal in your area.

REDUCE

It's a pretty simple concept, but it's often the most overlooked of the 3Rs. If you buy less stuff, then you will have fewer things to dispose of. It will also save you time, money, conserve natural resources, and reduce pollution, including greenhouse gases, which contribute to climate change. Consuming less is the first step in making a positive impact on the environment, according to Darby Hoover, senior resource specialist at the Natural Resources Defense Council (NRDC).

Here are some Internet resources to help you get out the clutter and avoid buying more stuff:

www.lendlist.org is a website where members post items they are willing to lend—everything from sports equipment to tools to books.

www.use-less-stuff.com offers additional tips on reducing.

Most of us have a lot more stuff than we could ever use. Since we live in such a consumer-oriented society, the possibilities for reducing are endless. Here are some ways to get started:

GREEN

- Buy reusable products. Try to avoid disposable products such as cameras, batteries, razors, water bottles, eating utensils, food containers, and paper cups.

- Do as many administrative tasks online as possible to cut down on paper. (See page 282 for more paper-saving ideas.)

- Cut down on the number of bags you take from stores. Put small items into your purse or into other shopping bags you may be carrying.

GREENER

- Borrow CDs, books, and DVDs from the library. Buy music on iTunes and rent movies from Netflix. Give old CDs in working condition to a charity or sell them back to a music store.

- Buy durable, long-lasting products, even if they cost a little more money.

- Purchase products with minimal packaging. Buy the largest package size you can use to cut down on the packaging that would be wasted by having to buy things more frequently in smaller quantities.

- Borrow items that you don't use frequently instead of buying them.

- Bring your own canvas bag shopping. For groceries, ask the store for a large used produce or dry-goods shipping box to bring your food home in.

GREENEST

- Break the shopping habit. Think twice before you buy. Buy only what you really need.
- Buy in bulk and share with neighbors or friends. This often cuts costs as well as reduces packaging.

REUSE

Reusing is preferable to recycling because the product doesn't need to be reprocessed before it can be used again. There are many ways to reuse items. Here is a sampling of online resources to help you buy, sell, and donate used items:

BookCrossing.com is an international online community whose goal is to make the "entire world a library." Members leave and look for registered books in public spaces and track their paths via the Web.

CraigsList, www.craigslist.org, is an online forum where you can post an item for sale or purchase in your region.

Dress for Success, www.dressforsuccess.org, is a nonprofit that provides professional clothing to disadvantaged women who are looking to get back into the workforce. You can donate suits, blouses, blazers, and professional shoes that are clean and in good condition.

eBay, www.ebay.com, is the world's largest flea market where you can buy and sell just about any old item. Be aware that many new items are sold on eBay, too.

The Freecycle Network, www.freecycle.org, was started in Tucson, Arizona, in 2003 specifically to reduce the waste that was clogging the city's landfills and now has chapters all over the country. You can list items for donation to other individuals on the website or look for free stuff.

The Flea Market Guide, http://fleamarketguide.com, lists flea-market sales nationwide.

Habitat for Humanity, www.habitat.org, and several other nonprofits will accept cars, trucks, motorcycles, boats, RVs, and other automobiles for charity. You can also donate partially used building supplies such as paint.

The Lions Clubs, collects and redistributes used eyeglasses to those in need. Visit the website, www.lionsclubs.org, for a drop-off location.

The ReUse People, www.thereusepeople.org, collects and sells building products to keep them out of landfills.

Novel Action, www.novelaction.com, allows you to exchange used books, paying only the price of shipping.

Planet Aid, www.planetaid.org, has drop boxes for clothing in many American cities. They sell items on eBay, and a portion of the profits help charity and development efforts in Asia and Africa.

Toy Swap, www.toyswap.com, members can buy, sell, or trade new and gently used toys for a small transaction fee.

Zunafish, www.zunafish.com, lets members of its online community barter books, DVDs, video games, and CDs for a small fee per transaction.

GREEN

- Call the pediatric ward of your local hospital to see if they accept toys and children's books.
- Donate to Salvation Army and Goodwill stores.
- Earth 911, http://earth911.org, lists many more organizations that will happily accept your unwanted items.

GREENER

- Spend your money repairing items instead of purchasing new ones.
- *ReadyMade* and *Real Simple* magazines both provide endless ideas about reusing household items in every issue. Better yet: search their websites for ideas instead of buying the magazines and adding to your clutter.
- Bring used egg cartons and boxes back to the farmers' market so they can be reused.

GREENEST

- Buy and sell vintage books, clothing, CDs, furniture, dishes, and other used items whenever possible.

- Get the next generation involved in a fun way: help kids organize a tag sale before buying a new toy; if you live in a state with the bottle bill, take a walk to a store for a treat and collect discarded bottles along the way to pay for it.

RECYCLE

Recycling whenever possible is a no-brainer. Recycling saves energy, water, and other natural resources, and reduces pollution, including the greenhouse gas emissions responsible for global climate change. The energy you save by recycling just one glass bottle, for example, is enough to light a 100-watt incandescent bulb for four hours. Recycling keeps cans, paper, and bottles out of landfills and oceans. We've come a long way since the early 1990s, but there is still room for improvement. In 2005, 24 percent of municipal waste was recycled. According to World Watch, in 2001 Americans failed to recycle about 51 billion aluminum cans—that's enough cans to circle the earth 153 times over.

Recycling options vary depending upon where you live. Your best bet is to visit http://earth911.org and enter your ZIP code to see what's available in your area. You might also want to check out www.obviously.com/recycle for ideas. A number of well-known manufacturers are devising ways to recycle the goods they create. Most major electronics companies now offer take-back programs (see "Electronic Waste," page 279). Here is a sampling of some other interesting programs in which consumers can participate:

Nike's Reuse-A-Shoe program, www.nike.com, accepts any brand of postconsumer (used) athletic shoes that don't contain metal. The shoes are recycled and the recovered material is then used to make athletic surfaces such as soccer fields, tennis courts, and playground matting.

Patagonia Common Threads program, www.patagonia.com/recycle, takes back and recycles fleece clothing, polyester long underwear, and other garments to make new items. The process saves around 70 percent of the energy and carbon dioxide emissions that would be used making clothing from virgin polyester.

Rechargeable Battery Recycling Corporation, www.rbrc.org, has 30,000 collection sites nationwide. Just enter your zip to find a location where you can drop off rechargeable batteries from a wide variety of products and cell phones.

Staples, www.staples.com, offers every-day in-store electronics and printer cartridge recycling. Other efforts to green its business include selling 100 percent recycled paper along with products made from postconsumer goods and materials and partnering with the EPA to promote EnergyStar certified office equipment.

GREEN

- Find out what the rules are for recycling in your area and comply. Set up a recycling area with color-coded receptacles in your kitchen, garage, or basement to make it easier.

GREENER

- Bring all electronic waste and hazardous waste to appropriate drop-off stations (see page 279).

- Avoid purchasing food and other items in nonrecyclable packaging. Buying local food at farmers' markets is a great way to cut down on packaging, among other resources.

- Compost your food scraps to make fertilizer (see Chapter 11).

● GREENEST

- Organize a recycling drive at your business or local school.

- If your community does not recycle, petition your local government to start a curbside program. "All plastic bottles" recycling programs have been shown to increase compliance. Go to www.allplasticbottles.org for more info.

- Try not to buy plastics that your city doesn't recycle, and write to manufacturers of your favorite products and ask that they switch to recyclable packaging. While you're at it, also ask them to cut down on packaging. Choose plastics that have been made from recycled materials.

The 3Rs don't stop at home. Hospitals, schools, and the other institutions we all visit generate vast amounts of waste. Here are some organizations that are tackling the issue:

Recyclemania, www.recyclemania.org, is an annual recycling competition between colleges and universities that aims to reduce waste generated on campuses and raise awareness. Schools compete to see who can collect the most recyclables per capita, the largest amount of total recyclables, the least amount of trash per capita, or have the highest recycling rate over a 10-week period. Over 200 schools participate each year.

Healthcare without Harm, www.noharm.org, is an international coalition of organizations working to reduce pollution in the health care industry.

Disposal FAQs

WHERE DOES OUR RECYCLED STUFF GO?

It all depends on where you live. Usually, the first stop after leaving your curb is a sorting facility where paper, metals, plastics, and glass are sorted and then sent along to remanufacturing facilities. Some plastics can be used in a number of products including carpet, clothing, and floor tiles. Repulped paper and cardboard can make its way back into your newspaper and other paper products. Aluminum cans are melted down and reused.

WHAT ARE BIODEGRADABLE PRODUCTS?

Biodegradable products, such as plates and cutlery, are making their way onto store shelves, which is a good development because most plastics are made from petroleum, a nonrenewable resource that's in short supply. That said, you'll need to take special care to make sure these products really do biodegrade (break down into smaller components), which is unlikely to happen in a landfill or even in your household compost facility. These products are fairly stable (which is a good thing in terms of being useful) so they need to be sent to commercial composting facilities. Call your local waste management authority to find out if this is an option in your community. Do not mix them in with regular plastics. If you don't have access to a commercial compost facility you should dispose of them with your garbage, says Hoover of the NRDC.

Even if you can't compost biodegradables properly you are doing a service by buying products that aren't made from petroleum and you're voting with your dollars for more of these kinds of products. It's up to you to decide whether they're worth any extra cost. Buying tips? Look for products that are entirely bio-based, or are labeled "biodegradable" and "compostable"; Hoover suggests that you choose products made from agricultural waste materials such as bagasse over others such as polylactic acid (PLA), which is made from corn, a more common option. If you want to do more, get active: ask your local management authority to provide compost pick up in your community.

WHAT CONSTITUTES HOUSEHOLD HAZARDOUS WASTE (HHW)?

Paints, cleaners, oils, pesticides, and batteries contain hazardous components, according to the EPA, which suggests using product labels as a clue. Labels that read "danger," "warning," "caution," "toxic," "corrosive," "flammable," and "poison" should be used and disposed of with care. The EPA says the best thing you can do is to give leftover materials to someone else to use, and if you still have leftovers see if your community has an HHM collection program. See pages 148–149 on disposing of compact fluorescent lightbulbs, which have a small amount of mercury in them.

HOW DO I KNOW IF A PLASTIC IS RECYCLABLE?

Some plastics are recycled more than others. Look for the recycling code—a number with arrows around it—located at the bottom of the package. It ultimately depends upon where you live, but in general code 1 and 2 plastics are recycled most often. These are usually beverage and food containers and other bottles. The others—codes 3, 4, 5, 6, and 7—are rarely recycled. To find out what your city recycles go to www.nrc-recycle.org and click on "Consumers" for links to your local government department of sanitation.

You can either throw the rest of your plastics in the garbage, or better yet inquire if there is a drop-off center nearby where you can dispose of the others, suggests Hoover. You can also ask manufacturers if they will take back their used products for recycling or composting. Reuse plastic shopping bags for shopping or as garbage liners, or see if your local grocery store will take them back.

ELECTRONIC WASTE

Technological trash, known as "e-waste," is the fastest-growing municipal waste issue in the country. Faster and more efficient high-tech products are introduced on a regular basis, and oftentimes buying a new computer or MP3 player can be cheaper than fixing what you already own. One problem with the relentless blitz of new gadgets is figuring out how to responsibly get rid of the old stuff.

This problem is likely to get worse before it gets better, and the ultimate answer is for manufacturers to make products that last longer and can be repaired easily and relatively inexpensively. The International Association of Electronics Recyclers projects that with current growth and obsolescence rates, an average of 400 million consumer electronics units a year will be tossed. Consumer electronics may contain lead, mercury, cadmium, polyvinyl chloride (PVC), and brominated flame retardants (PBDEs) as well as other toxic chemicals and metals that aren't harmful when products are intact but that can leach out chemicals and contaminate groundwater when they are thrown into landfills. Pollutants can be released into the air when they are burned in incinerators. Toxic chemicals also make recycling more complicated and expensive. Only about 12.5 percent of consumer e-waste is reclaimed. The majority of U.S. e-waste is shipped overseas to developing countries such as China and India where the labor is cheap and the materials are valuable.

Ultimately, regulations are needed to control this issue. Europe restricts the use of some toxic chemicals in electronics sold in the European Union and holds manufacturers responsible for recycling their products. (Advocacy groups say that this model of producer responsibility motivates manufacturers to build longer-lasting and less-toxic products since they are the ones who must deal with the disposal). It's more cost-effective for manufacturers to comply worldwide than to produce different products for different regions, so if you're buying new products from major manufactures they will most likely comply with European regulations. As of 2007, some progressive states in the United States such as California, Maine, and Washington have passed their own laws. So, for now, how you get rid of electronics depends very much on where you live.

GREEN

• Only buy from companies that are making efforts to make electronics with fewer toxins and that say they'll take back their old products. See Greenpeace USA's report card that ranks manufacturers based on recycling and chemicals policies at www.greenpeace.org/usa. The Computer TakeBack Program, www.computertakeback.com, issues an electronics report card that evaluates companies on green design and recycling programs. *Consumer Reports'* Electronic Reuse and Recycling Center, www.greenerchoices.org, gives great advice for purchasing electronics that may last longer.

GREENER

• Find new homes for your old products. eBay's Rethink Initiative, http://rethink.ebay.com, has many ideas on selling, donating, or recycling old cell phones, computers, digital cameras, and other products. The site helps you sell your old items or leads you to someone else who can do it for you, provides value guides so you know to price your goods, and also tells you how to erase all your personal data (a very important step!).

• Recycle responsibly. Your first step should be to check with the manufacturer of your current product or from whom you're buying a replacement product. Most companies have some kind of recycling policy, which may require you to pay a fee. See if a retailer, such as Staples, will take back your old product, or ask your cell phone wireless provider if it recycles. The Cellular Telecommunications Industry Association, www.recyclewirelessphones.org, offers information about drop-off and take-back programs for cell phones. If you have to find your own recycler, you'll find a list of recyclers that have agreed to follow environmental standards; go to the map on the www.computertakeback.com homepage and click on your state. The EPA, www.epa.gov/ecycling/index.htm, offers extensive information on recycling and has links to donation and recycling programs. Collective Good, www.collectivegood.com, recycles mobile devices and makes a contribution to a charity of your choice. (Recycling your cell phone has the added benefit of saving gorillas, which are seeing their habitat destroyed because of mining for coltan in the forests of the Congo.)

GREENEST

- Try to hold onto products for as long as you can. Add more memory to your laptop, for example, or clean up your hard drive. Repair items whenever possible instead of replacing them. Do you really need that fancy new cell phone? The fewer new products you buy the less you'll have to deal with down the line.

SAVING PAPER

You can get a lot of bang for your buck with smart paper consumption. You'll help preserve forests and reduce solid waste. You'll also curb pollution, including greenhouse gas emissions, the primary culprit in global climate change, since making paper from recycled content rather than virgin fiber creates about 75 percent less air pollution and 35 percent less water pollution. In a nutshell, use less, buy postconsumer recycled when possible, or try to find paper that's been certified according to the Forest Stewardship Council's standards. It's best to use paper that hasn't been bleached by chlorine to make it look whiter because the process contributes to the formation of harmful chemicals that pollute air and water. Chlorine-free products aren't exactly ubiquitous, but they are getting easier to find.

GREEN

- Always recycle paper. It's the item most frequently found in landfills, according to the EPA. If everyone recycled their Sunday paper 550,000 trees would be saved each week, according to Earth Day Network.

- Banish junk mail. Sign up with the Direct Marketing Association, www.the-dma.org. Visit www.obviously.com/junkmail for numerous tips. One easy one: Call up companies and cancel catalogues you don't use. Over 8 million tons of trees are used each year just to make catalogs. Don't have the time? Catalog Choice, www.catalogchoice.org, is a free service that will contact the catalog providers for you to request that your name be removed from unwanted lists. There are also services that you can pay to stop all of your junk mail. Try www.41pounds.org or www.greendimes.com.

- Print on both sides of paper and think twice before printing something out.

- Cancel phone book delivery and recycle old phone books that you don't need anymore.

• When you haven't used both sides of a page, cut up paper to make pads for jotting down notes.

• Reuse wrapping paper and ribbons. Wrap presents in kids' old artwork or brown recyclable paper that you have decorated. Greenest variation: adopt a no-wrapping policy.

GREENER

• Sign up for online banking to stop receiving paper statements.

• Shred old paper for packaging instead of using polystyrene peanuts. Take old peanuts to packaging stores for reuse. If you need to buy peanuts, then look for those made from vegetable starch, which dissolves in water.

• Buy or borrow preowned moving or shipping boxes. You can buy them online from Used Cardboard Boxes, www.usedcardboardboxes.com. This innovative company rescues and sells quality used boxes from businesses that might otherwise throw them out. They also sell new misprint and overrun boxes from box companies that no longer can use them.

• Cut down on subscriptions to newspapers and magazines. Read what you can online.

• Buy postconsumer recycled office paper. Staples sells recycled paper at reasonable prices, and it has other eco-friendly programs. But if you are looking for more options try Green Earth Office Supply, www.greenearthofficesupply.com.

- Use cloth napkins instead of paper, and rags instead of paper towels.

- Carry a portable mug for your coffee or tea.

● GREENEST

- Buy only recycled paper towels, napkins, and toilet paper, and cut down on use. See the NRDC's Shopper's Guide to Home Tissue Products, www.nrdc.org, for information on which brands use recycled content and other pertinent buying info such as whether chlorine was used to whiten it. The NRDC recommends that you look for products that are totally chlorine-free (TCF) or processed chlorine-free (PCF) when possible.

The website also offers ways to take action for those who want to do more. In the meantime, consider these facts from the NRDC. If every household in the United States replaced:

> One box of tissue paper (175 sheets) with 100 percent recycled ones we could save 163,000 trees.
>
> One roll of toilet paper (500 sheets) with 100 percent recycled rolls we could save 423,000 trees.
>
> One roll of paper towels (70 sheets) with 100 percent recycled rolls we could save 544,000 trees.

- Talk to your office manager about using recycled paper and instituting recycling at work. Check out the Environmental Defense's Paper Calculator, www.environmentaldefense.org/papercalculator, a tool designed to help people cut their paper use or increase recycled content. It's intended for large buyers, but consumers might find it useful as well.

Get Active

Basel Action Network, www.ban.org, is a nonprofit watchdog group aimed at ending the export of toxic waste to developing countries.

Center for Health, Environment and Justice, www.chej.org, aims to protect communities from exposures to dangerous environmental chemicals in the air, water, and soil. The center was founded by Lois Gibbs, known for her efforts at Love Canal (an environmental disaster in the late 1970s in which an upstate New York neighborhood was found to be built on a toxic dumping ground and residents suffered from frequent birth defects, miscarriages, and precancerous conditions). The center can help your community if faced with an environmental health risk from leaking landfills, incinerators, or hazardous waste sites, among others. There are also a number of national campaigns that you can support through the website's "Take Action" section.

RESOURCES

CHAPTER 1: FOOD

Produce

Demeter USA, www.demeter-usa.org

TransFair USA, www.trainsfairusa.org

Food Alliance, www.foodalliance.org

Rainforest Alliance, www.rainforest-alliance.org

Eco-Labels, www.greenerchoices.org/eco-labels/eco-home.cfm

Environmental Working Group, www.foodnews.org

Farmers' markets, www.ams.usda.gov/farmersmarkets

Local Harvest, www.localharvest.org

Robyn Van En Center at Wilson College, www.wilson.edu/csasearch/search.asp

Bionic Foods

True Food Shopping List, www.truefoodnow.org

Campaign to Label Genetically Modified Foods, www.thecampaign.org

Center for Food Safety, www.centerforfoodsafety.org

Greenpeace, www.greenpeace.org/usa

Union of Concerned Scientists, www.ucsusa.org

Chocolate

eChocolates, www.echocolates.com

K Chocolat, www.kchocolat.com

Birds and Beans, www.birdsandbeans.ca

Poultry and Eggs

Humane Farm Animal Care, www.certifiedhumane.org

Eco-Labels, www.greenerchoices.org/eco-labels/eco-home.cfm

Institute for Agriculture and Trade Policy, www.iatp.org/foodandhealth

USDA Safe Food Handling Fact Sheet, www.fsis.usda.gov/Fact_Sheets/Basics_for_Handling_Food_Safely/index.asp

Keep Antibiotics Working, www.keepantibioticsworking.com

Fish and Seafood

The Fish List, www.thefishlist.org

Oceans Alive, www.oceansalive.org

Eco-Labels, www.greenerchoices.org/eco-labels/eco-home.cfm

Environmental Working Group, www.ewg.org/tunacalculator

EPA Local Fish Advisories, www.epa.gov/waterscience/fish/states.htm

Seafood Choices Alliances, www.seafoodchoices.com

Monterey Bay Aquarium, www.seafoodwatch.com

Sierra Club, www.sierraclub.org

Greenpeace, www.greenpeace.org/usa

Meat and Dairy

Humane Farm Animal Care, www.certifiedhumane.org

Demeter USA, www.demeter-usa.org

USDA Safe Food Handling Fact Sheet, www.fsis.usda.gov/Fact_Sheets/Basics_for_Handling_Food_Safely/index.asp

Cornucopia Institute, www.cornucopia.org

American Grassfed Association, www.americangrassfed.org

Food Sourcing on the Net

Eat Well Guide, www.eatwellguide.org

Local Harvest, www.localharvest.org

GreenPeople, www.greenpeople.org

Food Preparation and Storage

Gaiam, www.gaiam.com

Cook's Illustrated, www.cooksillustrated.com

Consumer Reports, www.consumerreports.org

Klean Kanteen, www.kleankanteen.com

SIGG, www.mysigg.com

Institute for Agriculture and Trade Policy, www.healthobservatory.org

Food Activism

Center for Food Safety, www.centerforfoodsafety.org

Organic Consumers Association, www.organicconsumers.org

Slow Food Movement USA, www.slowfoodusa.org

Sustainable Table, www.sustainabletable.org

Union of Concerned Scientists, http://ucsaction.org

CHAPTER 2: BEVERAGES

Water

Environmental Protection Agency, www.epa.gov/safewater

Environmental Working Group National Tap Water Quality Database, www.ewg.org/tapwater

Natural Resources Defense Council, www.nrdc.org

Clean Water Action, www.cleanwateraction.org

Environmental Working Group, www.ewg.org

Sierra Club, www.sierraclub.org

Clean Water Network, www.cleanwaternetwork.org

Drink Clean: Finding the Best Filter

Environmental Protection Agency, www.epa.gov/safewater

"Making Sense of Your Right to Know Report," www.safe-drinking-water.org

NSF International, www.nsf.org/consumer

Greener Choices, www.greenerchoices.org

Healthwatch: Fluoridated Water

Fluoride Action Network, www.fluoridealert.org

Coffee and Tea

Smithsonian National Zoological Park, http://nationalzoo.si.edu

TransFair USA, www.transfairusa.org

Rainforest Alliance, www.rainforest-alliance.org

Boyd Coffee Company, www.boydscoffeestore.com

White Rock Coffee, www.wrcoffee.com

Café Sombra, www.cafesombra.com

Eco-Labels, www.greenerchoices.org/eco-labels/eco-home.cfm

Cusp Natural Products, www.cuspnaturalproducts.com

Organic Consumers Association, www.organicconsumers.org

Wine and Beer

Demeter USA, www.demeter-usa.org

Beer Advocate, http://beeradvocate.com

Brooklyn Brewery, www.brooklynbrewery.com

New Belgium Brewery, www.newbelgium.com

Wolaver's Organic Ales, www.wolavers.com

Butte Creek Brewing Company, www.buttecreek.com

Peak Organic Brewing, www.peakbrewing.com

Wild Hop Lager, www.wildhoplager.com

Stone Mill Pale Ale, www.stonemillpaleale.com

Bonterra, www.bonterra.com

Frog's Leap, www.frogsleap.com

Appellation Wine & Spirits, www.appellationnyc.com

Union Square Wines & Spirits, www.unionsquarewines.com

Astor Wines & Spirits, www.astorwines.com

Organic Wine Journal, www.organicwinejournal.com

Seven Bridges Cooperative, www.breworganic.com

CHAPTER 3: PERSONAL CARE

Skin Deep Cosmetic Safety Database, www.cosmeticsdatabase.com

Campaign for Safe Cosmetics, www.safecosmetics.org

Care2, www.care2.com

Coalition for Consumer Information on Cosmetics, www.leapingbunny.org

Eco-Labels, www.greenerchoices/eco-labels/eco-home.cfm

Hair Dye

Skin Deep Cosmetic Safety Database, www.cosmeticsdatabase.com

Oral Care

Skin Deep Cosmetic Safety Database, www.cosmeticsdatabase.com

Recycline, www.recycline.com

Drugstore.com, www.drugstore.com

Deodorants and Antiperspirants

Skin Deep Cosmetic Safety Database, www.cosmeticsdatabase.com

Sun Protection

Skin Deep Cosmetic Safety Database, www.cosmeticsdatabase.com

Solumbra, www.solumbra.com

Coolibar, www.coolibar.com

Feminine Products

Natracare, www.natracare.com

Seventh Generation, www.seventhgeneration.com

Drugstore.com, www.drugstore.com

Gaiam, www.gaiam.com

Lunapads, www.lunapads.com

Keeper.com, www.keeper.com

Healthwatch: Endocrine Disruptors

Environmental Health News, www.environmentalhealthnews.org

Collaborative on Health and the Environment, www.healthandenvironment.org

Silent Spring Institute, www.silentspring.org

Breast Cancer Fund, www.breastcancerfund.org

Get Active

Campaign for Safe Cosmetics, www.safecosmetics.org

Environmental Working Group, www.ewg.org

FDA complaints, www.csfan.fda.gov

State Efforts

Californians for a Healthy and Green Economy, www.cehca.org/projects.htm

Coalition for a Safe and Healthy Connecticut, www.safehealthyct.org

Alliance for a Clean and Healthy Maine, www.cleanandhealthyme.org

Alliance for a Healthy Tomorrow, www.healthytomorrow.org

Michigan Network for Children's Environmental Health, www.mnceh.org

Healthy Legacy, www.healthylegacy.org

Alliance for a Toxic-Free Future, www.toxicfreefuture.org

Toxic-Free Legacy Coalition, www.toxicfreelegacy.org

CHAPTER 4: BABIES AND CHILDREN

Baby Bottles and Training Cups

Newborn Free, www.newbornfree.com

Smart Plastics Guide, www.healthobservatory.org

Medela, www.medela.com

Klean Kanteen, www.kleankanteen.com

Healthwatch: Chemicals in Breast Milk

Making Our Milk Safe, www.safemilk.org

Natural Resources Defense Council "Healthy Milk, Healthy Baby" Report, www.nrdc.org/breastmilk

Diapers

Drugstore.com, www.drugstore.com

Ecobaby Organics, www.ecobaby.com

National Association of Diaper Services, www.diapernet.org

gDiapers, www.gdiapers.com

Diaper Free Baby, www.diaper-freebaby.org

Personal Care Products

Skin Deep Cosmetics Safety Database, www.cosmeticsdatabase.com

Hair Lice Solutions

National Pediculosis Association, www.headlice.org

Cribs, Mattresses, and Sleepwear

Consumer Products Safety Commission, www.cpsc.gov

Lifekind, www.lifekind.com

Dax Stores, www.daxstores.com

The Organic Mattress Store, www.theorganicmattressstore.com
Our GreenHouse, www.ourgreenhouse.com
Ecobaby Organics, www.ecobaby.com
Q Collection Junior, www.qcollectionjunior.com

Toys

Organic Gift Shop, www.organicgiftshop.com
Ecobaby Organics, www.ecobaby.com
North Star Toys, www.northstartoys.com

Persuading Your Child's School to Use Safer Products

Grassroots Environmental Education, www.grassrootsinfo.org
Environmental Health Perspectives, www.ehponline.org
Pesticide Action Network, www.pesticideinfo.org

Learn More

Healthy Child, Healthy World, www.healthychild.org
Institute for Children's Environmental Health, www.iceh.org
Healthy Schools Network, www.healthyschools.org
Environmental Protection Agency, www.epa.gov/children
The Green Guide, www.thegreenguide.com

CHAPTER 5: HOME BUILDING AND IMPROVEMENT

Green Building 101

U.S. Green Building Council, www.usgbc.org
Co-op America's National Green Pages, www.coopamerica.org

Insulation

Greenguard Environmental Institute, www.greenguard.org
Johns Manville Formaldehyde-Free Insulation, www.jm.com
Cellulose Insulation Manufacturers Association, www.cellulose.org
Icynene, www.icynene.com
BioBased, www.biobased.net
BondedLogic, www.bondedlogic.com

Roofing

Environmental Protection Agency Heat Island Effect, www.epa.gov/hiri
EnergyStar, www.energystar.gov
Database of State Incentives for Renewables & Efficiency, www.dsireusa.org
Green Roofs, www.greenroofs.com

Flooring and Carpeting

Carpet and Rug Institute, www.carpet-rug.com

Interface FLOR, www.interfaceinc.com

Shaw's EcoWorx, www.shawgreenedge.com

Rug Mark, www.rugmark.org

Wood Products

Forest Stewardship Council, www.fscus.org

Rainforest Alliance, www.rainforest-alliance.org

Paint and Wall Coverings

Natural Wall Covering, www.jadecor.com

American Clay, www.americanclay.com

Spotlight on PVC

Healthy Building Network, www.healthybuilding.net

Greenpeace PVC Alternatives Database, http://archive.greenpeace.org/toxics/pvcdatabase

Vinyl Institute, www.vinylinstitute.org

Ventilation

Air Conditioning Contractors of America, www.acca.org

Breathe Clean

EPA Mold Guide, www.epa.gov/mold/moldguide.html

EPA State Radon Contacts, www.epa.gov/iaq/whereyoulive.html

Green Home Shopping

Environmental Home Center, www.environmentalhomecenter.com

Livingreen, www.livingreen.com

The ReUse People, www.thereusepeople.org

Freecycle Network, www.freecycle.org

Craigslist, www.craigslist.org

For More Information

BuildingGreen, Inc., www.buildinggreen.com

Green Building Blocks, www.greenbuildingblocks.com

Green Building Resource Center, www.globalgreen.org/grbc/index.htm

U.S. Green Building Council, www.usgbc.org

The Green Home Guide, www.greenhomeguide.org

The Green Guide, www.thegreenguide.com

CHAPTER 6: ENERGY AND WATER CONSERVATION

Choosing a Green Energy Program

Green Power Options, www.eere.energy.gov/greenpower/buying/buying_power.shtml

Power Scoreboard, www.powerscorecard.org

Green-e, www.green-e.org

Water

EPA Water Sense Program, www.epa.gov/watersense

H_2OUSE: Water Saver Home, www.h2ouse.net

Water Heating

EnergyStar Home Advisor, www.energystar.gov/homeadvisor

Database of State Incentives for Renewables & Efficiency, www.dsireusa.org

Conducting an Energy Assessment

EnergyStar Home Energy Yardstick, www.energystar.gov

Office of Energy Efficiency and Renewable Energy, www.eere.energy.gov/consumer

The Lawrence Berkeley National Laboratory Home Energy Saver, http://hes.lbl.gov

Residential Energy Services Network, www.natresnet.org

California Home Energy Efficiency Rating Services, www.cheers.org

Heating and Cooling

Consumer's Guide to Energy Efficiency and Renewable Energy, www.eere.energy.gov/consumer

EERE "ENERGY SAVER$ Tips on Saving Energy and Money at Home," www.eere.energy.gov/consumer

Department of Energy's Insulation Fact Sheet, www.ornl.gov/sci/roof+walls/insulation/ins_01.htm

EnergyStar, www.energystar.gov

Windows, Doors, and Skylights

Office of Energy Efficiency and Renewable Energy, www.eere.energy.gov/consumer

EnergyStar, www.energystar.gov

National Fenestration Rating Council, www.nfrc.org

Lighting

Environmental Defense, www.environmentaldefense.org

Earth 911, http://earth911.org

EPA, www.epa/bulbrecycling

Appliances

EnergyStar, www.energystar.gov

Home Offices and Electronics

EnergyStar, www.energystar.gov

For More Information

Office of Energy Efficiency and Renewable Energy, www.eere.energy.gov

EnergyStar, www.energystar.gov

CHAPTER 7: APPAREL AND FURNISHINGS

Apparel

Bag Borrow or Steal, www.bagborroworsteal.com

Swap-O-Rama-Rama, www.swaporamarama.com

Organic Exchange, www.organicexchange.org

Co-op America National Green Pages, www.coopamerica.org

Green People Directory, www.greenpeople.org

Gaiam, www.gaiam.com

VivaTerra, www.vivaterra.com

Eco-Chic: Sustainable Designers

Anna Cohen, www.annacohen.com

Deborah Lindquist, www.deborahlindquist.com

Edun, www.edunonline.com

Linda Loudermilk, www.lindaloudermilk.com

Loomstate, www.loomstate.org

Patagonia, www.patagonia.com

Stewart+Brown, www.stewartbrown.com

The Green Loop, http://thegreenloop.com

Lazy Environmentalist, www.lazyenvironmentalist.com

Leather or Synthetic?

Beyond Skin, www.beyondskin.co.uk

Charmone Shoes, www.charmoneshoes.com

Stella McCartney, www.stellamccartney.com

MooShoes, www.mooshoes.com

Pangea, www.veganstore.com

Jewelry

Green Karat, www.greenkarat.com

Giving Back When You Buy

Maatiam, www.maatiam.com

iGive.com, www.igive.com

Mattresses, Bedding, and Towels

Under the Canopy, www.underthecanopy.com

Anna Sova Luxury Organics, www.annasova.com
Lifekind, www.lifekind.com
North Star Beds, www.northstarbed.com
The Organic Mattress Store, www.theorganicmattressstore.com
Good Night Naturals, www.goodnightnaturals.com
EcoChoices Eco Bedroom, www.ecobedroom.com

Spotlight On: Flame Retardants

Clean Production Action, www.cleanproduction.org

Furniture

Forest Stewardship Council, www.fscus.org
Greenguard Environmental Institute, www.greenguard.org
MBDC Design Firm, www.mbdc.com
Herman Miller, www.hermanmiller.com
Steel Case, www.steelcase.com
Sustainable Furniture Council, www.sustainablefurniturecouncil.com
Freecycle Network, www.freecycle.org
Co-op America National Green Pages, www.coopamerica.org

Buying Green Furniture

Q Collection, www.qcollection.com
Furnature, www.furnature.com
ABC Carpet & Home, www.abchome.com
Ikea, www.ikea.com
Vivavi, www.vivavi.com
Co-op America Woodwise Program, www.coopamerica.org

Candles

Green Feet, www.greenfeet.com
Bluecorn Naturals, www.beeswaxcandles.com

Get Active

Organic Consumers Association Clothes for a Change Campaign, www.organicconsumers.org/clothes
SweatShop Watch, www.sweatshopwatch.org

CHAPTER 8: CLEANING

General Household

Natural Resources Defense Council (NRDC), www.nrdc.org
Dr. B. C. Wolverton, www.wolvertonenvironmental.com
Ecoclean Services, www.ecocleanservices.com
Organic Cleaning, www.organiccleaning.net
The Green Mop, www.thegreenmop.com
ZENhome Cleaning, www.zenhomecleaning.com

Green and Clean: Safe Alternatives from Your Pantry

Arm & Hammer, www.armandhammer.com
Care 2, www.care2.com
The Green Guide, www.thegreenguide.com

Kitchen

Greener Choices, www.greenerchoices.org

Chemistry 101: Decoding Cleaning Product Labels

Eco-Labels, www.greenerchoices.org/eco-labels/eco-home.cfm
Greener Choices, www.greenerchoices.org
National Library of Medicine Household Products Database, www.householdproducts.nlm.nih.gov

Cleaning Equipment

Carpet and Rug Institute, www.carpetrug.org
Greener Choices, www.greenerchoices.org

Dry Cleaning

Hangers Cleaners, www.hangerskc.com
FindCO2.com, www.findco2.com

Get Active

Washington Toxics Coalition, www.watoxics.org
Environmental Working Group, www.ewg.org
Pollution in People, www.pollutioninpeople.org

CHAPTER 9: PEST CONTROL

How to Research Chemicals

American Lung Association, "How to Read a Material Safety Data Sheet," www.lungusa.org
Pesticide Action Network Pesticides Database, www.pesticideinfo.org
National Library of Medicine Household Products Database, www.householdproducts.nlm.nih.gov
Green Shield Certification, www.greenshieldcertified.org
Safety Source, www.beyondpesticides.org/safetysource

Ants

Northwest Coalition for Alternatives to Pesticides Carpenter Ant Management Fact Sheet, www.pesticide.org/carpeterants.html

Termites

University of California–Irvine IPM Program, www.ipm.ucdavis.edu

Rodents

Centers for Disease Control and Prevention, www.cdc.gov/ncidod/diseases/hanta/hps/noframes/FAQ.htm

For More Information

Beyond Pesticides, www.beyondpesticides.org

Northwest Coalition for Alternatives to Pesticides, www.pesticide.org

Pesticide Action Network North America, www.panna.org

University of California–Irvine IPM Program, www.ipm.ucdavis.edu

Washington Toxics Coalition, www.watoxics.org

CHAPTER 10: BACKYARD

Garden

Pesticide Action Network Pesticides Database www.pesticideinfo.org

H_2OUSE, www.h2ouse.net

Brooklyn Botanic Garden, www.bbg.org

Local Cooperative Extension, www.csrees.usda.gov/Extension

Gardener's Supply, www.gardeners.com

Companion Planting, www.companionplanting.net

Nearly Native Nursery, www.nearlynativenursery.com

High Country Gardens, www.highcountrygardens.com

A Consumer's Guide to Energy Efficiency and Renewable Energy, www.eere.energy.gov/consumer

Seeds of Change, www.seedsofchange.com

Organic Gardening, www.organicgardening.com

EPA GreenScapes Program, www.epa.gov/greenscapes

Gardens Alive, www.gardensalive.com

Peaceful Valley, www.groworganic.com

Planet Natural, www.planetnatural.com

Arbico, www.arbico-organics.com

Lawn Care

Grassroots Environmental Education, www.grassrootsinfo.org

SafeLawns, www.safelawns.org

Cornell University lawn care website, www.gardening.cornell.edu/lawn

Northeast Organic Farming Association, www.organiclandcare.net

National Coalition for Pesticide-Free Lawns, www.beyondpesticides.org/pesticidefreelawns

Composting

TerraCycle, www.terracycle.net

Planet Natural, www.planetnatural.com

Clean Air Gardening, www.cleanairgardening.com

Composting 101, www.composting101.org
U.S. Composting Council, www.compostingcouncil.org
Worm Digest, www.wormdigest.org
Mary Aphelof, www.wormwoman.com

Cut Flowers

Organic Bouquet, www.organicbouquet.com
Diamond Organics, www.diamondorganics.com
Local Harvest, www.localharvest.org

Furniture, Decks, and Play Structures

Healthy Building Network, www.healthybuilding.net
Eco Mall, www.ecomall.com

CHAPTER 11: TRANSPORTATION

Climate Change 101

Real Climate, www.realclimate.org

Cars

Fuel economy, www.fueleconomy.gov
Zipcar, www.zipcar.com
Flexcar, www.flexcar.com
City CarShare, www.citycarshare.org
HourCar, www.hourcar.org
EV Rental Cars, www.evrental.com
Bio-Beetle, www.bio-beetle.com
OZOcar, www.ozocar.com
PlanetTran, www.planettran.com
eRideshare, www.erideshare.com
Go Loco, www.goloco.com
NuRide, www.nuride.com
Better World Club, www.betterworldclub.com

Biofuels

Alternative fuel stations, http://afdcmap2.nrel.gov/locator

Spotlight On: Hybrid Cars

EPA Green Vehicle Guide, www.epa.gov/greenvehicle
Fuel economy, www.fueleconomy.gov
Hybrid Center, www.hybridcenter.org
Hybrid.com, www.hybrid.com
GreenerCars.org, www.greenercars.org
Yahoo! Autos Green Center, http://autos.yahoo.com/green_center

Diesel School Buses

Union of Concerned Scientists, www.ucsusa.org
Natural Resources Defense Council, www.nrdc.org
EPA Clean School Bus USA, www.epa.gov/cleanschoolbus

Healthwatch: Outdoor Air Pollution

Air Now, http://airnow.gov
American Lung Association, www.lungusa.org

Carbon Offsets

Fight Global Warming, www.fight globalwarming.com

NativeEnergy, www.nativeenergy.com

My Climate, www.my-climate.com

Atmosfair, www.atmosfair.edu

Clean Air—Cool Planet, "A Consumer's Guide to Retail Carbon Offset Providers," www.cleanair-coolplanet.org

Tufts Climate Change Initiative, "Voluntary Offsets for Air Travel Carbon Emissions," www.tufts .edu/tie/tci

Earth Day Network, www.earthday.net

Get Active

Environmental Defense, www.envi ronmentaldefense.org

Natural Resources Defense Council, www.nrdc.org

Sierra Club, www.toowarm.org

Union of Concerned Scientists, www .ucsusa.org

Clean Air—Cool Planet, www .cleanair-coolplanet.org

Stop Global Warming, www.stopglobal warming.org

U.S. House of Representatives, www .house.gov

U.S. Senate, www.senate.gov

League of Conservation Voters, www .lcv.org

Climate Crisis, www.climatecrisis.net

Earth Day Network, www.earthday.net

CHAPTER 12: THE 3Rs

William McDonough, www.mc donough.com

Earth911, www.earth911.org

National Recycling Coalition, www .nrc-recycle.org

Reduce

LendList, www.lendlist.org

Use-Less-Stuff, www.use-less-stuff .com

Reuse

BookCrossing, www.bookcrossing .com

CraigsList, www.craigslist.org

Dress for Success, www.dressforsuc cess.org

eBay, www.ebay.com

Freecycle Network, www.freecycle .org

Flea Market Guide, http://fleamarket guide.com

Habitat for Humanity, www.habitat .org

Lions Clubs, www.lionsclubs.org

The Reuse People, www.thereuse people.org

Novel Action, www.novelaction .com

Planet Aid, www.planetaid.org

Toy Swap, www.toyswap.com

Zunafish, www.zunafish.com

Earth 911, www.earth911.org

Recycle

Earth 911, www.earth911.org

Obviously.com, www.obviously.com/recycle

Nike's Reuse-A-Shoe Program, www.nike.com

Patagonia Common Threads Program, www.patagonia.com

Rechargeable Battery Recycling Corporation, www.rbrc.org/call2recycle

Staples, www.staples.com

Recyclemania, www.recyclemania.org

Healthcare without Harm, www.noharm.org

Disposal FAQs

NRC, www.nrc-recycle.org

Electronic Waste

Greenpeace USA's quarterly report card, www.greenpeace.org/usa

Computer Take Back Program, www.computertakeback.com

Consumer Reports Electronic Reuse and Recycling Center, www.greener choices.org

eBay Rethink Initiative, http://rethink.ebay.com

Cellular Telecommunications Industry Association, www.recyclewirelessphones.org

Environmental Protection Agency, www.epa.gov/ecycling/index.htm

Collective Good, www.collectivegood.com

Saving Paper

Direct Marketing Association, www.the-dma.org

Obviously.com, www.obviously.com/junkmail

41pounds.org, www.41pounds.org

Greendimes, www.greendimes.com

Green Earth Office Supply, www.greenearthofficesupply.com

Used Cardboard Boxes, www.usedcardboardboxes.com

NRDC Shopper's Guide to Home Tissue Products, www.nrdc.org

Environmental Defense Paper Calculator, www.papercalculator.org

Get Active

Basel Action Network, www.ban.org

Center for Health, Environment and Justice, www.chej.org

INDEX

ABOUT THE AUTHOR

Photo by India Baird

Lori Bongiorno is a journalist who was on staff at *BusinessWeek* magazine for six years before becoming a freelance writer. She has written about the environment for *The Green Guide*, and *Glamour*, *Verdant*, and *Plenty* magazines, among others. She lives in Brooklyn with her family.